A Jolly Folly?

A Jolly Folly?

The Propriety of the
Christian Endorsement of Christmas

Allan J. Macdonald

WIPF & STOCK · Eugene, Oregon

A JOLLY FOLLY?
The Propriety of the Christian Endorsement of Christmas

Copyright © 2017 Allan J. Macdonald. All rights reserved. Except for brief quotations in critical publications or reviews, no part of this book may be reproduced in any manner without prior written permission from the publisher. Write: Permissions, Wipf and Stock Publishers, 199 W. 8th Ave., Suite 3, Eugene, OR 97401.

Wipf & Stock
An Imprint of Wipf and Stock Publishers
199 W. 8th Ave., Suite 3
Eugene, OR 97401

www.wipfandstock.com

PAPERBACK ISBN: 978-1-5326-1791-1
HARDCOVER ISBN: 978-1-4982-4300-1
EBOOK ISBN: 978-1-4982-4299-8

Manufactured in the U.S.A.   JULY 20, 2017

Unless otherwise indicated, all Scripture quotations are taken from the ESV.

(The Holy Bible, English Standard Version®), copyright © 2001 by Crossway, a publishing ministry of Good News Publishers. Used by permission. All rights reserved.

A section of the chapter entitled *Significance for the Christian* includes an article published in an online Blog and authored by Dwight L. Longenecker. Used by permission.

Every effort has been made to credit the source of images used in this book and to discover any existing copyright holders. The author and publishers apologize if any have been missed and invite anyone claiming ownership not identified, to contact Wipf & Stock Publishers.

For
Jane my dear and
faithful in every way wife
and
my precious children
Lydia
Nathan
Susanna
Abigail
Daniel
Priscilla
&
Ruth
without whom this book
would have undoubtedly
been completed a very
long time ago!

Contents

List of Illustrations | viii
Preface | xiii
Introduction | xv

Historical Basis in Europe | 1
Down the Centuries | 23
New Year | 40
Historical Basis of Christmas in Modern Britain | 45
The Origins of Victorian Christmas Customs | 69
Biblical Misconceptions of the Nativity | 77
Significance for the Christian | 97
The Regulative Principle | 116
Twelve Reasons Justifying the Endorsement of Christmas | 151
Conclusion | 206

Bibliography | 217
Digital Sources | 225
Index | 227

List of Illustrations

1. *Pantheon, Rome: home to all of the Roman gods.* | 5
   [Source: www.freeimages.com/photo/pantheon-at-night-1451661]

2. *Section of ancient Rome model.* | 7
   [Source: www.commons.wikimedia.org/w/index.php?curid=24669233]

3. *Mother and child Hittite image.* | 9
   [Source: www.commons.wikimedia.org/HittiteGoddessAndChildAnatolia15th-13thCenturyBCE.jpg]

4. *Mother and child Roman frieze c. 20 BC.* | 9
   [Source: www.ldysinger.com/CH_501_Intro/01_Heln_World/01_txtbk_01_jes_hln.htm]

5. *Mother and child Egyptian image from Egypt.* | 10
   [Source: www.commons.wikimedia.org/wiki/File:Egyptian_-_Isis_Nursing_the_Child_Horus_-_Walters_2267_-_Three_Quarter.jpg]

6. *Mother and child image from Roman Gaul.* | 10
   [Source: www.commons.wikimedia.org/wiki/File:Déesse_Mère_gallo-romaine.JPG]

7. *Virgin Mary and child, Vatican, Rome.* | 11
   [Source: By Livioandronico2013-Own work, CC BY-SA 4.0, https://commons.wikimedia.org/w/index.php?curid=35513586]

8. *Denarius.* | 11
   [Source: www.commons.wikimedia.org/wiki/File:Early_Roman_coin,_silver_denarius_of_Julia_Domna_(FindID_197231).jpg]

LIST OF ILLUSTRATIONS ix

9. *Diana statue from Ephesus.* | 12

   [Source: www.commons.wikimedia.org/wiki/File:Fontana_di_Diana_Efesina-Tivoli,_Villa_d%27Este.jpg]

10. *Roman Probus coin.* | 13

    [Source: www.en.wikipedia.org/wiki/Marcus_Aurelius_Probus#/media/File:ProbusCoin.jpg]

11. *Mosaic of Christ as Sol from Rome.* | 14

    [Source: en.wikipedia.org/wiki/File:ChristAsSol.jpg]

12. *Jesus statue from the Vatican, similar to the depiction of Tammuz.* | 18

    [Source: www.mindserpent.com/American_History/religion/pope/rc_images.html]

13. *Constantine Coin.* | 19

    [Source: www.commons.wikimedia.org/wiki/File:Roman_coin;_nummus_of_Constantine_I,_Sol_reverse_(FindID_235287).jpg]

14. *Scudo (Vatican coinage) issued by Pope Innocent XII in 1698.* | 20

    [Source: aloha.net/~mikesch/sunburst.htm]

15. *Arch of Constantine, Rome.* | 25

    [Source: www.freeimages.com/photo/arch-of-constantine-1221077]

16. *Map showing the spread of Christianity from 300 to 800 AD.* | 28

    [Source: www.en.wikipedia.org/wiki/Early_centers_of_Christianity www.usu.edu/markdamen/1320Hist&Civ/slides/13xity/mapspreadofxity.jpg]

17. *Carnival masks.* | 31

    [Source: www.freeimages.com/photo/masks-1437827]

18. *Luther.* | 32

    [Source: www.freeimages.com/photo/martin-luther-statue-1415991]

19. *Geneva.* | 34

    [Source: www.commons.wikimedia.org/wiki/Genève#/media/File:Genf_panorama.jpg]

20. *Strasbourg.* | 35

    [Source: www.freeimages.com/photo/strasbourg-1227325]

21. *Coin of Janus, the Roman god of times.* | 40

    [Source: www.commons.wikimedia.org/w/index.php?search=janus+coin&title=Special:Search&go=Go&uselang=en&searchToken=7nhyhzxdkb8ksbrogcmujygm1#/media/File:Janus_coin.png]

22. *Big Ben at New Year.* | 42

[Source: www.flickr.com/photos/63930548@N04/16501630086]

23. *Queen Elizabeth I.* | 46

[Source: By The original uploader was Caro1409 at German Wikipedia-Transferred from de.wikipedia to Commons by Ireas using CommonsHelper., Public Domain, https://commons.wikimedia.org/w/index.php?curid=11605317]

24. *Josiah King's pamphlet on Father Christmas.* | 52

[Source: www.commons.wikimedia.org/w/index.php?search=josiah+king+pamphlet&title=Special:Search&go=Go&uselang=en&searchToken=5zsyiowot4h2hnjyfhshzem5l#/media/File:FatherChristmastrial.jpg]

25. *Benjamin Keach.* | 54

[Source: www.commons.wikimedia.org/w/index.php?search=benjamin+keach&title=Special:Search&go=Go&uselang=en&searchToken=6fjfbrr7usvugv5jd05eiuabo#/media/File:Benjamin_Keach.gif]

26. *Wesleys, Charles (left) and John.* | 57

[Source: www.commons.wikimedia.org/wiki/File:Charles_Wesley,_John_Wesley,_and_Francis_Asbury_(stained_glass_—_Memorial_Chapel,_Lake_Junaluska,_North_Carolina).jpg]

27. *Whitefield.* | 59

[Source: commons.wikimedia.org/wiki/File:George_Whitefield_(NYPL_Hades-247866-422729).jpg]

28. *Queen Victoria and Prince Albert Wedding Portrait.* | 63

[Source: commons.wikimedia.org/wiki/File:Wedding_of_Queen_Victoria_and_Prince_Albert.jpg]

29. *Dead Robin Christmas Card.* | 64

[Source: www.boingboing.net/2015/12/23/when-dead-birds-were-a-good-th.html]

30. *Spurgeon.* | 65

[Source: www.commons.wikimedia.org/wiki/Charles_Spurgeon#/media/File:Charles_Haddon_Spurgeon.jpg]

31. *Christmas tree on mountain-side, Italy.* | 70

[Source: http://tectonicablog.com/?p=103823]

32. *Saint Nicholas statue in Bari, Italy.* | 73

[Source: commons.wikimedia.org/wiki/File:Statue_Sankt_Nicolaus.jpg]

33. *Odin.* | 74

[Source: www. commons.wikimedia.org/wiki/File:Odin_rides_to_Hel.jpg.

LIST OF ILLUSTRATIONS xi

34. *Washington Irving.* | 75
    [Source: www.commons.wikimedia.org/w/index.php?curid=559325]

35. *Santa by Coca Cola.* | 76
    [Source: wikimedia.org/wikipedia/commons/thumb/1/1e/Cocacola_truck.jpg/
    1024px-Coca-cola_truck.jpg]

36. *Map of Judea, showing the topography of the area.* | 78
    [Source: © OpenStreetMap contributors—www.openstreetmap.org/copyright]

37. *Emperor Augustus statue.* | 80
    [Source: www.commons.wikimedia.org/wiki/Gaius_Iulius_Caesar_Octavianus_
    Augustus#/media/File:Statue-Augustus.jpg]

38. *Hill Country of Judah.* | 84
    [Source: breadforthebride.com/2013/11/06/lessons-from-the-wilderness-part-three/]

39. *Supernova.* | 93
    [Source: www.commons.wikimedia.org/wiki/File:M1-67_%26_WR124.png]

40. *Houses in the evening snow.* | 97
    [Sources: pixabay.com/en/photos/snow/?cat=buildings]

41. *Queen Elizabeth II.* | 100
    [Source: www.farnsworthexpress.com/palace-paramedic-buckingham/295/]

42. *Virgin Mary and child from the Church of the Holy Sepulchre, Jerusalem.* | 103
    [Source: www.commons.wikimedia.org/wiki/File:ירושלים,כנסיית_קבר.jpg]

43 *Joseph Ratzinger whilst Pope.* | 104
    [Source: www.wiki/wikipedia/commons/4/43/BentoXVI-51-11 05 2007 _ (frag).jpg]

44. *Christmas Eve Mass in St Peter's, Rome.* | 105
    [Source: www.flickr.com/photos/122627565@N05/16622120199/]

45. *'Santa snack.'* | 109
    [Source: the author, on Canon EOS 650D with Canon 70–200mm L USM]

46. *East–West Signs.* | 121
    [Source: www.flickr.com/photos/crcollins/273518047]

47. *Global Map of Asia.* | 121
    [Source: By Location_Asia.svg: Bosonic dressingLocation-Asia-UNsubregions.png:
    Shushruthderivative work: The Illusional Ministry (talk)-en:Image:Location-
    Asia-UNsubregions.png, CC BY-SA 3.0, https://commons.wikimedia.org/w/
    index.php?curid=8445916]

xii   LIST OF ILLUSTRATIONS

48. *Calvin's pulpit in St Peter's, Geneva.* | 136

    [Source: www.commons.wikimedia.org/wiki/File:Cathedral_St._Pierre,_Geneva_(6309177929)_(2).jpg]

49. *Music Notes.* | 140

    [Source: freeimages.com/photo/music-1161280]

50. *Hand on Mouth.* | 141

    [Source: waltbrite.files.wordpress.com/2012/08/how-can-i-keep-from-singing_std_t_nv.jpg?w=1024]

51. *Gammadion Cross in Granite.* | 160

    [Source: commons.wikimedia.org/wiki/File:Gammadion_in_granit.jpg]

52. *Ankh wall carving.* | 161

    [Source: www.flickr.com/photos/piaser/6795140207/]

53. *Esther's "Susa" or "Shushan," modern day Shush, Iran.* | 167

    [Source: www.heritageinstitute.com/zoroastrianism/susa/]

54. *Candles/Crucifix.* | 172

    [Source: cdn.pixabay.com/photo/2016/12/12/09/07/candles-1901047_960_720.jpg]

55. *Old State House, Boston.* | 179

    [Source: www.commons.wikimedia.org/wiki/File:Boston_Old_State_House_banner.jpg]

56. *Increase Mather.* | 180

    [Source: commons.wikimedia.org/wiki/File:Increase_Mather.jpg]

57. *Samuel Davies.* | 183

    [Source: www.commons.wikimedia.org/wiki/File:SamuelDaviesOfPrinceton.jpg]

58. *Zurich.* | 195

    [Source: www.commons.wikimedia.org/wiki/File:ZurichMontage.jpg]

59. *Fiddler on the Roof.* | 204

    [Source: www.flickr.com/photos/jumborois/7907996880]

60. *A. W. Tozer.* | 209

    [Source: www.flickr.com/photos/143852232@N06/28697626310/]

61. *Cartoon—Santa not in the Bible.* | 216

    [Source: christianfunnypictures.com/2014/12/a-great-question-for-santa-where-are.html]

Preface

THE CONTENTS OF THIS book probably contain little that readers have not considered in the past. The book's purpose is to stimulate further consideration and reflection on the subject—the religious endorsement of Christmas by Christian churches. The stimulus for the book itself arose out of my exposure to a whole new branch of Christ's church, after experiencing the repeated failure of Presbyterianism to govern churches righteously and having become convinced that the covenant theology of most Reformers (first and second Reformation periods) on the ordinance of Baptism was not based on a sound and logical interpretation of Scripture.

It appeared to me that they had, in a measure, been blinkered by the dogma and tradition of Rome, the non-Apostolic church-state connection they all grew up with and the fear of being viewed as too extreme, thus leading them into a position where they imposed an artificial presupposition on the Scriptural data, namely that Roman Catholic infant baptism had to be retained at all costs. This, I believe, not only resulted in the peculiar view that God's everlasting covenant of grace applied to both the elect and the non-elect,[1] but also in an ambivalence toward holy days because of the church-state connection.

Having abandoned Presbyterian convictions and embraced the Reformed Baptist world of autonomous, independent churches, I was struck by the widespread prevalence of Christmas and Easter services. It was not what I had expected and so began a search on my part to understand why this current practice prevailed and what its modern genesis was. I am not

---

1. Turretin, *Institutes*, 2:195; Blake, *Vindiciae Foederis*, 189; The outstanding exception to the majority view amongst Reformers, which these two references typify, is the covenant theology of John Owen (described by C. H. Spurgeon as "probably the most profound divine who ever lived").

suggesting that if the church were to discard holy days such as Christmas, it would bring a reviving work of God or solve all of the church's problems. The master sin of pride is what is to be discarded before such blessing can be expected and too many churches are too far from this to raise present expectations. However, is the discarding of holy days such as Christmas likely to please God and bring his favor? The suggestion we arrive at, in conclusion, is that from what we know of him in his Word, such a likelihood is very real.

You may not agree with the conclusions offered herein but we trust that even if that is your position, the book will nevertheless prove to be a useful analysis of and resource on this topic.

Soli Deo Gloria

Introduction

WHAT IS CHRISTMAS ALL about? Should the Christian endorse it with joy or reject it as folly?

A subject such as this is not fundamental to salvation, therefore, we have to bear that in mind when discussing it. It is a subject we are obliged to the Lord to discuss with toleration and respect for other Christians who adopt a view different to ours. The believer's sins are completely and eternally atoned for by Christ, yet the Day of Judgement will frustrate many present expectations regarding which believers lived their lives most pleasing to Christ.

The view held and presented here is that, on balance, Christmas is something that Christians should not recognize or practice in any religious sense. The view is founded upon a Reformed/Calvinistic interpretation of Scripture, with a mind-set which seeks to implement in every area of life the precept of Matt 28:18–20:

> And Jesus came and said to them, "All authority in heaven and on earth has been given to me. Go therefore and make disciples of all nations, baptizing them in the name of the Father and of the Son and of the Holy Spirit, teaching them to observe all that I have commanded you. And behold, I am with you always, to the end of the age."

In the minds of most people on earth, Christmas is the festival most people associate with Christianity. However, the Lord Jesus did not do Christmas, neither did his disciples and apostles. Following the ascension of the Savior, none of his followers that we know of celebrated his birth at any time of the year, or any "holy" day on December 25.

The earliest of the church fathers whose writings are extant and accepted as credible, had no such known practice. In other words, it was not something which Jesus had commanded his disciples to do or to teach other nations to do.

Following the Protestant Reformation in Scotland in 1560 it was banned and by the time of the second Reformation period of the 1640s it was banned and made a civil offense in England and also in New England, to which many of the Puritans emigrated. Although the ban was partly repealed in 1686 and then in 1712, December 25 remained a normal working day in Scotland until the late 1960s with normal league soccer matches played until the mid-1970s. Even in England national newspapers were published on this day until WWI and postal mail continued to be delivered until 1961. In the USA, it was as late as 1950 before the General Assembly of the PCUS formally sanctioned the religious observance of Christmas. Today some Christians still do not do it. This begs the question why Calvinist churches, which made so much of the Bible as the sole basis for their belief and practice, were so consistently opposed to Christmas!

We will look in the first instance at the historical basis for Christmas in Europe, from the pagan customs of the Roman Empire through its evolution in the new empire of the Roman Catholic Church. We shall then examine the development of Christmas down through the centuries. A chapter on New Year will examine how it has evolved in tandem with Christmas. Next we shall consider the evolution of Christmas in Britain, particularly from the Reformation to the present day. Then we shall reflect upon the source for all the familiar customs still practised today in much of the world—the great Victorian Christmas.

Having placed the whole issue in its historical context, we shall then contemplate the practical significance for the Christian, both in a social and religious context, including extensive reflection upon the Regulative Principle of worship. Reasons given by Christians to justify their endorsement of Christmas are considered and finally, we will draw a conclusion on the issue and pose some thought provoking questions. Sprinkled throughout are various excursuses, on Mithraism, Lutheranism, and Zurich and Geneva.

Historical Basis in Europe

Declension in the Church

WHAT IS CHRISTMAS AND where did it come from? To answer that question, we have to ask another one—what is Christianity? It is something very *personal*. The first man, Adam, was representing all mankind when he sinned and lost his personal relationship with God. Yet God in his grace took the initiative and in the person of his beloved Son and by his death on the cross, he atoned for the sins of all of Adam's descendants whose hearts he would subsequently open, whereby they would personally see and confess their sins and believe in Jesus Christ as Lord and Savior (see, for example, Nicodemus in John 3). Now personal responsibility is very important to note, if we are going to understand something of the concept of Christmas. Jesus and his apostles predicted repeatedly that the church would go bad—that people would come to believe a lie rather than the truth (Matt 7:15; Rom 16:17, 18; 1 John 2:18, 19; Jude 3, 4, 12). It happened! See Gal 1:6-8, written c. 50 AD. We know that Polycarp (c. 70-155 AD), a disciple of John and leader of the church in Smyrna, went to Rome shortly before his martyrdom there, in order to counteract prevailing heresy.

By 400 AD the New Testament doctrines respecting sin and salvation were being reinterpreted in the most influential part of the church. In a significant measure, true Christianity was being displaced by "Churchianity." Instead of the apostolic teaching that Jesus died for the individual person who subsequently believes personally in him (justification by faith), it began to be taught that Jesus died for the church, so that to know God, be saved and get to heaven, a person had to be part of the church and to believe with a general/catholic faith that there is remission for the sins of the church. The new doctrine would eventually teach that at a person's baptism the Holy Spirit infused grace into them and justified them, thus beginning a process of increasing or decreasing justification, dependent on the good or bad works performed by that person throughout their life (this see-saw of justification was even seen as continuing after death and became formulated in the doctrine of purgatory). So with a denial of the final definitive authority of Scripture, the clergy could formulate autonomous doctrines and worship as long as the new teaching had the blessing of the Pope and/or consensus of the church hierarchy. The result of this autonomous authority was a progressive corruption of worship and doctrine. The doctrine of justification by faith alone was replaced by human merit, sacerdotalism (human priests acting as a mediator to God), and works of righteousness. Doctrine always affects worship so, not surprisingly, worship degenerated into the gross, blasphemous idolatry of the mass, Mariolatry, saint worship, prayers for the dead, and so on.

During the early church period there were four centers of the faith—Jerusalem and Antioch in the east, Alexandria and Rome in the west. With the disintegration of the Roman Empire, the church at Rome gradually took over the wealth and influence of the emperors, even adopting some of their methods of administration. Eventually, Rome sent emissaries to all of the other churches, calling upon them to submit themselves to the authority of the Bishop of Rome, to whom was granted the title of "father" or "Pope." So the church in Rome was not concerned so much with pagans coming to an inward personal faith in Jesus, only that they joined the church and so became Christians outwardly through baptism. To encourage pagans to do this, the church allowed them to keep their old non-Christian traditions, gave them different names and called them Christian festivals! With the church's degeneration, it also began to become liturgical, with growing emphases on outward material matters as opposed to inner spiritual truths. Church leaders' dress-code, supposed locations of certain biblical events and their supposed dates assumed an importance that was void of any biblical warrant. Paul's warning to the Galatians was to avoid legalism. He sought to counter the plausible arguments of the Judaisers that, if adopted, would have resulted in a good-works religion, with a practical syncretism of following both Jesus and Judaism.

Some may not advocate as emphatically as their forefathers, that in 2 Thess 2:7, Paul's "mystery of lawlessness" is referring to the Roman Catholic Church, which came to prominence with the demise of the Roman Empire. However, the fact is that in Rome, Christianity was taken under the protection of the sovereign and an unnatural connection was formed between church and state, which subsists to the present day in so many countries around the world. What was this but a recurrence to the "*weak and worthless elementary principles"* (Gal 4:9) under which the church was placed in its minority? Roman Catholicism was simply Satan's attempt to return to Judaistic Israel of old. What is all the pomp and ceremony that have been introduced by the Church of Rome but an imitation of the Roman Emperors and before that, the Tabernacle worship? The splendid edifices are but imitations of the Jewish Temple. The ecclesiastical dignities that are so highly prized are but an imitation of the emperors and the institution of the Jewish priesthood. The same is true of the robes which distinguish the clergy, together with the titles they have assumed. As the power of the Roman Empire waned, the power of the Christian church waxed. The church, especially the Western church, also adapted the remnants of the Empire for its own purposes. Greek, the language of the gospels and the early church, was abandoned in favor of Latin, the language of the Western Empire. Bishops adopted the imperial purple, a color that they wear to this day. They also adopted secular symbols of power like the staff and mitre. They took to wearing special rings, which people would be expected to kiss. Each took over a diocese, which had been the jurisdiction of a Roman governor, previously set up by Diocletian (245–316 AD). Similarly, imperial provinces became the jurisdictions of metropolitans. Church ritual was borrowed from imperial court ritual, and church architecture from imperial architecture. Basilicas were originally secular buildings, large rectangular halls with columns down the side and an apse at one end. The emperor sat on a throne in the middle of the semicircular apse surrounded by his officials. Similarly, a judge would sit in the center surrounded by assessors. These basilicas were converted into Christian churches, and soon new basilica churches were being purpose built. Now a bishop sat in the apse, his throne (*cathedra*) at the center of a semicircle of his clergy. The apse of many high modern churches is a reminder of this arrangement. A modern day bishop still sits on a throne, called a *cathedra*, and the church in which he keeps his throne is thus known as a *cathedral* church. The thrones are now generally moved to the side, their original position now being occupied by the altar, but the bishop and his subordinates still wear their imperial court robes, a contemporary fashion from two thousand years ago. In the Western church, clerical robes are modeled on courtly robes from the time of Constantine, while in the Orthodox churches the vestments worn by bishops are the same as those once worn by the emperor in church.

What is the distinction between clergy and laity but a copy of the separation of the Levites from their brethren? On what does their claim of receiving tithes rest but the example of Israel? From where do they arrogate to themselves the exclusive right of dispensing ordinances, and endeavour to trace their genealogy as the successors of the apostles but because it was unlawful for any but the priests, the successors of Aaron, to offer sacrifice or burn incense? How do they assume the name of priests, seeing the office is exclusively held by the Son of God, as is shown at large in the epistle to the Hebrews? Correspondingly, what are the festivals of Lent, Easter, and Christmas, etc. but an imitation of those appointed by Moses and Roman pagans?[1] The Emperor Aurelius (c. 215–275 AD) had appointed himself *pontifex maximus*, high priest to the sun god Sol Invictus, and his successors had continued to use the title until 379. This title was applied to the Bishop of Rome originally as a criticism, because of its pagan associations but that was soon forgotten. Popes also appointed themselves *Bishops of Bishops*, another title borrowed from the emperor and which Constantine himself had once borne. So, too, popes decided that they should be addressed as *Your Holiness*, as emperors had been. Since the fourth century they have issued *decretals*, documents with the name and style of imperial edicts. They even invested selected bishops with a fur tippet (or pallium, a circular band about two inches wide, worn about the neck, breast, and shoulders, and having two pendants, one hanging down in front and one behind), just as emperors had previously invested their legates. In short, it will be found that the whole system of Roman Catholic worship is founded on the pagan Roman Empire and the Jewish law, the latter fulfilled and abrogated by Christ. If the instruction delivered by Paul to the Galatians, is understood and acted upon, it will destroy the very foundation of Rome's worship. The idea of dividing up Christ's life into events and sections and then attaching festival days or distinct holy days to each event, was brought into church practice in imitation of Roman emperor-worship. There was not a month in the Roman Empire's calendar that did not have its religious festivals.

Religion of the Romans

The Romans were polytheistic (with over sixty known gods), the greatest of their gods being Jupiter followed by Mars, Quirinus, Diana, Mercury, and Saturn. By the New Testament era, Roman emperors were themselves being worshipped as the embodiment of these gods. The Roman was, by nature, a very superstitious person. Emperors would tremble and even legions refuse to march if the omens were bad ones. The Pantheon in Rome was home to all their gods.

---

1. Haldane, *Reasons of a Change*, 50–51.

If anything, the Romans had a practical attitude to religion, as to most things, which perhaps explains why they themselves had difficulty in taking to the idea of a single, all-seeing, all-powerful god. Insofar as the Romans had a religion of their own, it was not based on any central belief but on a mixture of fragmented rituals, taboos, superstitions, and traditions they collected over the years from a number of sources. To the Romans, religion was less a spiritual experience than a contractual relationship between mankind and the forces which were believed to control people's existence and well-being. Every conquest by Rome of a new territory resulted in her adoption of that territory's gods with great pomp and ceremony, resulting in an absurd variety of religious worship. Provided that your choice was not to the exclusion of other deities from Rome's list, anyone could express their preference for the deity of their choice, just as later in the Middle Ages, Roman Catholics could express their preference of patron saint.[2,3] In spite of such polytheism and syncretism, Rome was a sacral society, where religion and state were indistinguishable. (This was true of Old Testament Israel, which was a church-state and a state-church, and both this model and that of pagan Rome would be subsequently mirrored in the Roman Catholic Church).

If the *pontifex maximus* (greatest pontiff) was the head of Roman state religion, then much of the organization rested with four religious colleges, whose members were appointed for life and with a few exceptions, were selected from among distinguished politicians. The highest of these bodies was the Pontifical College, which consisted of the *rex sacrorum, pontifices, flamines,* and the *vestal virgins*. *Rex sacrorum* (the king of rites) was an office created under the early republic as a substitute for royal authority over religious matters. Later he might still have been the highest dignitary at any

2. Goldsmith, *History of Rome*, 42.
3. Minucius Felix, *Octavius*, ch. 25.

ritual, even higher than the *pontifex maximus*, but it became a purely honorary post. Sixteen *pontifices* (priests) oversaw the organization of religious events. They kept records of proper religious procedures and the dates of festivals and days of special religious significance. The *flamines* were priests to individual gods: three for the major gods Jupiter, Mars, and Quirinus, and twelve for the lesser ones. These individual experts specialized in the knowledge of prayers and rituals specific to their particular deity. The *flamen dialis*, the priest of Jupiter, was the most senior of the *flamines*. On certain occasions his status was equal to those of the *pontifex maximus* and the *rex sacrorum*. The *vestal virgins* (numbering two to six) were priests to Vesta, the god of home/family. The only female priests permitted in the Roman system, they kept a sacred fire burning in her temple in Rome.

The temptation by some in the church to imitate the Roman calendar is understandable when we remember that the early church was composed of many converted Jews and Gentile proselytes to Judaism, all of whom had been used to following the Jewish calendar with its feasts and holy days throughout the different seasons of the year. Such imitation was not novel to the second and third centuries AD, as it was already happening during the Apostolic era. Paul addresses the issue in Galatians, to which we have already referred. He condemned such days when he rebuked believers who wanted to retain the old covenant shadows.

> But now that you have come to know God, or rather to be known by God, how can you turn back again to the weak and worthless elementary principles of the world, whose slaves you want to be once more? You observe days and months and seasons, and years! I am afraid I may have laboured over you in vain. (Gal 4:9-11)

James Bannerman writes:

> And in the context it is not difficult to gather the twofold ground on which the apostle condemned such observances. First of all, he grounded condemnation of ecclesiastical days on the fact that, in attaching importance to them, and regarding them as ordinary parts of the service due to God, the Galatians, like "children, were in bondage under the elements (*stoicheia*) of the world;" in other words, he stigmatises these appointments of days and seasons as rudimentary observances suited to the infancy of the church, but only fetters to it now, when it ought to have arrived at spiritual manhood.
>
> And again he characterises them as "the weak and beggarly elements (or rudiments) whereunto the Galatians desired again

to be in bondage." They were the empty and outward appointments of a carnal and worn-out dispensation.[4]

Since 500 BC (era of Esther), Roman pagans had kept the holiday of *Saturnalia*, a weeklong period of lawlessness celebrated between the 17th and 23rd of December, which had evolved out of worship of the mythological god Saturn, attributed with control of wealth and agriculture to name but a few of his supposed attributes. During this festival period, Roman courts were closed and Roman law dictated that no one could be punished for damaging property or injuring people during the weeklong celebration. It was largely wild, violent, and immoral. It was the only week of the year when gambling was permitted in public.

Costumes were worn and cross-dressing was common, as was role-reversal, where slaves were served by their masters and so on. All sexual prohibitions were lifted and erotic dancing in public was commonplace. The giving and receiving of presents was another feature (small dolls were a popular gift, although for an unpleasant reason, as they commemorated a myth that Saturn ate all his male children at birth to fulfill a pledge that he would die without heirs). All businesses were closed and the only vocations permitted to work were those of bakers and cooks. The festival began when Roman authorities chose "an enemy of the Roman people" to represent the Lord of Misrule. Each Roman community selected a victim whom they forced to indulge in binge eating and other physical pleasures throughout the week. At the original festival's conclusion, December 23, Roman authorities believed they were destroying the forces of darkness by brutally murdering this innocent man or woman. This violent ending became less common with the passage of time and the influence of Greek customs and practice, so that

4. Bannerman, *Church of Christ*, 1:414.

by the New Testament era the festival had become more light-hearted. The Lord of Misrule was selected by the drawing of lots and adopted the role of a mock king in charge of all the revelry, who was expected to order outlandish and scandalous actions to be performed by himself and others.

In the fourth century AD, Christianity imported the *Saturnalia* festival hoping to take the pagan masses in with it. Church leaders in the west succeeded in converting to Christianity large numbers of pagans by promising them that they could continue to celebrate the Saturnalia as Christians. As the church historian Philip Schaff noted, had the syncretism of winter festivals with the birth of Christ arisen during a period of Christian persecution by pagans, then everything pagan would have been abhorred and the idea of mixing the two, undoubtedly refuted. However, as the idea occurred "in the Nicene age, this rigidness of opposition between the church and the world was in a great measure softened by the general conversion of the heathen."[5] The problem was that there was nothing intrinsically Christian about Saturnalia. The weeks around December 25 coincided with a wide range of celebrations in earlier cultures, including the Midwinter Solstice (which at that time according to the Julian calendar fell on December 25), North European Yule, Celtic Samhain, Roman Saturnalia, and the Roman Birthday of Sol Invictus (or Invincible Sun), the official sun god of the Roman Empire, celebrating the rebirth of the winter-sun unconquered by the rigors of the season. In the third century AD this birthday was deemed to be December 25.

Excursus on Mithraism

The first empire after the Flood was that of Babylon (c. 2200 BC) under Nimrod, Noah's descendent via Ham and Cush (Gen 10:8–10). Ezekiel, prophesying to the Jewish captives in their Babylonian exile around 600 BC, condemns the worship of Tammuz (Ezek 8:13–18) the mythological son of Nimrod mothered by Semiramis, believed by pagans to have been born miraculously at the winter solstice. Numerous Babylonian monuments show the goddess-mother Semiramis with her son in her arms.

From Babylon this mystery religion spread to all the surrounding nations as the years went on and the world was populated by the descendants of Noah. Everywhere the symbols were the same and everywhere the cult of the mother and child became the basis of the ancient pagan religion's popular system. Their worship was celebrated with immoral practices and the image of the queen of heaven with the babe in her arms was seen

---

5. Schaff, *History of the Christian Church*, 3:396.

everywhere, though the names might differ as languages differed. It became the mystery religion of Phoenicia and by the Phoenicians was carried to the ends of the earth. In Egypt, the mother and child were worshipped as Isis and Osiris or Horus; in India as Isi and Iswara; in China, Japan, and Tibet, as the mother goddess Shing-moo with child (Jesuit missionaries to the East were astonished to find the counterpart of the Madonna and child as devoutly worshiped as they were in Rome); in Greece as Ceres or Irene and Plutus; in Rome as Fortuna and Jupitor-puer, or Venus and Adurnis; and in Scandinavia as Frigga and Balder. When Caesar invaded Britain, he discovered the Druid priests worshiping the "mother of god" as Virgo-Patitura.

The mother and child were worshiped in Babylon as Ishtar and Tammuz, and in Phoenicia as Ashtoreth and Baal. When Belshazzar was slain (Dan 5:30) and the Persians came to power under Cyrus and later Darius, the worship spread west into Anatolia which eventually by the first century BC, became the Roman province of Asia. As Imperial Rome was tied to Egypt by conquest and by necessity (the fertile lands around the Nile providing a major source of food for Rome), it is not surprising to discover that the Isis cult became fully integrated into Roman life. Ancient Egyptian depictions of Isis and Horus became replicated in Roman coinage of the third century AD.

Semiramis was worshiped in Ephesus as the pagan fertility goddess Diana, who represented the generative powers of nature. She was referred to as a fertility goddess because she mothered all the numerous pagan gods representing the god-incarnate Tammuz.

Diana was pictured with numerous teats so that she could nurse all the pagan gods, and she wore a tower-shaped crown symbolizing the Babylonian tower of Babel.

Sun worship is very central to Buddhism and Hinduism in which some of the doctrines are as follows: as the sun god (Nimrod) plunged into the waters of the Euphrates River, so the reincarnated son plunged into the waters of the womb to be worshiped as the savior; the cycle of the sun represents the sun rising (Brahma), the sun at the meridian (Siva), and the sun setting (Vishnu); at night, the sun rests in the womb of the ocean in the darkness of the underworld, representing the death and suffering of the sun god. As god of the ocean (Poseidon, Neptune), he was also worshipped as the fish god Dagon, who had plunged into the waters of the womb to be reborn. The most prominent form of worship in Babylon was dedicated to Dagon, later known as Ichthys, or the fish (Judg 16:23; 1 Chr 10:10; 1 Sam 5). Another name for sun worship is Mithraism. The Encyclopaedia Britannica calls Mithra "the Iranian god of the sun, justice, contract, and war" and states that this pagan deity (originating in Indo-Persia during Moses' era c. 1500 BC) was referred to as "Mithras" in the Roman Empire during the early centuries after Christ's death.[6] (It should be noted that from the eighteenth century onwards in the rise of modern human secularism, much has been published that emphasizes similarities between Mithraism and Christianity, arguing that the latter is but an imitation of the former. However, on closer

---

6. https://www.britannica.com/topic/Mithraism.

scrutiny, these claims are spurious and are void of any tangible evidence from the extant records of Mithraism.)

According to the Roman historian Plutarch (c. 46–120 AD), Mithraism began to be absorbed by the Romans during Pompey's military campaign against Cilician pirates around 70 BC. The religion eventually migrated from Asia Minor through the soldiers, many of whom had been citizens of the region, into Rome and the far reaches of the empire. Syrian merchants brought Mithraism to the major cities, such as Alexandria, Rome, and Carthage, while captives carried it to the countryside. By the third century AD Mithraism and its mysteries permeated the Roman Empire and extended from India to Scotland, with abundant monuments in numerous countries amounting to over 420 Mithraic sites so far discovered. The worship of the sun remained very prominent in Roman society and toward the end of the third century AD, the Lord Jesus was being referred to as the "Sun of Justice." There was without much doubt, a syncretism of the worship of the sun and the worship of the Son of God!

This Roman coin from the third century AD (Probus, AD 276–282) depicts, on the reverse, the pagan sun god driving a chariot drawn by four horses (Sol in Quadriga). The inscription reads SOLI INVICTO: "The Invincible Sun."

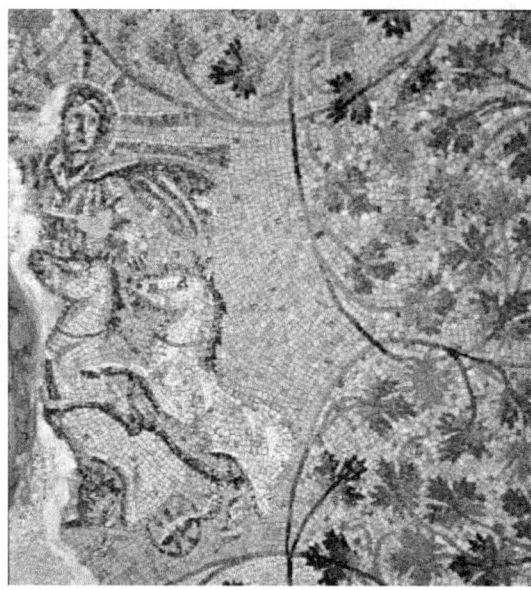

A similar mosaic found in the Vatican grottoes under St. Peter's Basilica, on the vaulted ceiling of the tomb of the Julii (also known as Mausoleum M), depicts Christ as the sun-god Helios/Sol riding in his chariot and is dated to the third century AD. The two left horses were destroyed when the hole was made to enter the tomb. This mosaic demonstrates that the pagan Roman culture of the day was incorporating Christ into the myriad of idols that they worshipped. An inscription by a T. Flavius Hyginus, dating to around 80–100 AD in Rome, dedicates an altar to Sol Invictus Mithras. These facts combine to explain why the Savior was honored by some in Rome with the title, "Sun of Justice." It is simply the attachment of a Mithraic title to Christ!

Many Romans simply preferred to worship the sun god that their ancestors had always worshiped. Their "god of light" was known by many names such as Mithra, Baal, and Sol Invicti. Now, another name was being connected to this pagan deity of the sun. That name was none other than Christ Jesus!

Syncretism

It appears that the church in Rome was willing, at the very least, to look the other way as the connection was being made. The intention of converting pagans to Christianity may have been a noble one. However, it appears that rather than converting pagans to Christianity, paganism was thoroughly incorporated into Christianity. The historian Clement A. Miles states:

The Dies Natalis Invicti was probably first celebrated in Rome by order of the Emperor Aurelian (270–275), an ardent worshiper of the Syrian sun-god Baal. With the Sol Invictus was identified the figure of Mithra, that strange eastern god whose cult resembled in so many ways the worship of Jesus, and who was at one time a serious rival of the Christ in the minds of thoughtful men. Mithraism resembled Christianity in its monotheistic tendencies, its sacraments, its comparatively high morality, its doctrine of an Intercessor and Redeemer and its vivid belief in a future life and judgment to come. Moreover, Sunday was its holy-day dedicated to the Sun.[7]

In 313, Emperor Constantine "converted" to Christianity and in 321, he enacted the first "Sunday" law, in the following terms:

On the venerable Day of the Sun let the magistrates and people residing in cities rest, and let all workshops be closed. In the country, however, persons engaged in agriculture may freely and lawfully continue their pursuits; because it often happens that another day is not so suitable for grain-sowing or for vine-planting; lest by neglecting the proper moment for such operations the bounty of heaven should be lost. (Given the 7th day of March, Crispus, and Constantine being consuls each of them for the second time).

Schaff goes on to explain that Constantine

enjoined the observance, or rather forbade the public desecration of Sunday, not under the name of Sabbatum or Dies Domini, but under its old astrological and heathen title, Dies Solis, familiar to all his subjects, so that the law was as applicable to the worshippers of Hercules, Apollo, and Mithras, as to the Christians. There is no reference whatever in his law either to the fourth commandment or to the resurrection of Christ. Besides he expressly exempted the country districts, where paganism still prevailed, from the prohibition of labor, and thus avoided every appearance of injustice. Christians and pagans had been accustomed to festival rests. Constantine made these rests to synchronize, and gave the preference to Sunday, on which day Christians from the beginning celebrated the resurrection of their Lord and Savior.[8]

As an aside, this event immediately preceded the medieval period of church history. Following Constantine's edict, regard for Sunday as a day of rest increased and continued through the Christianisation of barbarian nations.

7. Miles, *Christmas*, 23.
8. Schaff, *History of the Christian Church*, 3:380, n. 1, quoting Codex Justinianus.

Newly converted Germanic tribes recognized the similarities between the Jewish Sabbath and their own pagan taboo-days, therefore they willingly accepted a Sabbatarian Lord's Day.

The most important factor in the Lord's Day assumption of the requirements of the Sabbath came from the great scholastic theologian Thomas Aquinas. Aquinas developed a method of distinguishing between the moral and ceremonial aspects of the fourth commandment, which allowed the Christian to spiritually keep the Sabbath (with its moral aspects), without observing it on Saturday (the ceremonial aspect). Aquinas also articulated a doctrine which linked the Ten Commandments with the Natural Law, which he saw as binding on all men everywhere. This Thomist view of the Ten Commandments survived some challenges, to become the prevalent view of late medieval and traditional Roman Catholic theology, so was the leading view heading into the Reformation.[9]

We make mention of this, because later chapters will show how in the early church period, and also in the Reformation and the second Reformation periods, many theologians regarded the acceptance of Christmas as detracting from the Lord's Day. This was especially true of those who adopted the Puritan view that the Lord's Day was the Christian Sabbath, a creation ordinance binding on everybody, everywhere. It is unlikely that this Puritan view would have evolved, if the Reformers had made a complete break from the Roman Catholic position. Neither Luther nor Calvin believed that the Christian Sabbath of the Fourth Commandment was still in force and manifested in the Lord's Day.[10] (As we shall notice later, this inability of the Reformers to completely break from Roman Catholic practice, also had a significant impact on the whole issue of "holy days" such as Christmas.)

This was also the first use of a seven-day week in the Roman calendar.[11] The first and most important day of the week was Sun-Day, in honor of Sol Invictus/Baal. The six other days were all names of planets. The seventh day of the week, called Saturday (not Sabbath-day), represented the planet Saturn, which is furthest from the Sun and likewise on the calendar was day seven, the furthest day from Sun-Day, day one.[12]

The use of pagan names of the seven days was Constantine's way of erasing Sabbath and the Lord's Day. Hence, Christians conformed to the abolition of Sabbath as the day of rest, from an emperor who overtly chose a special day to honor his Sun-God, whom he patronized as being identical

---

9. Bauckham, "Sabbath and Sunday," 302–7.
10. www.bookofconcord.org, Art. 28; Calvin, *Selected Works*, 2:157–63.
11. *Journal of Calendar Reform*, 23:128n.
12. Weigall, *Paganism*, 231.

to Jesus. Sun-Day was central to Constantine's thinking and not only was the weekly holy day moved to Sunday, but Easter was moved to a Sunday as well. Easter had originally been celebrated on the fourteenth of the Jewish month of Nisan: the lunar month starting with the first full Moon after the spring equinox. Western Christians shifted it to the following Sunday, but it still depended upon the lunar cycle, which is why Easter falls at different dates in different years, and why it still causes so much confusion. A complicated set of tables is provided in the Anglican *Book of Common Prayer* for calculating the date of Easter for each year up to 2299.

Today in Christianity, we think that we can make a very clear distinction between worship of the *sun*, and worship of the *Son*. However, we can still commonly find a connection between Sol or Baal and Christianity in much of the Christian artwork of today. It is very common to see Christ, the apostles, prophets, Mary, lambs, and doves portrayed with a sunburst or halo of light surrounding their head. A halo or sunburst is also sometimes included in images of the cross. While some may make a link with the implausible theory of the star of Bethlehem shining directly onto Jesus' head, these halos and sunbursts are the same as those used in Mithraism or sun worship. Sadly, we can find this type of artwork today in the buildings of many Protestant denominations.

There were northern and southern European pagan winter festivals which extended from November 1 to January 10. The Celtic New Year began on November 1 and the Teutonic one on November 11. The idea was linked to the death of plants and the loss of leaves from trees. At this time of year there was an obsession with the cult of the dead. The pagan idea, widespread among many peoples, was that on one day or night of the year the souls of the dead return to their old homes and must be entertained. These and other superstitions marked this period up to and beyond the winter solstice. The number and regional variety of pagan folk customs and myths around Europe, based upon this time of year are too many to mention. As the Roman Catholic Church spread, there occurred a great medieval synthesis of paganism and Christianity. The church played a double role, at times an antagonistic one, forcing heathen customs into the shade and at other times one of adaptation, baptizing them into Christ, granting the pagan customs a Christian name and interpretation while often modifying their form. The church attempted to displace the pagan folk festivals with Saints days, in which the Mass was central. As a consequence of all of this, the pagans in the now apostate church could worship the queen of heaven and observe the birth of her son Tammuz, while the untaught, unsuspecting believers thought they were honoring Christ in the same ritual.

One may be forgiven for imagining that the gold statue (illustrated), is from a Hindu temple in India. However, this golden child is found in the Vatican treasury and like so many other images of the child in Roman Catholic churches, is reminiscent of the ancient worship of Tammuz as a child. Born on December 25, he represented the rebirth of the sun. In Europe alone, thousands of local female divinities transmogrified into the Virgin Mary, a fact that explains why even today she is represented in such conspicuously different ways in different areas of Italy, Spain, and Portugal.

We learn from Bede's "Historia Ecclesiastica" of a letter addressed in 601 by Pope Gregory I (the Great) to Abbot Mellitus, giving him instructions to be handed on to Augustine of Canterbury, which sheds a vivid light on the process by which heathen sacrificial feasts were turned into Christian festivals. This Pope opined of the Anglo-Saxons,

> Because they are wont to slay many oxen in sacrifices to demons, some solemnity should be put in the place of this, so that on the day of the dedication of the churches, or the nativities of the holy martyrs whose relics are placed there, they may make for themselves tabernacles of branches of trees around those churches which have been changed from heathen temples, and may celebrate the solemnity with religious feasting. Nor let them now sacrifice animals to the Devil, but to the praise of God kill animals for their own eating, and render thanks to the Giver of all for their abundance; so that while some outward joys are

> retained for them, they may more readily respond to inward joys. For from obdurate minds it is undoubtedly impossible to cut off everything at once, because he who strives to ascend to the highest place rises by degrees or steps and not by leaps.[13]

We see here very plainly the mind of the ecclesiastical compromiser. Direct sacrifice to heathen gods the church, of course, could not dream of tolerating—it had been the very center of her attack since the Apostolic era and refusal to take part in it had cost the martyrs their lives. Yet the festivity and merrymaking to which it gave occasion were to be left to the people, a policy which had clear advantages in making the church and therefore the church's form of Christianity popular. What we find is many pagan practices concealed beneath a superficial Christianity, often under the mantle of some saint, yet side by side with these are many practices obviously identical with heathen customs. With respect to the believer's attitude to the remnants of pagan idolatry, the biblical imperative is annihilation, not syncretism/incorporation! (see e.g., Deut 12:24, 30–31).

Roman emperors expected to undergo apotheosis and become gods when they died, therefore they were not too keen to learn that, according to Christian teaching, their fate was otherwise. To make Christianity more palatable, a compromise was achieved, by which newly expired Christian emperors became saints. Constantine thus became St. Constantine. Not taking any chances, the Senate recorded their gratitude after his death for the "divine" memory of Constantine, as they were to do for a string of subsequent Christian emperors. Constantine was a sun-god worshipper. He began in 309 his vast homogenous series of coinages inscribed "Soli Invicto Comiti."

These coins had Constantine's image on one side, and on the reverse "Soli Invicto Comiti," meaning "Sol (Sun), Invincible, Comrade (of Constantine)." Sol Invictus is depicted as the sun-god with a rayed solar crown. One hand gives a blessing and the other holds a globe. Note the cross on his right, another indication of syncretism with Christianity. Constantine's coinage

---

13. Bede, *Ecclesiastical History*, 1:30.

to honor Sol Invictus was a huge scale operation, unmistakably intended to implant an idea in the minds of the population of the empire.[14]

Incidentally, compare the scudo from 1698 of Pope Innocent XII, which depicts a very similar image of Sol Invictus as Christ—with a rayed solar crown, one hand giving a blessing and the other holding a globe!

All Saints Day, ("All Hallows" in old English) on November 1, was certainly observed in England, France, and Germany in the eighth century. Pope Gregory III (731–741) moved All Saints Day (originally celebrated on the first Sunday after Pentecost, signalling the official end of Easter) from May to November 1. The day, which involved a vigil kept the night before (October 31) was set aside to commemorate all saints too numerous to be given their own feast day and was observed in Rome, before being extended by Gregory IV to the rest of the church a century later. It coincided with the Celtic New Year, "Samhain," when pagans believed the boundary between this life and the next could be more easily crossed. However, there exists no evidence that either Pope had any knowledge of Samhain.

Note that the 'occult' aspects of modern Halloween (all-hallows-eve) have their roots firmly in Roman Catholic belief, not in ancient paganism! Both the vigil and day remain Roman Catholic holy days of obligation. It would seem that the people needed something more tangible for their own dead and therefore All Souls' Day, on November 2, with its solemn Mass and prayers for the departed was introduced to supply this need. The special liturgical features of the church's celebration are the Vespers, Matins, and Lauds of the Dead on the evening of November 1, and the solemn Requiem Mass on November 2. Throughout Europe various customs continue to prevail, from making meals for the dead to eat in the night, to baking "soul-cakes," given originally to the living as a reward for their prayers for the dead in purgatory.

St. Hubert's Day, was concocted for November 3; St. Martin's Day or Martinmas was concocted for November 11 by Pope Martin I (649–654); St. Clement's Day for November 23; St. Catherine's Day for November 25; St. Andrew's Day for November 30; St. Nicholas's for December 6; St. Lucia for December 13; and St. Thomas the Apostle for December 21. The three

14. Grant, *Collapse and Recovery*, 51.

saints' days immediately following Christmas are St. Stephen's for December 26; St. John the Evangelist's for December 27; and the Holy Innocents' for December 28.

The number of fantastic superstitions which built up around those days, part pagan and part Roman Catholic in origin, not to mention those associated with Christmas Eve and the twelve days thereafter, are legion in number. In light of all of the Saints Days established, we can understand how the feature of Advent evolved, with a few churches commencing it the sixth Sunday before Christmas Day but most on the fourth Sunday before. While Advent was ratified at the Council of Tours in 567, it is attested to have been in existence since 480.

From our historical review, it can be gathered that while we associate Christmas with December 25, on its pagan side it cannot be separated from the folk-feasts of November and December. In the Hampton court of Charles I (d. 1649), Christmas was reckoned to commence on All Hallow Tide, (All Saints Day) on November 1.[15] As November 1 was considered by many to be the start of Christmas, so Candlemas on February 2 was considered to be the end of Christmas. There had existed in Roman society a festival called the *Amburbium*, which took place at the beginning of February and consisted of a procession around the city of Rome with lighted candles to purify it. Candles or other lights were also placed in graves with dead bodies, the thought being that they would have light in the next world! This was displaced by Pope Liberius in the fourth century with Candlemas. Candles were blessed in church and then taken on procession as a symbol of Christ as a light to lighten the Gentiles. As with all of these "Christian" holy days concocted by the papacy, with the passage of time there was assimilation with the pagan myths and practices which the church festivals were intended to displace.

It was commonplace in some areas to remove the winter evergreens such as holly and ivy on Candlemas Eve, replacing them with spring plants such as snowdrops. Miraculous powers came to be associated with the candles, so that they would be lit and kept burning during times of storms or illnesses or at a death. Candlemas was believed by some to be the lighting of a partially burned stick from the Yule log of Christmas, therefore considered to be the last farewell to Christmas. Linked with this was Mary's forty days of purification after she gave birth (Lev. 12:1–8) before she could offer a sacrifice in the Temple in Jerusalem, therefore with the assumption that the Lord was born on December 25, forty days later brings us to February 2–3 (Candlemas).

---

15. Dyer, *British Popular Customs*, 396.

When it came to Christianising the pagan festivals, the church encountered a particular problem with New Year and the varied forms of paganism which evolved from the Romans *Kalends* celebrations. Their attempts to change it proved less successful, as we shall see in a subsequent chapter on New Year. The earliest Christmas holidays were celebrated by drinking, sexual indulgence, singing naked in the streets (a precursor of modern carolling), etc. We conclude this section with a quote from an American historian. Stephen Nissenbaum, history professor at the University of Massachusetts, Amherst, writes,

> In return for ensuring massive observance of the anniversary of the Savior's birth by assigning it to this resonant date, the church for its part tacitly agreed to allow the holiday to be celebrated more or less the way it had always been.[16]

---

16. Nissenbaum, *Battle for Christmas*, 4.

Down the Centuries

T. K. Cheyne's *Encyclopædia Biblica* cites a famous learned Jesuit—A. Lupi—declaring in 1785 that there is not a single month in the year to which the Nativity has not been assigned by some writer or other.[1] This ought to remind us of the great ambiguity in establishing Christ's birth, an ambiguity purposed by God in his providential sovereignty.

The first date connected with the birth of the Lord Jesus, was not December 25 but January 6. The origin of this Epiphany festival is very obscure, neither can we say with certainty what its meaning was at first, the date probably having a pagan origin in connection with the birth of the world (the Egyptians celebrating the winter solstice on this date since 2000 BC). The Alexandrian Gnostic heretic—Basilides—teaching between 117 and 138 AD, and his followers, appear to be the first in the church to link this date with the Lord's birthday. Epiphany had come to be regarded as referring to two different events: the appearance of the wise men to worship Jesus and his appearance to be baptized in the Jordan River by John the Baptist, although it also alluded to his birth/nativity. (In the Greek Church to this day, Epiphany remains of greater significance than Christmas, and in the Armenian Church, December 25 is not recognized at all.)

Respecting the early church fathers, Irenaeus (130-202) from Polycarp's hometown of Smyrna in Asia Minor, Origen (184-254) from Alexandria in Egypt, and Tertullian (160-225) from Carthage, modern Tunisia, do not include Christmas or Epiphany, or their dates on their lists of feasts and celebrations (although Origen's teacher—Clement of Alexandria (d. 215)—recorded that some Christians believed Jesus to have been born in April). Tertullian (dogmatic in his belief that Christ had been crucified on March

---

1. Cheyne, *Encyclopædia Biblica*, 3:351, n. 1.

25, a date also believed by some to be the sixth day of Creation when Adam was made) rebuked Christians for partaking in pagan festivals.

Writing probably between 200 and 210, he states, "The Saturnalia, the feasts of January, the Brumalia and Matronalia, are now frequented; gifts are carried to and fro, new year's day presents are made with din and sports, and banquets are celebrated with uproar."[2] We do not know if those referred to were believers brought up as Christians or those who had more recently come into the church. In any event, they obviously were still attached to the prevailing festivals of paganism in their society. (Brumalia was the month-long pagan feast centered upon crop sowing that immediately preceded Saturnalia; Matronalia at the beginning of March, celebrated the goddess of childbirth.)

Origen, who spent the last twenty-five years of his life in Palestine, writing around 248, laments that in spite of Paul's criticism of believers in Galatia and elsewhere observing Jewish festal days, Christians were still "observing" different days such as Preparation, Passover, and Pentecost. There is, however, no mention of pagan days and Origen makes it clear that the most important day to be observed is the Lord's Day.[3] Sextus Julius Africanus (c. 160–240) was a Christian traveller and historian who wrote *Chronographiai* in 221, popularizing the belief that Christ was conceived on March 25 and therefore born on December 25. In coming decades this led some in the church to desire the recognition and celebration of December 25 as Christ's birthday, something that Origen emphatically denounced in 245, not on the basis of the date chosen but on the principle that such birthday celebrations lacked biblical warrant, as he said himself, as if Christ "were a king Pharaoh."[4] (Pharaoh and Herod being the only examples in the Bible where birthdays are recorded, both days characterized by murder: Gen 40:20; Matt 14:6.)

As we noted in the preceding chapter, in 313 Emperor Constantine legalized Christianity (he claimed to have been converted but his policies and lifestyle merely display a recognition of Christianity's importance in the politics of his empire, not of any saving change in his heart). Paganism was not banished but all religions tolerated. This legalization made it easier to establish universal dates of feasts and organize their celebration; indeed, some historians credit Constantine with replacing the pagan events on December 25 with what would later become known as Christmas or the Nativity.

---

2. Tertullian, *On Idolatry*, ch. 14.
3. Origen, *Against Celsus*, vol. 4, 8:32.
4. Origen, "Homily Eight," 156.

The Arch of Constantine I, Rome, built in 315 AD.

Constantine established the capital of the eastern part of the empire in Byzantium, which was renamed Constantinople in his honor. With the exception of Julian, who in 362 sought to displace Christianity and restore the empire's former power by embracing polytheism (including Mithraism), the subsequent emperors after Constantine all observed Christianity.

In the East, the concelebration of the two events of Christ's birth and baptism continued for some time after Rome had instituted the separate feast of Christmas. Gradually, however, as the church in Rome grew in its power and influence, the Roman use spread: at Constantinople, December 25 was introduced in about 380 by the theologian Gregory Nazianzen; at Antioch it appeared in 388; and at Alexandria in 432 (the church of Jerusalem refusing to adopt the new feast until the seventh century).

Moreover, the Arian controversy raging at this time over Christ's Divinity (debated in several convened councils, from Nicaea, just south of Constantinople in 325, to Constantinople in 381) may well have lead some believers to place an overemphasis on Christ's birth and the events surrounding it, as they sought to prove that he was truly man, truly God, and truly one. The Alexandrian school argued that Christ was the Divine Word made flesh (see John 1:14), while the Antioch school held that he was born human and infused with the Holy Spirit at the time of his baptism (see Mark 1:9–11). A feast celebrating Christ's birth gave the church an opportunity to promote the intermediate view that Christ was Divine from at least the time of his incarnation.

There are no extant records (minutes) of the Council of Nicaea and Constantine appears to have been the decision-maker. He decreed that Jesus was divine and coequal with God the Father. While his decision is theologically correct, one wonders if he made it in part because it suited him to merge Jesus with his sun-god!

We quote Schaff, whose source is Eusebius of Caesarea (c. 275–339):

> The moment the approach of the emperor was announced by a given signal, they all rose from their seats, and the emperor appeared like a heavenly messenger of God, covered with gold and gems, a glorious presence, very tall and slender, full of beauty, strength, and majesty. With this external adornment he united the spiritual ornament of the fear of God, modesty, and humility, which could be seen in his downcast eyes, his blushing face, the motion of his body, and his walk. When he reached the golden throne prepared for him, he stopped, and sat not down till the bishops gave him the sign. And after him they all resumed their seats. . . .
>
> There are supposed numerous accounts of the events of Nicea (the twenty Canones, the doctrinal Symbol, and a Decree of the Council of Nicaea, and several Letters of bishop Alexander of Alexandria and the emperor Constantine (all collected in Greek and Latin in Mansi: Collect. sacrorum Conciliorum, tom. ii. fol. 635–704). Official minutes of the transactions themselves were not at that time made; only the decrees as adopted were set down in writing and subscribed by all (comp. Euseb. Vita Const. iii. 14). All later accounts of voluminous acts of the council are sheer fabrications.[5]

The first reference to December 25 as a Christian feast day in ancient documents is in *The Chronography of 354* (also known as the *Calendar of 354*), which was an illustrated manuscript produced in 354 for a wealthy Roman Christian named Valentinus. The work refers to the year 336 when it was recognized by some that the birth of Christ took place in Bethlehem, Judea, on December 25.[6] Vatican records reveal that Christmas was instituted in Rome by Pope Liberius at some time during his period in office (352–366). Ambrose (340–397) records in a letter to his sister that when she was consecrated as a nun by Liberius on December 25, 360, he addressed her as follows: "Thou seest what multitudes are come to the birth-festival of thy bridegroom," which appears to imply the existence of the Christmas feast day.[7]

---

5. Schaff, *History of the Christian Church*, vol. 3, sec. 120.

6. "Part 12: Commemorations of the Martyrs," *The Chronography* of 354 AD, www.tertullian.org.

7. Ambrose, *De Virginibus*.

A few decades later it had become established in the eastern part of the church also. Writing in 400, John Chrysostom, from Antioch, who had become the chief or "arch" bishop of Constantinople, was aware of the date being associated with pagan gods but clearly saw no problem in adopting the date as a celebration of Jesus' supposed birthday, commenting:

> But Our Lord, too, is born in the month of December . . . the eight before the Kalends of January [December 25]. . . . But they call it the "Birthday of the Unconquered." Who indeed is so unconquered as Our Lord . . . ? Or, if they say that it is the birthday of the Sun, He is the Sun of Justice.[8]

Earlier in 386, he delivered the Christmas homily in his home town of Antioch on December 25 and called the festival, "the fundamental feast, or the root, from which all other Christian festivals grow forth."

Rome fell to the Barbarians in the fifth century and the Roman Empire in the west effectively came to an end (although continuing in the east for another millennium until falling to Sunni Muslim Turks in 1453). Its end began with the sacking of Rome by the Goths in 410. Into this vacuum, the papacy provided continuity with the past and continued to establish both religious and secular influence.

Pope Innocent I was followed by Pope Leo ("the Great"), who is credited with saving Rome from physical destruction by his diplomacy with Attila the Hun in 452 (the Huns being Eurasian nomads who had migrated west into Europe around 370 AD) and the Vandals (from North Africa) in 455. Pope Gelasius I was the first to take to himself the title, "Vicar of Christ," in 494 and he also invented St. Valentine's Day on February 14, in an attempt to combat the persistent legacy of the Roman festivals of *Lupercalia* and *Juno Februata*, the most sexually promiscuous of all the Roman festivals. Of great significance is the fact that the victorious Barbarians adopted Christianity (i.e., either Roman Catholicism or Arianism) as their own religion. The first to do so was Clovas I, king of the Franks who became a Roman Catholic in 492.

In 567, Pope John III called the Council of Tours, France, at which the celebration of Christmas in the West on December 25 was formally combined with the celebration of the Epiphany in the East on January 6, to form the "Twelve Days of Christmas."

At the Council of Mâcon (581) it enjoined that from Martinmas (November 11), the second, fourth, and sixth days of the week should be fasting days. At the close of the sixth century, Rome, under Pope Gregory ("the Great"), adopted the rule of the four Sundays in Advent.

---

8. Chrysostom, *del Solst. Et Æquin*, II, 118.

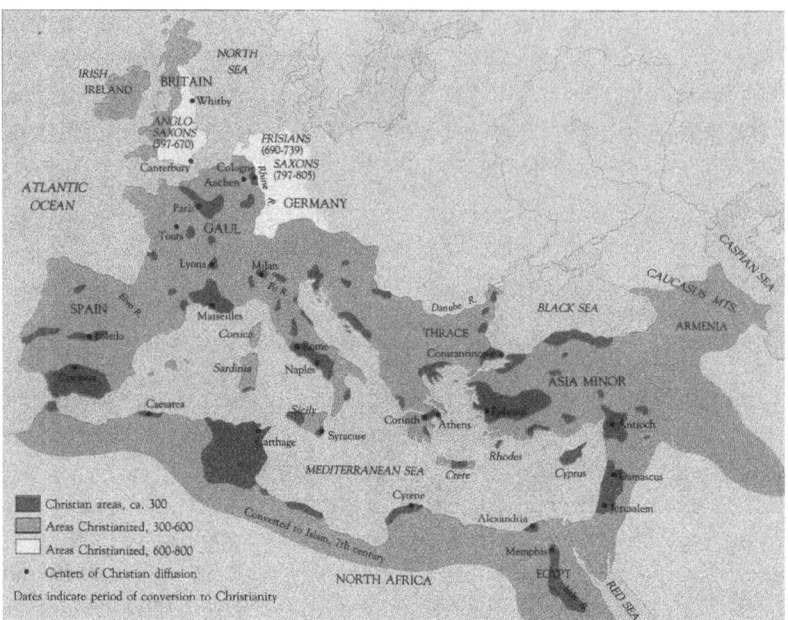

Augustine of Canterbury (not to be confused with Augustine of Hippo, N. Africa, 354–430), had been a Benedictine monk in Rome, when in 595 he was chosen by Pope Gregory I to Christianize England. Whether or not the Celtic Church further north had already introduced Christmas, Augustine certainly did. On Christmas Day 598, he is said to have witnessed the baptism of 10,000 converts to Christianity.

Christmas Day began to achieve Europe-wide prominence after Charlemagne's coronation as Holy Roman Emperor on December 25, 800, by Pope Leo III in Rome. Charlemagne was a Frank and inaugurated the Carolingian Dynasty, laying the foundations for the modern states of France and Germany. (The Holy Roman Empire encompassed the Netherlands, Belgium, Luxembourg, present-day Germany, western Poland, the Czech and Slovak Republics, Austria, Switzerland, as well as parts of eastern France, northern Italy, and Slovenia. It developed a complex legal and political structure. Its central figure was the emperor, whose position combined ancient Roman pretensions of universal and divinely sanctioned rule, with the Germanic tradition of elected kingship. By 1600 it was a mere shadow of its former glory, as its German heartland had been split into a mass of princes and states. It would continue in name until 1806 when it and its coalition of states were defeated by Napoleon.)

In Germany, Christmas was formally established by the Synod of Mainz in 813.

The synod or Council of Chelsea in 816 was called by the King of Mercia (the kingdom of Mercia incorporating all of Britain south of the Humber, minus Wales and the west of Cornwall). The Council enforced the observance of Christmas on December 25, this date formerly being called "Mothers Night," a vigil in honor of the rebirth of the new sun. King Edmund the Martyr (of East Anglia) was anointed on Christmas Day in 855.

By the ninth century, priests, deacons, and choirs with antiphonal singing were acting the parts of the magi and shepherds during mass on Christmas Day, some churches even suspending a star from the roof which was then pulled to make it move!

Around 950, Christmas was adopted in Norway by King Hakon the Good. There had existed a pagan Yule feast that had been celebrated in the eighth century, if not earlier, and occurred in mid-January throughout most of Scandinavia. King Hakon transferred it to December 25th. King Æthelred of England, who reigned from 978 to 1016, ordained in his laws that Christmas was to be a time of peace and concord among Christian men, when all strife must cease. King William I of England ("the Conqueror") was crowned on Christmas Day 1066. The anglicized word Christmas, a contraction of "Christ's mass," first appeared in writing in 1038 but did not assume common usage in Britain until after the Norman invasion. Prior to that, the festival was always referred to as "In Festis Nativitatis," the Feast of the Nativity. (It has also been called Noël or Nowel. As to the derivation of the word Noël, some say it is a contraction of the French *nouvelles* (tidings), *les bonnes nouvelles*; that is, "The good news of the Gospel"; others take it as an abbreviation of the Gascon or Provençal *nadaü, nadal*, which means the same as the Latin *natalis*; that is, *dies natalis*, "the birthday." Others say Noël is a corruption of *Yule, Jule*, or *Ule*, meaning, "The festival of the sun." The name *Yule* is still applied to the festival in Scotland and some other places. Christmas is represented in Welsh by *Nadolig*, which signifies "the natal, or birth" and in Italian by *Il Natale*, which, together with its cognate term in Spanish, is simply a contraction of *dies natalis*, "the birthday.")

In central Italy, St. Francis of Assisi in 1223 held a midnight mass on Christmas Eve with a nativity scene and live animals. The people in the plays sang songs or "canticles" that told the story during the plays. Although generally credited as being the first nativity play, as we have noted above, something similar had occurred in earlier centuries.

However, where biblical truths from the Apostolic era had been retained, in isolated groups in the region of the Alps such as those who subsequently became known as the Albigenses and Waldenses, Christmas was rejected. This became evident during the Inquisition by Rome, set up by

Pope Innocent III around 1200 and initially enforced by Pope Gregory IX in 1233, in order to identify and eradicate "heretics."

A Romish Inquisitor, in speaking of the Waldenses, tells us:

> They . . . affirm that the traditions of the church are no better than the traditions of the Pharisees, insisting, moreover, that greater stress is laid on the observance of human tradition than on the keeping of the law of God.

Seisselius, Archbishop of Turin, states:

> They receive only what is written in the Old and New Testaments.

Reinerius Saccho, who provided condemning evidence against them to the Inquisition in a 1254 report entitled, "Of the Sects of the Modern Heretics," reports:

> Whatever is preached that is not substantiated by the text of the Bible they esteem fables. They hold that none of the ordinances of the church which have been introduced since Christ's ascension ought to be observed, as being of no value.[9]

The French Inquisitor Bernard Gui, writing in 1320, sweepingly describes the Waldenses as having rejected all the traditions of the Roman Catholic Church, namely ecclesiastical authority, especially by their conviction that they were not subject to the pope or his decrees of excommunication. He goes on to complain how all Catholic feast-days, festivals, and prayers were rejected by them as man-made and not based upon the New Testament.[10]

King Richard II of England hosted a Christmas feast in 1377, at which twenty-eight oxen and three hundred sheep were eaten. "Misrule," with drunkenness, promiscuity, and gambling, remained an important aspect of the festival.

Some of the customs of the Saturnalia carnival appear to have been transferred into Carnival in February, first celebrated in the thirteenth century and commencing after Candlemas is over (although in some countries such as Germany and the Netherlands, it commences at Martinmas in November). It is largely a Roman Catholic or Orthodox festival. The selection of modern Venetian Carnival masks, shows one feature of Carnival which remains to this day with its spread globally, which is that of "masking," often as part of cross-dressing.

---

9. Armitage, *History of Baptists*, 308.
10. Finucane, "Waldensians," 316.

We noted above how the practice of parading naked in the streets formed a part of Saturnalia, whether the act was voluntary or forced at the behest of the Lord of Misrule. As part of Carnival, the Mardi Gras commences on Epiphany or the Twelfth Night (January 6 when traditionally all Christmas decorations are to be removed). Mardi Gras is French for "Fat Tuesday" and is synonymous for parades, immorality, and excessive partying and feasting immediately before the fasting period of Lent commences. We noted that in the Saturnalia, binge eating, including by force, was also an intrinsic part of the festival. In any event, in Rome in 1466 during Carnival, Pope Paul II forced Jews to run naked along the main street, the *Via Lata*, for the entertainment of non-Jews. An eyewitness account reports:

> Before they were to run, the Jews were richly fed, so as to make the race more difficult for them and at the same time more amusing for spectators. They ran . . . amid Rome's taunting shrieks and peals of laughter, while the Holy Father stood upon a richly ornamented balcony and laughed heartily.[11]

(Interestingly, as part of the Carnival throughout the eighteenth and nineteenth centuries, Jewish rabbis of the ghetto in Rome were forced to wear clownish outfits and march through the city streets to the jeers of the crowd, pelted by a variety of missiles. When the Jewish community of Rome sent a petition in 1836 to Pope Gregory XVI, begging him to stop this annual abuse of the Jewish community, he responded, "It is not opportune to make any innovation.")[12]

---

11. Pastor, *History of the Popes*, 4:16, 20.
12. Kertzer, *Popes Against the Jews*, 74.

By 1500 the festival of Christmas was firmly established wherever the Roman Catholic Church held sway, including in Scotland. The annual indulgence in eating, dancing, singing, sporting, and card playing escalated in England and by the seventeenth century, the Christmas season featured lavish dinners, elaborate masques, and pageants.

Following his protest in 1517 and with that the initializing of the Reformation, Luther in subsequent years saw little problem with Christmas and very much encouraged the celebration. Luther appeared initially to take a unified stance with Calvinists against holy days, writing in 1520 in his "Address to the Nobility of the German Nation:"

> One should abolish all festivals, retaining only the Lord's Day.
> But if it were desired to keep the festivals of Our Lady and the greater saints, they should all be held on Sundays, or only in the morning with the mass; the rest of the day being a working day. My reason is this: with our present abuses of drinking, gambling, idling, and all manner of sin, we vex God more on holy days than on others. And the matter is just reversed; we have made holy days unholy, and working days holy, and do no service; but great dishonor, to God and his saints will all our holy days. There are some foolish prelates that think they have done a good deed, if they establish a festival to St. Otilia or St. Barbara, and the like, each in his own blind fashion, whilst he

would be doing a much better work to turn a saint's day into a working day in honor of a saint.[13]

However, Luther's reasoning appears to have been motivated by pragmatism in order to counter "the present abuses" he identified.

Excursus on Lutheranism

Standing on the doctrine of *sola Scriptura*, Martin Luther (1483–1546) was very successful at eliminating many of the perverse teachings of Romanism (e.g., the Roman Catholic mass, auricular confession, pilgrimages, the saints as mediators, the sacerdotal priesthood, etc.). As Brian Schwertley suggests, unfortunately, perhaps as a result of his conservative personality, or his comfort with medieval style worship, or even a simple error in logic, he never made the connection between Scripture alone and the need of Divine warrant for worship ordinances, in the way that Calvin and others did. Luther held that human traditions in worship are valuable and should be respected as long as they do not contradict the Bible. In other words, only rites and ceremonies that are expressly forbidden by Scripture should be disallowed. As a result of the inconsistent application of *sola Scriptura* to only some matters relating to worship, the Lutherans retained many ceremonies, rites, and practices that were not derived from the Bible. It is then hardly surprising that a large portion of the ceremonial, ritualistic, and governmental structures of the Roman Catholic Church manifested themselves in Lutheranism. For whatever reason, Luther and his successors seem not to have realized that the very structures they were retaining, were the original causes of the historical corruption in the church against which Luther had rebelled in the first place![14]

The Anglican or Episcopal Church also gave the church the power to decide and establish ecclesiastical rites and ceremonies not derived from Scripture. While in many ways the Lutheran and Anglican churches became a vast improvement over Rome (e.g., regarding justification by faith alone), they both denied the absolute authority of Scripture in the area of worship.

Fifty years before Luther, the first ever Protestant Church (the Moravians), led by Jan Hus (John Huss, 1370–1415) also tolerated Christmas. *Der Haus-Christ*, meaning "the House Christ," was a term used in sixteenth century Germany for the gift-bringer. German Protestants, who wished to abolish the Catholic cult of saints, needed a replacement for St. Nicholas as the traditional bearer of presents at Christmas. Clergymen chose to speak of

---

13. Luther, "Open Letter to the Christian Nobility," 127.
14. www.reformedonline.com/uploads/1/5/0/3/15030584/chapter_1_christmas.pdf.

Christ himself as the bringer of good things at Christmas and his collection of gifts as the "Christ-bundle." This shows how Protestants recognized the pagan roots of the gift-giving practice during the Reformation. However, rather than abandoning the pagan practice, some chose to attempt to "Christianize" it. Ironically, this is exactly what the Roman Catholic Church had done twelve centuries earlier. The Reformers were condemning the Roman church for incorporating paganism into the church, but some of the Reformers themselves were unwilling to completely walk away from the cult-like behavior.

In Zurich, Zwingli abolished the vast majority of the Roman Catholic holy days but several, including Christmas, were retained. William Farel (1489–1585) arrived in Geneva (pictured) in 1532 and ministered there as a Reformed pastor with Peter Viret (1511–1571). Calvin joined Farel in 1536 and both sought to move the city toward a more biblical lifestyle.

Farel instigated a ban on all holy days, including Christmas, which caused uproar in the city. In so doing, he followed the example of Martin Bucer in Strasbourg, two hundred miles to the north. Bucer had assumed leadership of the Reformation there in 1529, and in 1535 he eliminated all holy days from the church calendar, except the weekly Lord's Day.[15]

Calvin supported Farel but adopted a more conciliatory approach to the matter, declaring that "little will be said about ceremonies before the judgement-seat of God."

There was a struggle between those who wanted the magistrates firmly in control of the clergy and others, like Calvin, who wanted a city where the clergy were free to preach what they wanted from the pulpit and administer the sacraments as they wished.

Matters came to a head over several practical issues demanded by the Council, including the reintroduction of Christmas and other holy days. In 1538, Geneva's city elections resulted in a demand to the pastors to imitate Bern (where Bernhold Haller and then Caspar Hedio pastored) and re-adopt Christmas and other holy days, among other things. Calvin and

---

15. Manetsch, *Calvin's Company*, 125.

others refused to comply with what they viewed as unwarranted interference in spiritual matters.

After they ignored an order banning them from their pulpits, in April 1538 Farel and Calvin were forced by the Council to leave the city, which they did, going to Strasbourg (pictured). It was there, while agreeing to pastor a group of French refugees, that Calvin experienced the power of congregational song on a regular basis, which stimulated his preparation of a complete French psalter.

Farel never returned to Geneva, ministering in Strasbourg and Neufchatel, but Calvin returned for an intended stay of a week in 1541 and to great acclaim from most in the city, only to remain there for the rest of his life!

Calvin progressively endeared himself and his teaching to the influential families in the city and Geneva's City Council became increasingly Reformed. The functions of the church in Geneva and its relationship to the state were embodied in the Ecclesiastical Ordinances, which were officially adopted and promulgated by the General Council on November 20, 1541. Calvin insisted that the Lord's Day was the Christian's true holiday. In 1545 and after much campaigning, the Genevan Company of Pastors persuaded the magistrates to follow Bucer's example in Strasbourg, outlawing all holy days. They feared that the retention of days such as Christmas would reinforce the long-standing superstition as to the sacred value of certain days and seasons.[16]

According to the *Register of the Company of Pastors*, in 1546, Calvin and his fellow pastors issued an edict to the effect that "those who observe the Romish festivals or fasts shall only be reprimanded, unless [i.e., if] they remain

16. Ibid.

obstinately rebellious."[17] On Sunday, November 16, 1550, an edict was issued by the pastors reaffirming a ban on holy days: "Respecting the abrogation of all festivals, with the exception of Sundays, which God had ordained." Holy days were to be treated as a normal working day.

A church member in Geneva, Antoine Cadran, was suspended from the Lord's Table for "impertinence and lies," for maintaining that Geneva was wrong for not practicing Christmas, which, he maintained, was a mandatory requirement of Scripture as a commemoration of Noah's flood! It had been the custom to hold the Lord's Supper four times a year, including on Christmas Day, but this was now changed and moved to the Sunday closest to December 25.[18]

Calvin was more relaxed on the issue of holy days than Farel or Bucer. He and others viewed the "evangelical feast days,"[19] as they called them, not as a part of the Christian's accomplishment of his or her salvation, as viewed by the Church of Rome, but as celebrations of the salvation that Christ had already accomplished for them in his incarnation (Christmas), death (Good Friday), resurrection (Easter), ascending to the Father (Ascension), and giving of his Spirit (Pentecost). He subsequently recommended that Christmas Day be observed in the morning only and that shops and trades resumed work as normal in the afternoon. These views are expressed in two different letters he sent, one from Geneva, dated January 2, 1551, to John Haller, pastor in Bern (previously an understudy to Bullinger in Zurich),[20] and the other from Lausanne, dated March 1555, to the leaders of Bern.[21] However, although Calvin permitted the retention of Good Friday, Easter, Pentecost, and Ascension, the Council of Geneva disagreed with him and subsequently reintroduced the ban on all these "holy days" once again. Although the Council, during and after Calvin's life, sought at times to reintroduce former practices, including reintroducing holidays such as Christmas into the church calendar, the Company of Pastors consistently rebuffed the attempts.[22]

Calvin's Commentaries on the Bible are appreciated the world over; however, we only have them because he did so much consecutive preaching, selecting a Bible book then preaching through it week by week, chapter by chapter, and verse by verse. One of the benefits that Calvin received

---

17. Hughes, *Register of the Company of Pastors*, 66.
18. Manetsch, *Calvin's Company*, 125.
19. Nichols, *Corporate Worship*, 100.
20. Calvin, *Selected Works*, 5:299–300 (no known relation to Bern's Reformer Bernhold Heller referred to earlier).
21. Ibid., vol. 6, part 3, 162–69.
22. Manetsch, *Calvin's Company*, 301.

in Geneva was the appointment of a stenographer to record his sermons. As Calvin worked his way slowly and systematically through one book of the Bible at a time, he produced 123 sermons on Genesis, 200 sermons on Deuteronomy, 159 sermons on Job, 176 sermons on First and Second Corinthians, and 43 sermons on Galatians.[23] Often, each year when it came to December 25, Calvin did not take a break from the book he was preaching through but continued unabated, irrespective of how relevant or irrelevant the verses were to Christ's birth.

Following Calvin's death in 1564, there was growing pressure from the Genevan population to reinstate holy days, including Christmas. This occurred in the context of a Roman Catholic resurgence that had a significant military dimension to it.

The Second Helvetic Confession (1566), composed by Heinrich Bullinger (Zwingli's successor in Zurich) and received by many Reformed churches, did not disapprove of Christmas, leaving it as a matter of liberty of conscience for churches to decide.

Theodore Beza (Calvin's successor in Geneva who visited Zurich to liaise with Bullinger in compiling the *Confession*) wrote to Knox, requesting Scottish approval for the *Confession*. The General Assembly in Scotland replied with a letter of "general" approval. Nevertheless, the

> Assembly could scarcely refrain from mentioning, with regard to what is written in the 24th chapter of the aforesaid *Confession* concerning the "festival of our Lord's nativity, circumcision, passion, resurrection, ascension, and sending the Holy Ghost upon his disciples," that these festivals at the present time obtain no place among us; for we dare not religiously celebrate any other feast-day than what the divine oracles prescribed.[24]

The Dutch Reformed churches had been in the habit of keeping Christmas, Easter, and Whitsuntide (Pentecost) as days of religious worship. The Provincial Synod of Dort, 1574, enjoined the churches to do this no longer, but to be satisfied with Sundays only for divine service. One common factor that the Reformers constantly had to address was the attitude of the populace and the secular governments, who desired and stipulated respectively that certain feast days such as Christmas had to be observed. This often was not the preference of the church, but the church had to accommodate itself to the secular authority (another upshot of the unnatural relationship between church and state created by Rome).

23. Old, *Worship*, 75.
24. Knox, *Works*, 6:547. See "Excursus on Geneva and Zurich" in the penultimate chapter "Twelve Reasons Justifying the Endorsement of Christmas."

In April 1605, the two-hundred strong Genevan Council requested the Company of Pastors to clarify their view respecting Christmas reinstatement. The Company responded by rejecting any such reinstatement and appealing to the happy memory of Calvin. They warned that the reinstatement of religious festivals would cause scandal and give the impression that Geneva was sliding back toward the Papal Church.[25]

This tension over holy days is evidenced by the following quote from the Dutch Calvinist theologian, Gisbert Voetius (1589–1676), in 1659 on Christmas and Good Friday:

> Such articles are not characteristic or intrinsic or voluntary impulses proceeding from the heart of the church; but occasional, extrinsic (just as an eclipse is a characteristic phenomenon of the moon), imposed from the outside, burdensome to the churches, in and of themselves and in an absolute sense unwelcome. Synods were summoned, compelled and coerced to receive, bring in and admit these articles, as in the manner of a transaction, in order to prevent worse disagreeable and bad situations. . . .
>
> Synods did not willingly furnish or institute [the annual observance of days] because they saw in them a better way or more edification. But they were instituted because of the necessity and imposition of them by the magistrate and the people, when after all attempts at stopping the observances, and the decree of Synod of 1574 to lay them aside, at a certain point of time they were not able to abrogate them—a fact they admitted in 1578.[26]

Francis Turretin (1623–1687), the acclaimed Reformed theologian in Geneva did not oppose Christmas, adopting a similar view to Bullinger. Both on the continent and in Britain, a struggle was emerging in Protestantism between those who viewed holy days as positively unscriptural and those who viewed them as convenient. The Anglican Church (in large part an artificial creation by Henry VIII to facilitate the success of his marital aspirations) also retained Christmas. As we noted in the Lutheran excursus above, although it developed a Protestant theology, the Anglican Church kept much of Roman Catholic liturgy, including festivals celebrating aspects of Christ's life and the feast days of many saints. It gave special emphasis to the celebration of Christmas. In a subsequent chapter, we focus more closely on the attitude to Christmas in the church in Britain. The sixteenth and seventeenth centuries produced many Christmas hymns in German. Among the most famous is, "Fröhlich soll mein Herze springen" ("All My Heart This

---

25. Manetsch, *Calvin's Company*, 127.
26. Voetius, *De Sabbatho et Festis*, app. 2.

Night Rejoices"), which was written by Paul Gerhardt (1607–1676). In addition, music by Johann Sebastian Bach (1685–1750), George Frideric Handel (1685–1759), and Felix Mendelssohn (1809–1847) was adapted and used in Christmas carols. As an aside, the term "carol" is derived from Latin and from the old French "carole" meaning a circle-dance. In the Middle Ages, the use of these dance songs expanded in the religious realm as processional songs at Roman Catholic festivals. Their use fell into sharp decline following the Reformation, until being revived again in the nineteenth century by prominent composers.

In colonial America, the practice of Christmas all depended on the origin of the settlers. Those from Puritan England banned it and so it was outlawed in Boston from 1659 to 1681. The ban by the Pilgrims was only revoked in 1681 by an English governor and it was not until the 1850s that celebrating Christmas became fashionable in the Boston region. In contrast, other parts such as New York, Pennsylvania, and North Carolina, that were predominantly Moravian, openly kept the festival.

Rev. Increase Mather of Boston observed in 1687 the metamorphoses of the pagan holiday into a Christian one, in a pamphlet he published criticizing Christmas in his own day, *A Testimony against Several Prophane and Superstitious Customs Now Practiced by Some in New England*. During the seventeenth and well into the eighteenth century, most New England congregations used the so-called *Bay Psalm Book*, a rhymed version of the Old Testament Psalms, with additional hymns taken from various biblical sources (this was the first book published in New England). None of these hymns dealt with the Christmas story. By the 1750s, however, the *Bay Psalm Book* had largely been replaced in New England churches by a pair of new verse translations of the Psalms, both of which contained Christmas hymns. Between 1760 and 1799, at least thirty different Christmas songs were published in New England. Yet Christmas was still not that popular in colonial America in comparison to parts of Europe, especially Germany and Bohemia/Moravia (modern Czech Republic). This was illustrated during the American Revolution of 1765–1783. The British had hired thirty thousand troops from the Hesse region of Germany to increase their military might. On December 26, 1776, George Washington launched a major offensive against Hessian troops in New Jersey. Central to the choice of the date to attack was the belief that the German troops would be intoxicated and drowsy after their zealous celebrations of the previous day!

New Year

DIFFERENT CULTURES AND SOCIETIES have always adopted different calendars, as they do today, and so the commencement of the New Year has always varied (from spring, to autumn, to winter). The ancient pagans believed that the world operated within an eternal framework of oscillating and recurring cycles. Some early cultures such as the Sumerian, Indian, and Chinese, universally held to the notion of never-ending, repeating, cyclic time. The Babylonians, Persians, and Greeks all held to 36,000 year cycles while the Hindus believed that the cycles were as long as 4.3 million years. The Mayans (Central America) taught that the world had been created, destroyed, and recreated at least four times, with the last recreation occurring on February 5, 3112 BC. The pagans understood time as a circle rather than an arrow. The earliest recorded New Year celebration is in Mesopotamia in Abraham's day, when the vernal equinox (equal day and night) of mid-March was used. The Israelites' New Year commenced in late September/early October, as did the Egyptians, Phoenicians, and Persians. Later, the Greeks recognized it at the winter solstice (December 21/22).

There is, of course, no biblical warrant for a religious commemoration of the New Year. Some of the same principled reasons that find fault with Christians endorsing Christmas in a religious sense could equally be applied to an overtly religious endorsement of New Year.

The Romans gave each other New Year gifts of branches from sacred trees. In later years, they gave gold-covered nuts or coins imprinted with pictures of Janus, the god of gates, doors, and beginnings. January was named after Janus, who had two faces—one looking forward and the other looking backward. By the Roman Republican calendar, the year began on March 1; after 153 BC the official date was January 1 and this was confirmed by the Julian calendar in 46 BC, named after Julius Caesar. It was at the Council of Tours in 567 that the Roman Catholic Church abolished January 1 in favor of different days during the subsequent centuries (March 1st; March 25; December 25, and Easter). For most of the following millennium, March 25 was used and also called Lady Day in honor of Mary and the annunciation (we noted in the preceding chapter, the link between March 25 and December 25). The Gregorian calendar, named after Pope Gregory XIII, was introduced in 1582 as it was more accurate (only one day out every 3,236 years, while the Julian calendar was one day out every 128 years). It was immediately adopted by Roman Catholic nations. Countries with less Roman Catholic influence gradually followed suit: Scotland in 1660; Germany and Denmark about 1700; England in 1752; Sweden in 1753; and Russia in 1918. This new calendar changed the commencement of the New Year back to January 1.

Kalends, the Roman New Year festival, began on January 1 and lasted until January 5. The Romans celebrated Kalends in much the same way they did Saturnalia. Early Christian writers condemned the carousing crowds. Nevertheless, some of the customs associated with Kalends were eventually absorbed into the celebration of Christmas. Called "kalends" (or "calends"), the Romans also used this word to refer to the first day of each month, within the framework of lunar phases. On this day, Roman officials posted the calendar for each month. The English word "calendar" comes from the old Latin term "kalends." New consuls were inducted into office and for at least three days high festival was kept. The houses were decorated with lights and greenery, another precursor to the modern Christmas tree. As at the Saturnalia, masters drank and gambled with slaves. *Vota*, or solemn wishes of prosperity for the Emperor during the New Year, were customary and the people and the Senate were even expected to present gifts of money to him.

Emperor Caligula (ruling 37–41 AD) excited much disgust by publishing an edict requiring these gifts and by standing on the porch of his palace to receive them in person. Such gifts, not only presented to the emperor, but frequently exchanged between private persons were called *strenae*, a name still surviving in the French étrennes (New Years presents). A sprig of greenery taken from the groves dedicated to the goddess Strenia was considered a very traditional gift. Later, the Romans added cakes and honey (symbolizing a sweet New Year), and coins (symbolizing wealth) to the roster of traditional

New Year gifts. Feasting, drinking, and merrymaking rounded out the festival. Kalends Eve celebrations resembled our own New Year's Eve festivities. A fourth century Greek scholar named Libanius (314–393) wrote that almost everyone stayed up on Kalends Eve to usher in the New Year with drinking, singing, and revelry. Instead of spending the evening at home, crowds of people roamed through the streets, returning to their houses near daybreak to sleep off the night's overindulgence. Sound familiar?

It will, therefore, be no surprise to discover that the present day Scottish traditions of Hogmany, staying up to "the bells" at midnight and New Year's Day feasts, are no modern invention but mirror very closely the pagan practices in Roman times.

Indeed, the feast of Saturnalia and the Roman Kalends festival of New Year had only two days between them, and over time the customs of each became intertwined.

The Roman Catholic Church established the Feast of Mary, the Mother of God, on New Year's Day. Moreover, on the same day, the Anglican and Lutheran churches celebrate the Feast of the Circumcision of Christ (based on the belief that if Jesus was born on December 25, then his circumcision on the eighth day of his life (Luke 2:21) was on January 1/2).

However, in spite of these new "Christian" holy days the church found itself unable to root out of people the immoral practices of Kalends, which is not a surprise given that the vast majority of those under Roman Catholic influence were not new creatures in Christ, changed within by the Holy Spirit but merely those who acknowledged the church's religion outwardly. With the prominence given to Christmas, what happened over time was that most of the Kalends practices transferred into the Christmas festivities. The church's recorded denunciations of such pagan festal practices are numerous, ranging in date from the fourth century to the eleventh and coming from Spain, Italy, Antioch, northern Africa, Constantinople, Germany, England, and various districts of what is now France. Attempts were made to root the practices out by making the first three days of the year a solemn fast with litanies (set, audible prayers, often chanted in processions). What disturbed the church most was the continued Kalends practices of cross-dressing, dressing as animals with animal skins and heads, auguries (interpreting the will of the gods by examining flight patterns of birds), the superstitions about fire, the giving of presents, and the excess of feasting, drunkenness, and general riot.

In a letter written in 742 by St. Boniface (born in England but missionary to Germany where he remains Germany's patron saint) to Pope Zacharias, Boniface complained that certain:

> Alamanni, Bavarians and Franks refused to give up various heathen practices because they had seen such things done in the sacred city of Rome, close to St. Peter's and as they deemed, with the sanction of the clergy. On New Year's Eve, it was alleged, processions went through the streets of Rome with impious songs and heathen cries, tables of fortune were set up and at that time no one would lend fire or iron or any other useful article to his neighbour.
>
> They recount also that they have seen women wearing pagan amulets and bracelets on their arms and legs and offering them for sale.[1]

The Pope replied that these things were odious to him, should be so to all Christians and so in 743, all such practices at the January Kalends were formally forbidden by the Council of Rome. Most of the customs associated with either the modern New Year or the Roman one were anticipated by earlier festivals. As noted earlier, many of the Kalends practices shifted to Christmas. Most of the observances surrounding New Year rest on the principle that "a good beginning makes a good ending," that as the first day is, so will the rest be. For example, if you would have plenty to eat during the year, dine lavishly on New Year's Day, or if you would be rich, see that your pockets are not empty at this critical season. This is by no means exclusive to Europeans but is common among Hindus also. To this day in Scotland, visitors on New Year's Day would be considered rude not to bring a gift with them.

Many ancient peoples performed rituals to do away with the past and purify themselves for the New Year. For example, some people put out fires they were using and started new ones (hence the Scottish custom for

---

1. Tangl, *Letters of Saint Boniface*, 50.

"first-footers" to bring with them a piece of coal as a gift). The Celts (as we noted earlier) celebrated the New Year (Samhain) on November 1, marking the end of summer and the harvest and the beginning of the cold, dark winter ahead (this was a precursor to Halloween). They built "sacred" bonfires to scare off evil spirits and to honor their sun god. Throughout Britain even to recent times, pagan superstitions lay behind many odd traditions and rituals. For many centuries among Slavs, the first visitor to one's house on Christmas Day was considered very important and may be compared with "first-footing" in Scotland on January 1. The character of the first visitor was believed to determine the welfare of the household throughout the coming year and the superstitions surrounding the event are many and varied in number from region to region. Due to the fact that Christmas was abolished in Scotland during the late sixteenth century, New Year assumed a greater significance in Scotland than in probably any other European country. It is only through the spread of Anglicanism, the resurgence of Roman Catholicism, and the demise of Protestant Church attendance throughout the twentieth century, that Christmas has come to rival New Year in popularity.

Historical Basis of Christmas in Modern Britain[1]

We have noted the development of Christmas in Britain during the Middle Ages under the guidance of the Roman Catholic Church. We now want to trace its course into the modern world, commencing with its examination upon the rediscovery of scriptural truth at the Reformation.

The reign of Elizabeth I (1558–1603) provides a point of cohesion for evaluating the Reformation in England but only because of its longevity, rather than the ease of widespread generalizations. We quote at length the comments of the historian Christopher Haigh:

> With a reign that lasted over four decades, Elizabeth accomplished what neither of her predecessors could do: she enforced a politico-religious vision. Her methods were not markedly different than any tried before but she incorporated a sensitivity to opposing forces that Edward VI and Mary had not granted.
>
> Her success, originally political and then slowly religious, resulted as much from this approach and her devotion to uniting the realm as it did from her longevity; had she died after five or six years, like her predecessors Edward VI and Mary, indeterminacy would likely have reigned again.

---

1. We give attention to the development of Christmas in North America in Reason 8 in the penultimate chapter, "Twelve Reasons Justifying the Endorsement of Christmas."

Elizabeth clearly sought to reverse the Marian religious direction, yet competing for her attention and consequently her care in theological decisions, was a fractured domestic scene and tenuous foreign relationships. England was still at war with France and allied with Spain, both Catholic states.

The French were supporting Mary Stuart's rival claim to the English throne and, if needed, Elizabeth could tap Lutheran states as prospective allies to ward off potential French aggression. Her personal theological preferences; some favoring Protestant thinking, some favoring Catholic ritual, helped shape the religious settlement she fashioned in 1558–59 and the resulting, enduring Anglican Church.

As an institution, the church's favorable acceptance of the principles of adiaphora (things indifferent) and via media (a middle way), allowed religious liberty and toleration to manifest themselves as never before welcomed. Anglicanism was English, patriotic and not firmly Calvinist. It rejected what was, in its eyes, the bibliolatry of the hard-line Protestant in favor of a more broadly based appeal to tradition, reason, and history, as well as Scripture. It embraced adiaphora and came to tolerate various church polities. By the mid-1550s these values formed the seeds of seventeenth century English Congregationalism and Independency. These ideas emerged both in the exiled congregations, especially at Frankfurt, and in the remaining underground Protestant congregations in England. This religious atmosphere had profound historical consequences as it allowed the growth of various nonconformist groups and the development of Puritan thought, which itself would create an atmosphere conducive to political developments that likely would not have happened in a Catholic society. In the 1560s, London became the center of a movement to accomplish a truly reformed church.

Despite its accomplishments, Elizabeth's broadly accommodating church had not completely satisfied the urge to purify the church and nowhere was this unquenched thirst for purification felt more strongly than in London. In reaction to Elizabeth's compromises, viewed as unacceptable and even threatening to those with strong Protestant convictions, the godly moved among parishes seeking one that was more than half-reformed. Puritan movements and separatist tendencies found vitality among the varieties of faith in the city. Believers now faced choices, not only about how to reach salvation, but where, and with whom they could consciously commune. It effected a shift from a religion of symbol and allegory, ceremony and formal gesture to one that was plain and direct: a shift from the visual to the aural, from ritual to literal exposition, from the numinous and mysterious to the everyday. It moved from the high colors of statue, window and painted walls to whitewash; from ornate vestments and altar frontal to plain tablecloth and surplice; from a religion that, with baptismal salt on lips, anointings and frankincense as well as image, word and chant, sought out all the senses, to one that concentrated on the word and innerliness.

There was a shift from a religion that often went out of doors on pilgrimage and procession to an indoor one; from the sacral and churchly to the familial and domestic; from sacrament to word; from the objectivity of ex opere operato and Real Presence, for instance, to the subjectivity of feeling faith and experience. Consequently, the Reformation had produced a Protestant nation, but not immediately a nation of Protestants. Catholic behaviours and doctrines had been removed from worship via political statute but Catholic views of life and salvation took time to die out.[2]

In *Anatomy of the Abuses in England in Shakespeare's Youth* by the Cheshire Calvinist, Philip Stubbes, first published in 1583, he bewails the vain pastimes of the Christmas season.

2. Haigh, *English Reformations*, 20–21.

"Especially," he says, "in Christmas time, there is nothing else used but cards, dice, tables, masking, mumming, bowling, and such like fooleries; and the reason is, that they think they have a commission and prerogative at that time to do what they want, and to follow what vanity they will. But (alas!) do they think that they are privileged at that time to do evil? The holier the time is (if one time were holier than another, as it is not), the holier ought their exercises to be. Can any time dispense with them, or give them liberty to sin? No, no; the soul which sins shall die, at whatever time it offends . . . Notwithstanding, who knows not that more mischief is at that time committed than in all the year besides?"[3]

During the Elizabethan Period poets wrote carols of a more polished character but still dealt with the life of the Christ Child. One of the best known of this era would be Nahum Tate's "While Shepherds Watched Their Flocks." This work was more of a transitional piece from true carols to hymns and paved the way for such Methodist Revival hymns as "Hark The Herald Angels Sing," "Angels From the Realms of Glory," or "It Came Upon the Midnight Clear." These were made widespread over the years by careful editors and enterprising publishers. On Christmas Day in England, these and other carols took the place of psalms in the churches, especially at afternoon service with the congregation joining in. At the end of the service the parish clerk would usually declare in a loud voice his wishes for "a Merry Christmas and a Happy New Year."

Puritan Era

When the Puritans had gained the upper hand they proceeded with the suppression not only of seasonal abuses but of the season itself. On September 2, 1642, the largely Puritan Parliament outlawed the performance of plays, including Christmas pageants and plays, and the theaters were closed.[4] On June 12, 1643, Parliament abolished the offices of Archbishops, Bishops, their Chancellors, Commissaries, Deans, Deans and Chapters, Archdeacons, declaring "and other Ecclesiastical Officers depending upon the Hierarchy, is evil, and justly offensive and burthensome to the Kingdome."[5]

---

3. Stubbes, *Anatomy of Abuses*, 173.
4. Firth and Rait, *Acts and Ordinances*, 1:26–27.
5. Ibid., 180–84.

On August 26, 1643, legislation was passed which included a bill entitled, "An Ordinance for the utter demolishing, removing and taking away of all Monuments of Superstition or Idolatry."

The aim was to facilitate an improved observation of the Lord's Day, and thereby the "better advancement of preaching God's Holy Word in all parts of the kingdom."

Communion tables were to be moved from their customary location on the east side of churches, to be fixed in some convenient place in the body of the church. All altars and rails, tapers, candlesticks, basins, crucifixes, crosses, images, pictures of saints or the Virgin Mary or depicting the Persons of the Trinity, and superstitious inscriptions in churches or churchyards, were to be taken away or defaced.[6] Church organs were also moved from many churches.

An excellent opportunity for turning the annual Christmas feast into a fast, as the church had done earlier with the Kalends festival, came in 1644. It had been the practice in the past to preach a sermon to the Lords in Westminster Abbey on Christmas Day, something that a growing number of Puritans were uncomfortable with. The issue came to a head in that year, when Christmas Day happened to fall upon the last Wednesday of the month, a day already appointed by the Lords and Commons for Fasting and Humiliation. Parliament published the following "Ordinance for the better observation of the Feast of the Nativity of Christ," on December 19, 1644:

> Whereas some doubts have been raised whether the next Fast shall be celebrated, because it falleth on the day which, heretofore, was usually called the Feast of the Nativity of our Savior; the lords and commons do order and ordain that public notice be given, that the Fast appointed to be kept on the last Wednesday in every month, ought to be observed until it be otherwise ordered by both houses; and that this day particularly is to be kept with the more solemn humiliation because it may call to remembrance our sins and the sins of our forefathers, who have turned this Feast, pretending the memory of Christ, into an extreme forgetfulness of him, by giving liberty to carnal and sensual delights; being contrary to the life which Christ himself led here upon earth, and to the spiritual life of Christ in our souls; for the sanctifying and saving whereof Christ was pleased both to take a human life, and to lay it down again.[7]

---

6. Ibid., 265–66.
7. Ibid., 580.

This, in effect, banned the celebration of Christmas that year, 1644. Edward Calamy (1600–1666) from London, preached the Lord's sermon on December 25. He stated:

> This day is commonly called The Feast of Christ's nativity, or, Christmas-day; a day that has formerly been much abused to superstition, and profaneness. It is not easy to say, whether the superstition has been greater, or the profaneness. . . .
>
> And truly I think that the superstition and profanation of this day is so rooted into it, as that there is no way to reform it, but by dealing with it as Hezekiah did with the brazen serpent. This year God, by his Providence, has buried this Feast in a Fast, and I hope it will never rise again. . . .
>
> I have known some that have preferred Christmas Day before the Lord's Day. I have known those that would be sure to receive the Sacrament on Christmas Day though they did not receive it all the year after. This was the superstition of this day, and the profaneness was as great. There were some that did not play cards all the year long, yet they must play at Christmas.[8]

In 1645 the English Parliament approved the *Directory for the Public Worship of God*, which stated, "There is no day commanded in Scripture to be kept holy under the gospel but the Lord's day, which is the Christian Sabbath. Festival days, vulgarly called Holy-days, having no warrant in the word of God, are not to be continued" (this document is examined in more detail below in the penultimate chapter, "Twelve Reasons Justifying the Endorsement of Christmas"). It was on June 8, 1647, that Christmas, along with all other holy days, was formally banned by an ordinance or Act of Parliament.

> Forasmuch as the feast of the nativity of Christ, Easter, Whitsuntide, and other festivals, commonly called holy-days, have been heretofore superstitiously used and observed; be it ordained, that the said feasts, and all other festivals, commonly called holy-days, be no longer observed as festivals; any law, statute, custom, constitution, or canon, to the contrary in anywise notwithstanding.[9]

The Puritan parliament was concerned, however, that this would deprive many people, especially those employed as servants, of having this as a day off work in accordance with past custom (just as the Genevan Reformers were similarly concerned a hundred years previously). To mitigate the loss of the day, they stipulated in another ordinance three weeks later that all

---

8. Neal, *History of the Puritans*, 2:284–85.
9. Firth and Rait, *Acts and Ordinances*, 1:954.

servants were to have "with the leave of their masters, such convenient reasonable recreation, and relaxation from labour, every second Tuesday in the month throughout the year."[10] The ban on Christmas was reiterated in 1652 and 1657, with all shops in London required to remain open as usual for business on December 25. Research based on the records of 367 English parishes reveals that between 1645 and 1649, the vast majority ceased to observe Christmas "festival communion," but the records do not always represent reality, especially outside London.[11]

As an aside, it is a complete myth without any documentary evidence that Oliver Cromwell or any of his peers banned the eating of mince pies, even though some pamphleteers of his day on the Christmas topic speak as a matter of fact of Parliament formally banning them.[12] The myth has been perpetuated to this day, particularly by those opposed to the godliness reflected in the lives of the Puritans. The myth possibly arose as a consequence of the monthly fast. This was instituted by Act of Parliament in August 1642, due to the perceived low state of true religion in England and Wales. The Act required that on routinely set days, once a month, the public should engage in acts of humiliation and prayer, enjoined with public worship, with abstinence from the normal eating routine. As we noted above, in December 1644 this fast day fell on the twenty-fifth day of the month, so that the normal Christmas Day feasting (which would undoubtedly have included the consumption of minced pies) was forbidden. No legislation was ever passed during the Puritan Interregnum outlawing mince pies or any other particular food!

All these measures were insufficient and celebrations continued, often covertly, despite the penalties of fines and imprisonment. The English people's love of Christmas could not be destroyed. This is not surprising, given that the Christmas season was traditionally the longest calendar period of celebration and that many felt that this meteorological time of year was when joy was most needed.

---

10. Ibid., 985–86.
11. Hutton, *Rise and Fall*, 213–14.
12. *Arraignment*, 1.

A satirical pamphleteer, Josiah King, put it this way in his fictional personification of Christmas:

> Christmas is a very kind and loving man; inoffensive to all: a hater of strife, a lover of harmless mirth. . . . He uses all means to bring us together, & to renew friendship: he is a great Peacemaker.

In his account of Christmas's trial before the Puritan courts, a needy man gives the following evidence:

> I dwell at the Town of Want, in the Country of Needs . . . poor in estate: and had it not been for old Christmas I had been poorer. . . . If you take away this merry old Gentlemen from us, you take away all our Joy, and comfort that we have.[13]

Various protests were made against the suppression of the festival. Although Parliament sat every Christmas Day from 1644 to 1656, the shops in London did not always open and those that did were often roughly harassed. In 1647 evergreen decorations were put up in the city, and the Lord Mayor and City Marshal had to ride about setting fire to them! There were even riots in country places, notably Canterbury, Bury St. Edmunds, and Norwich. The following account from Canterbury, although undoubtedly biased and pro-Christmas, gives a flavor of the unrest:

13. King, *Examination and Tryall*, 30–31.

> The mayor, endeavouring to keep the peace, had his head broke by the populace and was dragged about the streets; the mob broke into diverse houses of the most religious in the town, broke their windows, abused their persons, and threw their goods into the streets, because they exposed them to sale on Christmas Day. At length, their numbers being increased to above two thousand, they put themselves into a posture of defence against the magistrates, kept guard, stopped passes, examined passengers, and seized the magazine and arms in the town-hall, and were not dispersed without difficulty.[14]

A petition with more than ten thousand signatures from the Kent region demanded either the restoration of Christmas or else the king back on the throne. The unpopular laws banning Christmas likely played some part in the English cry for the restoration of the crown.

With the restoration in 1660, Christmas naturally came back to a position of full recognition but most English Calvinist ministers still disapproved of Christmas celebration. Misson, the French traveller, reported as follows:

> From Christmas Day till after Twelfth Day is a time of Christian rejoicing; a mixture of devotion and pleasure. They . . . make it their whole business to drive away melancholy.[15]

Seventeenth Century Baptists

During this period, English Protestants were still working out what practices were acceptable and unacceptable in worship. Take, for example, Benjamin Keach (1640–1704), a Particular Baptist pastor in London. *The Child's Delight* was written by Keach as a primer for children and reveals in clear terms Keach's antagonism to the corruption, as he saw it, of the Roman Catholic Church. First published in 1664 as *The Child's Instructor*, this handbook stirred up a controversy and landed Keach at the Assizes in Aylesbury before Lord Chief Justice Hyde, on the charge of violating the 1662 Licensing Act, the law regulating the content of printed books.

---

14. *Canterbury Christmas*, 1.
15. James and Hill, *Joy to the World*, 114.

Keach eventually served two weeks in prison and saw the primer burned in an effort to purge the land of heresy. Among other things, the Licensing Act forbade the printing of any:

> heretical, seditious, schismatical or offensive books or pamphlets, wherein any doctrine or opinion shall be asserted or maintained which is contrary to the Christian faith or the doctrine or discipline of the Church of England.

It is interesting to note which issues Keach chose to be of fundamental importance in writing the primer. He presented lessons on the character of God, the child's place before God, and a series of Solomon's proverbs. He also set the Ten Commandments into verse form for ease of learning. Part 2 of the manual's catechism refuted the Roman church, teaching a rejection of any priest or vicar other than Christ and of the sacrifices by priests of the Roman church. We note with particular interest his view of worship, taking a strict constructionist view of acceptable worship, arguing that elements of worship are acceptable only as long as they are directly authorized by Scripture.

Keach's religious position, strongly Protestant and unashamedly anti–Roman Catholic is clear. His pro-Reformation writing may not differ much from other separatists and nonconformists of the time but he was clearly operating from the mentality of the Reformation as the most important guiding force in recent history.[16]

16. Brooks, *Benjamin Keach*.

The Breach Repaired, Keach's exposition to prove congregational singing, serves as another example of how he intertwined the Reformation with his aim of purifying the church. When Keach wrote *The Breach Repaired* in 1691, twenty-seven years after his initial primer appeared, he explicitly affirmed the vitality and relevance of the Reformation to his cause. He depicted the church as still in the process of Reformation, newly come out of "the Wilderness, or Popish Darkness and not so fully neither, as to be clear as the Sun, as in due time she shall." Reformation, he argues, is and ever was a hard and difficult work, it being no easy thing to restore lost ordinances.

How then did Keach and other seventeenth century Baptists, such as Hercules Collins and John Spilsbury, treat Christmas in their worship? This is not easy to answer as there are virtually no extant writings on this subject by any seventeenth century Baptist. There are several passing references to events which took place on December 25, where the term "Christmas Day" is used, but as this was the social norm among the majority of the populace, it tells us little. Clearly, the scarcity of any written treatment of the subject tells us that it simply was not an issue in their church life. Arguments from silence must always be handled with caution, but what does this written silence imply? Was it the case that Christmas services formed an integral part of worship throughout their congregations and therefore was not an issue for discussion, or was it the case that Christmas services formed no part of worship throughout their congregations and so there existed unanimity on the issue? It is extremely likely to have been the latter. Baptists had consistently received a very bad press from paedo-baptists, whether Anglicans, Presbyterians, or Independents. It was commonplace for them to be portrayed as a threat and likened to the radical Zwickau Prophets and Thomas Müntzer, from the era of Luther and who appeared to have influenced the emerging Anabaptist movement. Throughout the seventeenth century, Baptists, especially Calvinistic Baptists, sought to demonstrate their orthodoxy to their paedo-baptist counterparts and this was one of the main reasons lying behind *The First London Baptist Confession of Faith*, published in 1644 prior to the *Westminster Confession of Faith*. There is no known dissent from Baptists to the Puritan outlawing of Christmas in Parliament. There is much in Baptist writings, such as Keach's just referred to, which show their aversion to all things Roman Catholic.

The General Baptist, Thomas Grantham (1633–92), spoke of the suspicious nature of "festival days" including Easter:

> And indeed the variety of the usages of Ancient Christians touching the Lent Fast, shews it to be an Innovation, and not of Divine Authority: No, the Observation of Easter itself is

acknowledged by Socrates Scholasticus to have crept into the churches.[17]

Grantham followed with a lengthy quote from the early historian thus making his case against Easter and Lent. Although Grantham did not mention Christmas, if he was rejecting the propriety of Lent and Easter as popish inventions, it is safe to assume that he would have regarded Christmas similarly. A contemporary of Keach, Thomas Delaune was a converted Roman Catholic from Cork, Ireland, who settled in London as a Baptist writer. Responding to criticism from Anglicans for separating from the Church of England, he published '*A Plea for the Non-Conformists, Shewing the True State of Their Case: In a Letter to Dr Benjamin Calamy*,' in 1683. This was a very risky business prior to the 1688 'Glorious Revolution,' for which Delaune was imprisoned with his wife and children until their death from ill-health in 1685. In the book he compares Papal Rome to ancient Rome, cathedrals like St. Paul's in London to Roman temples, national saints to Roman gods and holy days to Roman feast days. Respecting the latter, he states of Roman Catholicism: " . . . some of their capital feasts are these, viz. Christmas (their Saturnalia) observed both in time and manner as theirs was, with yulegames . . . adorning their houses and temples with green leaves . . . being all pagan or papal inventions."[18] Taking all these facts together, it seems virtually certain that the seventeenth century Baptists did not practice Christmas in their congregations.

Eighteenth Century

John Wesley (1703–1791), the father of Methodism, said virtually nothing about Christmas and in all of his collected sermons there are no Christmas sermons. He did compile, and his brother Charles (1707–1788, left, with John centred, and Francis Asbury, in next picture) did compose hymns on the birth of Christ.

---

17. Grantham, *Christianisimus Primitivus*, book 2, part 2, 148.
18. Delaune, *Plea for the Non-Conformists*, 170–71.

The most famous of them today is "Hark the Herald Angels Sing" but this was not the original wording of the hymn. Charles Wesley had published it in 1738 as, "Hark, how all the welkin rings, glory to the king of kings." Welkin is an old fashioned word that has passed out of use but means "vault of heaven." Wesley had written that, in response to Christ's birth, heaven rang or proclaimed loudly "glory to the king of kings." Clearly, he was seeking to reflect the text of Luke 2:14, "Glory to God in the highest."

In 1753, the same year he began construction on the London Tabernacle church, George Whitefield compiled his own hymnal, "Hymns for Social Worship." It included twenty-one hymns from the Wesleys', including the aforesaid hymn, but with a significant alteration: "Hark! the Herald Angels sing, Glory to the newborn King!"

It is said that Charles Wesley was incensed and refused to sing the hymn throughout the rest of his life. Making changes to the Wesleys' hymns was not new but the brothers did not appreciate such changes. Over a period of forty years, they had published numerous different hymn collections but in 1779, they succumbed to requests to publish a large, single compilation of them.

The new hymnal was entitled *A Collection of Hymns for the Use of the People called Methodists*, and comprised 560 hymns. In the preface John Wesley wrote:

> Many gentlemen have done my brother and me (though without naming us) the honor to reprint many of our hymns. Now they are perfectly welcome to do so, provided they print them just as they are. But I desire they would not attempt to mend them, for they are really not able. None of them is able to mend either the sense or the verse. Therefore, I must beg of them these two favors: either to let them stand just as they are, to take things for better or worse, or to add the true reading in the margin, or at the bottom of the page, that we may no longer be accountable

> either for the nonsense or for the doggerel of other men [doggerel being another old word, probably derived from "dog" and used to indicate something crude or poor].[19]

Whether it is a fact or not that Charles Wesley refused to sing the hymn, what *is* factual is that the hymn, "Hark How all the Welkin Rings" / "Hark the Herald Angels Sing," did not appear in the new hymnal! Charles died in 1788 and John in 1791 and the hymn did not appear in this hymnal until fifty years later, when a two-hundred hymn supplement was added, published in London by John Mason in 1830.[20] As we point out in a subsequent chapter, "Biblical Misconceptions of the Nativity," the attributing of song to the angels is conjecture, as the Bible does not state whether the declaration was sung or spoken. That Whitefield himself kept Christmas is no surprise, given that he was an ordained Anglican deacon. The following is an abbreviated excerpt from his diary on a 1739 tour of North America:

> Monday, December 24. (1739) Crossed Pamplico River, about Five Miles wide, Yesterday Evening. Set out by break of Day; crossed New River about Four in the Afternoon, and reached Newborn Town, Thirty-Two Miles from Bath Town, by Six at Night had a sweet Communion in Spirit, after I came to the Inn, with my dear Friends at England, who I supposed were joining with one Accord in fervent Prayer, and ushering in the Festival of our dear Lord's Nativity, by singing of Hymns and Spiritual Songs....
>
> Tuesday, December 25. Endeavoured still to keep my Mind as much as possible in Union with all those pious Souls who I knew were rejoicing in the Glad Tidings of Salvation by Jesus Christ ... The People were uncommonly attentive, most melted into Tears, and shewed what a great Impression the Word made upon their Hearts....
>
> The Woman where we lodged would take nothing for our Christmas Dinner, and wished we could stay with them longer ... Oh how will it rejoice me to hear that some poor Soul this Day was born again! Then it would be a Christmas Day indeed![21]

In a sermon on Matt 1:21, "And she shall bring forth a Son," and entitled, "The Observation of the Birth of Christ, the Duty of all Christians; or the True Way of Keeping Christmas," Whitefield states:

---

19. Wesley, *Collection of Hymns*, preface, para. 8.
20. Ibid., 1–520.
21. Whitefield, *George Whitefield's Journals*, 5th journal.

I. My brethren, I am to show when your celebration of this festival is not of the right kind. And first, you do not celebrate this aright, when you spend most of your time in cards, dice, or gaming of any sort; Secondly, they cannot be said truly to celebrate this time, who spend their time in eating and drinking to excess; Thirdly, nor can they, my brethren, be said to keep, or rightly observe the commemoration of the birth of our Redeemer, the Lord Jesus Christ, who neglect their worldly callings to follow pleasures and diversions. II. I come now, in the second place, to show you, who they are who do rightly observe, and truly celebrate the birth of our Redeemer. And I shall show you who they are in two particulars, directly opposite to the others; and then, my brethren, take your choice: you must choose the one or the other, there is no medium, you must either serve the Lord or Baal; and, therefore, my dear brethren, let me beg of you to consider, First, that those spend their time aright, and truly observe this festival, who spend their hours in reading, praying, and religious conversation. Secondly, let the good things of life, you enjoy, be used with moderation. Thirdly, let me beg of you not to alienate too much of your time from the worldly business of this life, but have a proper regard thereunto, and then you may be said rightly to observe this festival.[22]

---

22. Whitefield, *Works of Reverend George Whitefield*, 5:251–61, sermon 16.

Scotland

The Church of Scotland discouraged the observance of Christmas from the Reformation in 1560. Knox's *First Book of Discipline* outlawed it in the church and suggested that it ought to be outlawed publicly by the courts. In 1607, King James I insisted that a play be acted on Christmas night and that the royal court indulge in games. This is no surprise from the monarch who introduced the Book of Sports declarations (initially in Lancashire in 1617 and then nationally in 1618), to force his citizens to play sport on Sunday in an era of a six-day week, one purpose of which was to prevent them from keeping Sunday as the Lord's Day (the Puritans would abolish the law in 1643).

King James IV commanded Christmas celebration in 1618 (one of the Five Articles of Perth he imposed) at the Church of Scotland Assembly in St John's Kirk, Perth, earlier that same year; however, attendance at church services was very scant.

Responding to this with a publication, David Calderwood echoed the sentiment of his fellow Calvinist ministers in stating:

> If it had been the will of God that the several acts of Christ should have been celebrated with several solemnities, the Holy Ghost would have made known to us the day of his nativity, circumcision, presentation in the temple, baptism, transfiguration, and the like.... This opinion of Christ's nativity on the 25th day of December was bred at Rome.

Calderwood then notes inconsistent claims made in previous centuries for other dates on the calendar, as the day of the Savior's nativity:

> The diversity of the ancients observing some the 6th day of January, some the 19th day of April, some the 19th of May, some the 25th day of December, argues that the Apostles never ordained it.... You see then as God hid the body of Moses, so has he hid this day, and other days depending on the calculation of it, wherein he declared his will concerning the other days of his notable acts: to wit, that not Christ's action, but Christ's institution makes a day holy.... Nay, let us utter the truth, December-Christmas is a just imitation of the December-Saturnal of the ethnic [heathen] Romans, and so used as if Bacchus, and not Christ, were the God of Christians.[23]

During the twenty years between the 1618 adoption of the Five Articles of Perth and the Calvinistic protests culminating in the Solemn League and Covenant in 1643, the Church in Scotland officially became

---

23. Calderwood, *Perth Assembly*, ch. 5, sec. 2.

Episcopalian and with that came the restoration of all of the old Roman Catholic holy days. This religious calendar was again abolished in 1638 by the Glasgow Assembly of the Church of Scotland, declaring that it was to be "utterly abolished," as it is "neither commanded nor warranted by Scripture." In 1640 the Scottish Parliament officially abolished the observance of Christmas, the "Yule vacation and all observation thereof in time coming."

The act was partly repealed in 1686 but the view of the church remained the same, therefore Christmas had little recognition among most of the populace. (This followed the failed attempt by Charles I to impose Anglicanism on Scotland, his subsequent defeat in battle to the Scots near Newcastle, and his insincere concession to the restoration of Presbyterianism in Scotland, a period when from 1660 to 1688, thousands died because they refused to acknowledge Episcopal church government and worship practices.)

Social Change

The suppression of Christmas by the Puritans did have a long-lasting effect. Some aspects of Christmas such as carol-singing remained out of fashion well after the Puritan era and until its revival in Victorian times. The fact that the cultural momentum had been broken is also illustrated in the fact that from 1790 to 1810, the December issues of *The Times* makes no reference to Christmas whatsoever and those from 1810 to 1835 refer to it in passing, in the briefest of terms.

What the Puritans could not do, the Industrial Revolution, which began in the mid-1700s, nearly accomplished! During this time, English society underwent a marked change. Worldwide commerce was becoming a reality: James Watt invented the steam engine and Edmund Cartwright invented the power loom. Factories and industrial towns sprang up to meet the demand and from a largely rural lifestyle, many were now drawn to the city in search of greater economic gains in the factories. There was a mass migration from the Old World to the New World which coincided with a massive expansion in the urban population across the Northern hemisphere during the nineteenth century. Excepting the opening of massive new ranches and farms in the American Midwest, the countryside in many places was in the process of becoming depopulated.

Increased mechanization obliged many people to undertake activities that were to some extent dehumanizing, with the result that a collective nostalgia for a rural idyll arose—a yearning for what were imagined to have been softer attitudes and certainties. The nostalgia included what one might call a wish for the return of the "good old days."

This happened alongside a genuine fear among the intelligentsia, politicians, and churchmen, that societies across what we would now call the Western World, were being disconnected from a combination of their history, social values, culture, and religious roots: what Karl Marx labelled "the alienation of labour." Moreover, there was a series of foreign wars of succession that seemed to have little relevance to domestic needs.

In Scotland, enclosures, the clearances of land for sheep-grazing, repression and exile for many dissidents (especially after the 1745 Jacobite rising) brought about even more social impoverishment in what few rural communities survived.

The sum total of this was, that other than as a time of eating and drinking, based on the need to slaughter livestock that could not be fed in the winter months and for perishable crops to be eaten, Christmas was not observed in any sense that we would recognize today.

As all of this happened, the old traditions of the "twelve days of Christmas," from December 25 to January 6, began to disappear and nothing was put in place to replace it. In the first two decades of the nineteenth century, Christmas was hardly celebrated in Britain and most businesses were open for work on December 25. That would soon change. The scene was set for a well-intentioned "revival" of the Christmas festival by part-time scholars and well-intentioned amateurs working from relict folk memory, a few old written accounts and a tendency to draw links and comparisons, that would not really stand up to any serious research into the historical and archaeological evidence available today. It was the Victorians who largely introduced the traditional Christmas we have become so familiar with.

The Victorians

The Christmas tree first came to England with the Georgian Kings who came from Germany. Following the death in 1714 of Queen Anne of Great Britain, George I from Hanover, Germany, ascended the British throne (although over fifty Roman Catholics bore closer blood relationships to Anne, the Act of Settlement, 1701, prohibited Roman Catholics from inheriting the British throne and George was Anne's closest living Protestant relative). At this time also, German merchants living in England decorated their homes with a Christmas tree. However, the British public were not fond of the German Monarchy (many of the royals not even bothering to speak in English) so they did not copy the fashions at Court, which is why the Christmas tree did not establish itself in Britain at that time.

In 1761 King George III married Queen Charlotte from Germany. She introduced the Christmas tree into the royal household and Queen Victoria (the last of the Hanoverian monarchs) adopted this practice as a teenager. Victoria, in 1832 as a thirteen-year-old princess, records in her journals preparing a "Christmas box" for her German-born mother in Kensington Palace.[24]

Queen Victoria's marriage to her first cousin, the German Lutheran Prince Albert in 1840 was very significant, as Albert encouraged Victoria to develop the custom in Windsor Castle with greater decorations and presents (prior to this, gift-giving had traditionally occurred at New Year). The British and American public was entranced by the young queen and when this practice in the royal household was published internationally between 1848 and 1850 with drawings in newspapers, the practice went viral in Britain and North America! Victoria also regularly donated Christmas trees to schools and barracks for children's parties. Other commercial enterprises soon took off, such as wrapping sweets in a cracker and sending cards. The first known period of sending Christmas cards was in 1846, instigated by Sir Henry Cole who owned an art shop in London. The card sending accelerated greatly with the introduction of the half-penny postage stamp and by 1880, nearly twelve million cards were being sent. The majority of these cards were depicting what we would class as normal Christmas/winter scenes; however, a significant minority were deliberately cynical, portraying

---

24. Victoria, *Journals of Queen Victoria*, 2:201.

violence, dead animals, and evil spirits, with the intention to shock and frighten. This highlights what the essence of Christmas was to most of the Victorians—a time of fun and a welcome escape from the realities of life.

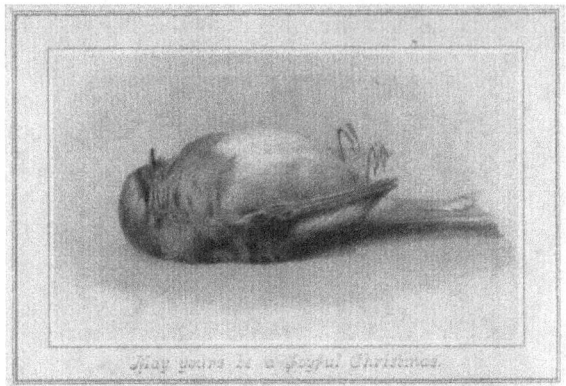

The text on the dead robin card, a mild example of the genre, reads, "May yours be a joyful Christmas." Candles were lit on the tree to represent the stars shining on an assumed cloudless night when Jesus was born in Bethlehem (see the subsequent chapter titled "Biblical Misconceptions of the Nativity").

C. H. Spurgeon's viewpoint is an interesting one to note on this question. Spurgeon (1834–1892) had little time for ecclesiastical traditions and decrees; nevertheless, he was willing to preach on the birth of Christ during the Christmas season. His rationale for this was that Christmas Day was as good a day to celebrate Christ's birth as any other. In a sermon on Luke 2:10 he writes:

> As the thoughts of a great many Christian people will run at this time towards the birth of Christ and as this cannot be wrong, I judge it meet to avail ourselves of the prevailing current and float down the stream of thought. Our minds will run that way, because so many around us are following customs suggestive of it, therefore let us get what good we can get out of the occasion.[25]

On this basis, had Spurgeon preached immediately after the Apostolic era and alongside men such as Timothy and Titus, or indeed in the mid-eighteenth century, he would not have preached from Luke 2 in December, as the "prevailing current" and the "customs" being followed would not then have "ran at this time toward the birth of Christ." Prevailing currents of thought, as well as customs, change from generation to generation and from place to place. In some parts of the world formerly regarded as Christian, it

---

25. Spurgeon, *Metropolitan Tabernacle Pulpit*, 22:709–10.

is today in fact a post-Christian society where human secularism prevails. In such societies, there exists a majority wish to move away from a religious emphasis at every time of year and replace it with a secular emphasis. This includes Christmas where the religious element is removed and it becomes termed a "winter festival" or "festive season." Where this is the prevailing current of thought and custom and comes to be reflected in the churches, then on the basis of Spurgeon's principle we should no longer preach Christ's birth in December.

Spurgeon cannot be reasonably criticized for his actions. The birth of Christ is a real event and a biblical event. No more reasonable criticism would be warranted if that event was the subject of a sermon preached in July. The death of Christ was undoubtedly in the spring but to preach on it in the autumn is beyond reasonable criticism.

For the avoidance of doubt on Spurgeon's position, however, we should also note what else he said about Christmas:

> We have no superstitious regard for times and seasons. Certainly we do not believe in the present ecclesiastical arrangement called Christmas: first, because we do not believe in the mass at all but abhor it, whether it be said or sung in Latin or in English; and, secondly, because we find no scriptural warrant whatever for observing any day as the birthday of the Savior

> and, consequently, its observance is a superstition because not of divine authority.[26]

> When it can be proved that the observance of Christmas, Whitsuntide, and other Popish festivals was ever instituted by a divine statute, we also will attend to them but not till then. It is as much our duty to reject the traditions of men, as to observe the ordinances of the Lord. We ask concerning every rite and rubric, "Is this a law of the God of Jacob?" and if it be not clearly so, it is of no authority with us who walk in Christian liberty.[27]

In his message on December 24, 1881, Spurgeon preached against Christmas as:

> a religious superstitious event that no Christian should celebrate because it is of no divine origin or commandment.... No doubt all of its observance and inception is of Pagan origin.

While Charles Dickens (1812–1870) did not invent the Victorian Christmas, his 1843 book, *A Christmas Carol*, is credited with helping to popularize and spread the traditions of the festival throughout the English speaking world. Its themes of family, charity, goodwill, peace, and happiness encapsulated the spirit of the Victorian Christmas. Prior to 1834, the Bank of England observed thirty-three 'saint's days' and religious festivals as holidays, then they were reduced to four, including Christmas Day. Christmas Day was not made the subject of any legislation in England, unlike other days, as it had been recognized as a common-law holiday since before modern records began.

In Scotland, change was longer in coming. In the 1700s and the early 1800s Christmas had little meaning and significance for most in Scotland.

By the 1900s Christmas had begun to infiltrate Scotland. It arrived in small pockets, from Anglicans following English customs, to more liberal-minded churchgoers interested in the customs of their neighbors down south and across the Atlantic. Stockings were hung on mantelpieces and carols sung in the national Church of Scotland. In 1875 Leishman, latterly a Church of Scotland General Assembly moderator, argued in *The Ritual of the Church* that, as the superstitions surrounding festival days had been purged with time, the church could now observe them again.

---

26. Spurgeon, *New Park Street Pulpit*, Sermon on Dec. 24, 1871.
27. Spurgeon, *Treasury of David*, on Psalm 81:4.

Twentieth Century

John F. Moncrieff, a prolific pamphleteer from Edinburgh who had been a member of several Presbyterian churches, wrote in 1912:

> It is noticeable that, with the lessening regard for the sanctity of the Sabbath, there has been an increasing desire among Presbyterians to keep other days, such as Christmas, Good Friday, and Easter.

That point ought to resonate with us, as we recall the concern for the Lord's Day expressed both by the early church fathers and then 1,500 years later by some Reformers and Puritans, in the context of their opposition to feast/holy days such as Christmas. In 1922 the Church of Scotland General Assembly formally permitted the celebration of the "more important festivals," while also retaining the *Westminster Confession* as the principle subordinate standard! Yet New Year remained the preeminent festival and in many homes presents were still swapped on Hogmanay rather than Christmas Day. The following childhood recollection of a 1930s Scottish Christmas is typical of many:

> Most of the presents in our family were given by Gran, because we were quite poor and she would always give them on New Year's morning. They'd be wrapped in brown paper—no decorative paper in those days. I once, in all innocence asked her: "Why do we not celebrate Christmas?" Her answer still staggers me; she said, "We're no heathens, laddie."[28]

The influence of World War II was pivotal. Abroad and in the company of English soldiers, many Scots experienced their first proper Christmas dinner and once tasted it was never forgotten. On their return home, these servicemen began to celebrate the festival with some style and gradually their ideas took root. The advent of radio and the spread of national newspapers, both carrying foreign ideas of Christmas, changed attitudes. George V had been the first British monarch to broadcast a Christmas Day message in 1932, by radio. While Christmas Day was a holiday in England, the Scot worked on. One kilt-maker from the Royal Mile in Edinburgh remembers:

> It was a regular working day, nothing special. I remember coming into work and they [the city workers] were digging up the street, you know, repairing it. The street was all torn up; it was just another business day.

---

28. Weightman and Humphries, *Christmas Past*, 29.

Visitors from the south were visibly bemused at such sights but these sights were not to last much longer. In 1954, the minister of St. Giles Church of Scotland in Edinburgh preached an impassioned Watch Night Service calling for industrialists to make Christmas Day a public holiday. Four years later, in 1958, his wish was granted.

It was official acknowledgment of a quiet revolution that had been taking place throughout the century but from its early manifestations, nobody could have anticipated the speed with which the festival would develop.

In the space of a few years, the thrifty, low-key, still largely religious festival had turned into a commercial merry-go-round. It was a measure of increasing wealth and the need for distraction and comfort, as well as an indication of declining interest in the Christian religion. Since the 1980s, with the fading of the church's influence and the increased influences from the rest of the UK and elsewhere, Christmas and its related festivities in Scotland are now nearly on a par with Hogmanay and New Year's Day.

It is, therefore, important to note that the adoption of the traditional Christmas season into British society in the nineteenth century, together with its massive growth and importance throughout the twentieth century, was not instigated by any focus on the Bible or desire to bring God glory. While the motives behind the season's reinvention and the subsequent outcome were, for the most part, wholesome in motive, they were, however, secular in origin and not biblical.

Charles Dickens *A Christmas Carol*, which we have just referred to, has no explicit reference to religion at all, bar three words where he tells us that before Scrooge acquired the new Christmas spirit, he, too, "went to church." It is an interesting thought for those Christians who today endorse Christmas, whether or not they view Dickens as a villain because he wrote *A Christmas Carol* with virtually no reference to the birth of Christ. Dickens's "spirit of Christmas" was and remains one that the unregenerate atheist could heartily endorse just as much as the born-again Christian!

The adoption of the modern Christmas season was secular and something to which the Protestant churches contributed very little. Those churches that had endorsed Christmas historically, such as the Anglican Church, were as surprised as anyone when their pews began to fill up for Christmas services and most of those churches that had rejected Christmas historically, very gradually assimilated it into their own church life. The re-emergence of the Roman Catholic Church into a place of national influence, together with the displacement of Christianity with human secularism, has occurred concurrently with the growth of Christmas.

The Origins of Victorian Christmas Customs

The Origin of the Christmas Tree

PAGANS HAD LONG WORSHIPPED trees in the forest, or brought them into their homes and decorated them (Jer 10:1–4) and this observance was adopted and painted with a Christian veneer by the church. The practice of adorning houses with evergreens at the January Kalends was common throughout the Roman Empire, as we learn from Libanius, Tertullian, and Chrysostom. A grim denunciation of such decorations and the lights which accompanied them may be quoted from Tertullian in the second century:

> "Let them," he says of the heathen, "kindle lamps, they who have no light; let them fix on the doorposts laurels which shall afterwards be burnt, they for whom fire is close at hand; meet for them are testimonies of darkness and auguries of punishment. But thou," he says to the Christian, "art a light of the world and a tree that is ever green; if thou hast renounced temples, make not a temple of thy own house-door."[1]

---

1. Tertullian, *Book of Apology*, ch. 25.

Wherever the Bible did not transform communities, pagan superstitions prevailed as they do to this day. One superstition was that in winter, when trees shed their leaves, it was the spirits living in the trees that were departing. The fear was that the trees would not grow leaves again; therefore, to encourage the tree spirits to return, people dressed the trees with strips of colored cloth hoping that by making them attractive to the spirits, they would return in the spring! When, of course, new leaves grew on the trees in spring, the people believed their efforts had been successful so they continued the practice each winter.

Winfred Boniface (referred to earlier) originally from Wessex in England and missionary to Germany, is reliably recorded in 725 as being involved in the cutting down of an oak tree in the region of Hesse, from which a chapel was built to evangelize the pagans. However, Roman Catholic legend quickly embellished the event, claiming that the tree was miraculously blown down by God, whereupon the pagans all converted to Christianity. Boniface is said to have then cut down a small fir tree beside the oak, used its branch formation to highlight the Trinity and encouraged the new converts to use such trees to remind them of God. This legend in subsequent centuries resulted in a strong relationship between the fir tree and the German church. Taking fir trees inside the house began in Germany and colored cloths were replaced with strings of beads with fruit and sweets on them. So there appears to be an affinity with other "vegetation spirits" and there is probably a union of several elements: the old Roman custom of decking houses with laurels and green trees at the Kalends of January, and the popular belief that every Christmas Eve apple and other trees blossomed and bore fruit. Added to this is the Roman Catholic tree legend of Boniface.

The Origin of Mistletoe

Mistletoe, holly, and ivy plants are the most prominent green plants in British native woodland during the winter. There are many varied traditions and myths surrounding these plants. Norse mythology recounts how the god Balder was killed using a mistletoe arrow by his rival god Hoder, while fighting for the female Nanna. Druid rituals use mistletoe to poison their human sacrificial victim. The white sticky viscin seeds from the mistletoe berries were believed to be the semen of the gods! The custom of "kissing under the mistletoe" is a later synthesis of the sexual license of Saturnalia with the Druidic sacrificial cult. With the passage of time, numerous other customs centered around it. Some examples of Christmas iconography have been discovered in engravings from the Nottingham Guild of Alabasters in the fifteenth century. From these we discover that it was the practice to hang carvings of the nativity family outside many northern homes, frequently held within hoops of greenery among which would be mistletoe, a "magical" plant believed to have come from Heaven because it only grew high amid the trees! The custom was to give a kiss of peace under the holy family and leave any weapons by the threshold, which probably was a refinement of the earlier Norse custom of not bringing weapons into a banqueting hall. (Not a custom that helped the Welsh Princes who were weaponless and massacred by William de Braose during a Christmas banquet at Abergavenny Castle in 1175.)

The Origin of Holly and Ivy

Ivy was sacred to the worship of Bacchus, the Greek god of wine and a part of sun worship. During the Middle Ages it was adopted by the Roman Catholic Church and assumed a Christian symbolism as a Christmas decoration. The Druids celebrated the winter solstice by wearing holly wreaths on their heads and the Romans considered it to be the plant of their god Saturn. In Scandinavia, holly is known as the "Christ Thorn," the prickly leaves representing the crown of thorns that Jesus wore before he was crucified and the berries, the drops of blood that were shed by Jesus because of the thorns. There was a midwinter custom of holding singing contests between men and women, where the men sang carols praising holly (for its "masculine" qualities) and disparaging ivy, while women sang carols praising the ivy (for its "feminine" qualities) and disparaging holly. The contest was amicably resolved by the introduction of mistletoe, under which the competing men and women kissed each other.

The Origin of Christmas Presents

In pre-Christian Rome, the emperors compelled their most despised citizens to bring offerings and gifts during the Saturnalia (in December) and Kalends (in January). Later, this ritual expanded to include gift-giving among the general populace.

> The Kalends is celebrated everywhere as far as the limits of the Roman Empire extend. . . . The impulse to spend seizes everyone. He who the whole year through has taken pleasure in saving and piling up his pence, becomes suddenly extravagant. He who erstwhile was accustomed and preferred to live poorly, now at this feast enjoys himself as much as his means will allow. . . . People are not only generous toward themselves, but also toward their fellow-men. A stream of presents pours itself out on all sides. . . . The highroads and footpaths are covered with whole processions of laden men and beast. . . . As the thousand flowers which burst forth everywhere are the adornment of Spring, so are the thousand presents poured out on all sides, the decoration of the Kalends feast.[2]

The Roman Catholic Church gave this custom a Christian flavor by re-rooting it in the supposed gift-giving of Saint Nicholas.

The Origin of Santa Claus

Nicholas was born in Parara, Turkey, in 270 AD and later became Bishop of Myra. He died in 345 AD on December 6. He was only named a Roman Catholic Saint in the nineteenth century. Nicholas was among the most senior bishops who convened the Council of Nicaea in 325 AD, where the discussion centered on the Arian controversy of whether or not Jesus as the Son of God was eternally divine and coequal with the Father. Following his death, a cult idolizing him was established with the tradition that Nicholas had been in the regular habit of anonymously giving gifts to people (most notably to a family with three daughters, thus enabling them to escape the necessity of becoming prostitutes). He became the patron saint of boys and the patron saint of seafaring men. In 1087, a group of sailors who idolized Nicholas moved his bones from Turkey to a sanctuary in Bari, an Adriatic coast city in southeast Italy. There, Nicholas supplanted a female boon-giving deity called "The Grandmother," or "Pasqua Epiphania," who used to fill the children's stockings

---

2. Libanius (fourth century AD Greek sophist), as cited in Dyer, *British Popular Customs*, 1:407.

with her gifts. The Grandmother was ousted from her shrine at Bari, which became the center of the Nicholas cult. Members of this group gave each other gifts during a pageant they conducted annually on the anniversary of Nicholas's death, December 6. An annual festival in Bari continues to the present day, organized around a model of Nicholas.

The Nicholas cult spread north until it was adopted by German and Celtic pagans. These groups worshipped a pantheon led by Woden—their chief god and the father of Thor, Balder, and Tiw. Woden was depicted as having a long, white beard and rode a horse through the heavens one evening each autumn.

When Nicholas merged with Woden ("Odin" in Norse), he shed his Mediterranean appearance, grew a beard, mounted a flying horse, rescheduled his flight for December, and donned heavy winter clothing! It is interesting to note that the Roman god Saturn was said to travel through the heavens on a quadriga (Roman chariot) pulled by horses or in some cases winged serpents. We noted earlier how Roman coins from the second century BC show Saturn being pulled by horses.

In a bid for pagan adherents in Northern Europe, the Roman Catholic Church adopted the Nicholas cult and taught that he did (and they should) distribute gifts on December 25 instead of December 6. We also noted that at the Reformation in Germany, Martin Luther wanted to get rid of the devotion to Saint Nicholas and invented the theory of "The Christ Child," picturing it as a representation of Christ at his incarnation as God's gift. Luther's aim appears to have been in shifting the emphasis of the established practice of giving gifts away from its association with Roman Catholic superstition to something more biblical.

In 1809, the novelist Washington Irving (pictured, whose father was from Orkney, Northern Scotland, and whose most famous works are *The Legend of Sleepy Hollow* and *Rip Van Winkle*) wrote a satire of Dutch culture entitled *Knickerbocker History*. The satire refers several times to the white bearded, flying-horse riding Saint Nicholas using his Dutch name, Santa Claus. Irving was an acquaintance of Charles Dickens, having met him on one of Dickens's several American tours. Dr. Clement Moore, a professor and founding member of a large Episcopalian Seminary in New York, read *Knickerbocker History* and in 1822 he published a poem estimated by some to be the most famous verses ever penned by an American. It was entitled *A Visit from St. Nicholas* and was based on the character Santa Claus:

> Twas the night before Christmas, when all through the house, not a creature was stirring, not even a mouse. The stockings were hung by the chimney with care, in the hope that Saint Nicholas soon would be there...

Moore innovated by portraying a Santa with eight reindeer who descended through chimneys. The Bavarian illustrator Thomas Nast almost completed the modern picture of Santa Claus. From 1862 through 1886, based on Moore's poem, Nast drew more than 2,200 cartoon images of Santa for *Harper's Weekly* (the very influential American political magazine based in New York). Before Nast, Saint Nicholas had been pictured as everything from a stern looking bishop to a gnome-like figure in a frock. Nast also gave

Santa a home at the North Pole, a workshop filled with elves, and a list of the good and bad children of the world. All Santa was missing was his red outfit.

In 1906 there was a common depiction of Santa dressed in red with white fur linings and soft drinks companies were using this by 1915, but this image of him took off in 1931. It was then that the Coca Cola Corporation contracted the Swedish commercial artist, Haddon Sundblom, to create a Coke-drinking Santa. Sundblom drew inspiration from Moore's 1822 poem and presented a plump, happy character, in order to promote the idea that Coke could be drunk all year round. In 1936, Sundblom revised the image and modeled his Santa on his friend Lou Prentice, chosen for his cheerful, chubby face. Sundblom continued to create new versions for the company until 1964.[3] So, the modern day Santa was born—a blend of early church Bishop later venerated by Rome, pagan god, and commercial idol!

---

3. "Coca-Cola and Father Christmas: The Sundblom Santa story." Coca-Cola Journey. www.coca-cola.co.uk/stories/history/advertising/coca-cola-and-father-christmas-the-sundblom-santa-story.

Biblical Misconceptions of the Nativity

MAKE BELIEVE ON THE part of the unconverted is to be expected. If one does not know God, or the purpose and destiny of life, then to invent and perpetuate fictional concepts and characters is natural. Anything which obscures or distracts from the "truth as it is in Jesus" is the trademark of Satan, "the god of this world" (2 Cor 4:4). Of much greater concern are erroneous beliefs and biblical misconceptions tolerated by some of the Lord's people. Nowhere do they abound more than on the subject of Christ's birth.

The Bible does not say that the angels sang, nor that the special star was visible to the shepherds, or that Mary traveled to Bethlehem on a donkey, or that she arrived the day or night Jesus was born, or that he was born in a stable, or that any animals were present at the birth, or that he was born in the middle of the night; neither does it say that there were three men from the East, or that they were kings, or that they rode on camels.

The Prelude to the Birth

In spite of Mary probably being a fit teenager, it is doubtful that Joseph and Mary would attempt to make the eighty mile trip from Nazareth in the final stages of her pregnancy (the usual route for Jews was the in-direct one to the east of the Jordon in order to avoid Samaria and it would normally take four or five days to complete on foot). Luke, in stating in 2:5 the fact that they commenced the trip when Mary was pregnant uses a term (*egkyos*), which does not indicate which pregnancy stage or trimester. Also, Luke 2:6 strongly implies that the couple were already residents in Bethlehem for at least some short time and that during their stay Mary gave birth to Jesus ("And while they were there, the time came for her to give birth").

We can easily assume a few weeks have passed, perhaps even a month or more. Thus, the birth took place in shelter found by Joseph during those weeks. Was Joseph so totally incompetent that he could provide nothing by way of adequate housing after a significant number of days in the district?

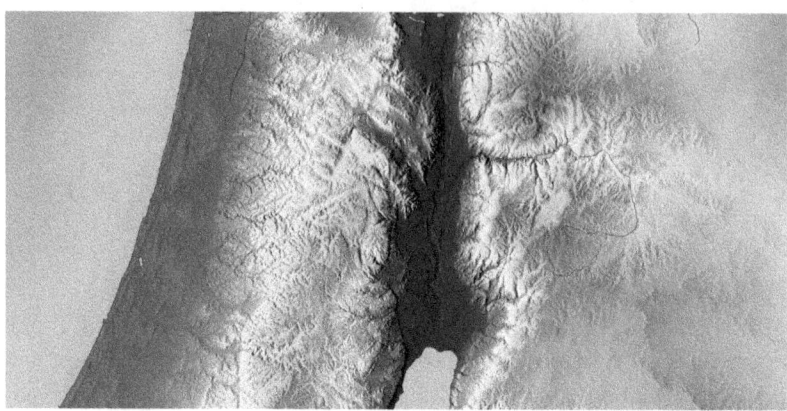

Elizabeth and Zacharias

Elizabeth and Zacharias lived relatively near to Bethlehem. The pictured relief map shows the area of the hill country of Judah, extending due south of Jerusalem. The "hill country of Judah" (Luke 1:39, 65) is a well-defined area south of Jerusalem, extending thirty-five miles long by fifteen miles broad, protected on three sides by natural frontiers: the Negeb desert to the south; steep hills to the west separating it from the Shepelah Plain; and the Judean wilderness and Dead Sea on the east.[1] Mary had already visited them during the third trimester of Elizabeth's pregnancy (probably the first trimester of her own pregnancy—Luke 1:36, 39, 56), when she would have grown intimately close to her elder cousin domestically but especially spiritually, with an intense, intimate communion in the Spirit. Given this fact, it is very possible that Mary and Joseph visited again while in the vicinity of Bethlehem. (As an aside, it is debatable whether or not Mary remained until the birth of John the Baptist or left just before. It would, in all of the circumstances, be odd for her to be with her elder cousin throughout the more difficult period of the pregnancy and then leave when the birth was imminent. Luke's description of events gives no certainty regarding Mary's absence.)

---

1. Beitzel, *New Moody Atlas*, 35

Both Elizabeth and Zacharias were descendants of Levi and his great-grandson Aaron (whose wife was also called Elizabeth—Exod 6:23). Her father was a priest and her brothers and uncles, and so on. Zacharias was not only a Levite but also a priest (since all priests descended from Aaron, all priests were Levites, yet all Levites were not priests, although they served the priests). There were twenty-four divisions of priests and most estimate that each division contained a thousand men. Zacharias would have served in the Jerusalem temple for two separate weeks annually. Lots were cast to determine which duties would be performed. The Talmud (written version of Jewish oral law and legend) states that the glorious privileged duty of going in with the incense before the altar of incense, to offer it before the Lord for the people, was a once-in-a-lifetime duty. No priest having performed it was allowed to perform it again. This year, this week, providence chose Zacharias! It was during this duty that the revelation from Gabriel was given to him, respecting the birth of John the Baptist, fulfilling the promise given the last time God had spoken to man four hundred years earlier, in the last two verses of Malachi:

> Behold, I will send you Elijah the prophet before the great and awesome day of the Lord comes. And he will turn the hearts of fathers to their children and the hearts of children to their fathers, lest I come and strike the land with a decree of utter destruction.

(Interestingly, Zacharias means "God remembers," and Elizabeth means "his oath," so taken together their names mean, "God remembers his oath"!) The Levites had no tribal area of their own but were permitted to live in forty-eight cities throughout Israel (Num 18:20; 35:18). Of these forty-eight, thirteen were specifically allocated to the priests (Josh 21:4–19), with six of these being cities of refuge. The only Levitical priestly cities in the hill country of Judah were Hebron, Juttah, Debir, Eshtemoa, and Jattir. The closest city, Hebron, (and sole city of refuge in this district) is about twenty miles walking distance from Bethlehem, a distance accomplished in a day (eight to nine hours), while the furthest was Jattir, ten miles further south. Most of the historical experts link Zacharias with Hebron. Elizabeth and Mary were within a day's travel of each other at the most, whenever Mary was in the vicinity of Bethlehem.

The registration process ordered at the behest of Caesar Augustus and Quirinius (who served two different terms as governor) was known in Judea as much as in Galilee. The process was either to facilitate an oath of allegiance to Augustus, or a census for tax purposes. If calling for a worldwide oath of allegiance, Augustus ordered his government officials and clients (which included Herod) to "make this happen" regardless of the social or civic status of their constituencies. Such an oath would have been highly offensive to Jews and there may well have been reluctance on Herod's part to implement it. The campaign to create an Augustus-centric image of the Roman world came at the worst possible time for Herod, the years 13–4 BC being times of intense difficulty and problems for him, largely due to his own family but there were external crises as well. So this enrolment was not about taxes (at least not at first), but about knowing the resources of the world and aligning those resources for the achievement of Augustus's personal ambitions and vision for what he thought the empire should become.[2]

If it was a census, then it was likely one which was preparatory to taxation, to identify non-Jewish males suitable for military service, and as such was conducted every fourteen years right up until 270 AD (which is why Luke refers to it as "the first census" in Luke 1:2).[3] Therefore, we can work back and identify the year that the first census was taken, which was in 8 BC. The Roman method was to take the census of a city or community of the persons living there but Judæa, not yet being a Roman province, took the census according to the Jewish method, which was based on the tribes and their families.

2. Barnett, "Apograhe and Apographesthai."
3. Cranfield, "Some Reflections," 182.

There is evidence, however, that Herod and the Jews stalled in their compliance with this inaugural census for two to four years, as they resented paying taxes to the Romans.

Toward the end of his life, Herod was not at all in high favor with Rome.[4] Even the Romans themselves resisted participation in censuses.

Whatever the real purpose behind the "decree" of Augustus, it could have been issued some years before it filtered down to Herod, and thus to Joseph and Mary. The enrollment may have eventually proceeded under final ultimatums from Rome and occurred sometime between 6 and 4 BC.[56] The point to note is that Elizabeth and Zacharias would have been well aware of the necessity for Joseph to come to Bethlehem, knowing that his father/family were from there and it was his ancestral home. Given the intense personal and spiritual interest that Elizabeth and Zacharias held in the birth of Mary's child, no less than "my Lord" to Elizabeth (Luke 2:43), enhanced by Mary's recent three-month stay in their home, plus the close proximity of Joseph and Mary to Elizabeth at the time of the Savior's birth, it is very likely that Elizabeth and Zacharias were well aware of Mary's movements as her pregnancy developed. It is quite possible that they were present at Jesus' birth.

Mary and Joseph

There was no necessity for Joseph to take Mary with him from Nazareth in order to complete the obligatory Roman registration process; however, it is understandable that he would have wanted to protect her from social shame and scorn in Nazareth due to her pregnancy. To appreciate this point, we need to reflect on their Jewish marriage customs before proceeding further.

Mary and Joseph were fully and legally married when Mary became pregnant, indeed they may have been married since early childhood. There were three stages to Jewish marriage: first, the written contract between the bride's father and the groom (or the bride's father and the groom's father if the groom was a child); second, the physical consummation in the bride's home; and third, the celebrations that immediately followed the consummation, commencing with a procession to the groom's home and all of the festivities therein in the days that followed.

First, the contract was a legally binding document, the primary purpose of which was to protect the bride, even though she did not even sign

4. Bock, *Jesus according to Scripture*.
5. www.gty.org/Resources/Print/Sermons/42-23.
6. Drane, *Introducing the New Testament*, 57.

it. The bride was seen as being completely under her father's control and the father of the bride would use his wisdom to look out for the best interests of his daughter:

> So then both he who gives his own virgin daughter in marriage does well, and he who does not give her in marriage will do better. (1 Cor 7:38—NASB)

The groom and the father of the bride would negotiate a legal document with conditions clearly laid out. There was the dowry money to be paid to the father by the groom:

> Ask me for as great a bride price and gift as you will, and I will give whatever you say to me. Only give me the young woman to be my wife. (Gen 34:12)

The bride price was usually set at fifty shekels of silver and was a cash penalty for divorce without cause. The contract also included an accounting of assets (cash, property, livestock, businesses, etc.) whereby the bride contributed to the new husband's estate when she married him. The contract was signed in triplicate where the father and groom each got a copy and a third one was filed with the court (synagogue) with a seal to be broken only by a judge. Once signed, a legal divorce was required to dissolve the marriage or betrothal.[7]

In the second stage, once the contract was signed, the couple did not have sexual relations until the groom fulfilled his financial obligations to the father of the bride (usually at least twelve months later). The bride's parents would arrange for a wedding room within the bride's house (the custom varied with the room sometimes being in the groom's new home). Sometimes the delay between the signing of the contract and consummation was because arranged marriages were signed when the bride was a child and the groom had to wait until she reached puberty. The "virginity cloth" that lay under the bride when she consummated the marriage (the common belief being that the bride's hymen would break causing bleeding) was of great importance. The bride and the groom might have up to ten friends who would act as witnesses to the event. Both the groom's parents and the parents of the bride would assign several formal witnesses to the event and would wait outside or in an adjoining room while the couple consummated the marriage in the wedding bed. Note John the Baptist's likely reference to this custom as he answers the concerns of his disciples and the wider public about Jesus' growing prominence:

---

7. Bruce and Rohrbaugh, *Social-Science Commentary*, 26–31.

> The one who has the bride is the bridegroom. The friend of the bridegroom, who stands [outside the wedding room] and hears him [announcing the satisfactory consummation which then legitimizes the marriage and the festivities to follow], rejoices greatly at the bridegroom's voice. Therefore, this joy of mine is now complete. (John 3:29)

The groom would hand the proof, the virginity cloth, to the witnesses in the room outside and the cloth would be validated and kept by the father of the bride as proof of her virginity. (This practice, although biblical, may appear unseemly to us, but it was also commonplace in the Middle Ages and up to the eighteenth century in Europe, especially among royalty and the nobility, where bilateral treaties were involved and evidence of the consummation deemed vital. With time, the emphasis shifted from rituals connected with betrothal, to that which we are familiar with today, connected with the wedding celebrations.)[8]

Deuteronomy 22 deals with a man who, following his wedding, spreads the charge that he found his wife not to have been a virgin. He probably does so in order to get out of the marriage, because should he simply divorce her without cause, he would probably forfeit the bride-price. The bride's parents produce physical evidence of her virginity, namely, a sheet or garment that was spotted with blood when the marriage was consummated. Upon this evidence the slandering husband is flogged, fined, and prohibited from ever divorcing the bride:

> If any man takes a wife and goes in to her and then hates her and accuses her of misconduct and brings a bad name upon her, saying, "I took this woman, and when I came near her, I did not find in her evidence of virginity," then the father of the young woman and her mother shall take and bring out the evidence of her virginity to the elders of the city in the gate. And the father of the young woman shall say to the elders, "I gave my daughter to this man to marry, and he hates her; and behold, he has accused her of misconduct, saying, 'I did not find in your daughter evidence of virginity.'
>
> And yet this is the evidence of my daughter's virginity." And they shall spread the cloak before the elders of the city. Then the elders of that city shall take the man and whip him, and they shall fine him a hundred shekels of silver and give them to the father of the young woman, because he has brought a bad name upon a virgin of Israel. And she shall be his wife. He may not divorce her all his days. But if the thing is true, that evidence

---

8. Gies and Gies, *Marriage and Family*, 97–100.

of virginity was not found in the young woman, then they shall bring out the young woman to the door of her father's house, and the men of her city shall stone her to death with stones, because she has done an outrageous thing in Israel by whoring in her father's house. So you shall purge the evil from your midst. (Deut 22:13–21)

If a wife became pregnant before the formal consummation ceremony, it was not a major problem and the child was not considered illegitimate. However, this left the bride vulnerable to future accusations of not being a virgin, since she would have no virginity cloth attested by her father.

This is the case of Mary, when she confirmed to Joseph that she was pregnant.

Prior to the angelic appearance to him in a dream, ordering him to cast away his fears, Joseph was intending to divorce Mary. Matthew 1:19 states, "And her husband Joseph, being a just man and unwilling to put her to shame, resolved to divorce her quietly."

He did not want to disgrace her, even though he at first believed she was an adulterer. He was going to divorce her secretly by merely handing her the divorce certificate, without making an accusation of adultery. This meant that Joseph was required to return the inventory of assets the bride had brought into the marriage and pay the bride-price to her father. He was described as righteous or 'just' because he had lawful grounds to accuse her, keep her inventory of assets, and not have to pay the fifty-shekel bride-price, all of which he was prepared to forego. A man in Joseph's position had everything to gain by openly accusing his bride, as it was going to cost much to divorce her secretly.

In conjunction with Joseph taking Mary away from the gossiping tongues of Nazareth, where else might Mary desire most to go but into the company of Elizabeth, who understood her and what God was doing in her life, more than anyone else?

Elizabeth and Zacharias knew that Mary had neither committed adultery nor engaged in premature sexual relations with Joseph. The prospect of returning into their company in the Bethlehem area (probably with several months of the pregnancy left) must have been a great encouragement to Mary. Moreover, Mary too was from the lineage of David and had relatives (like cousin Elizabeth) in the district, possibly still in David's birthplace of Bethlehem itself. Most travel in New Testament times was done on foot. Mary and Joseph knew the route south well, having traveled to the temple in Jerusalem at least three times each year from early childhood. Moreover, Mary had just recently made the return trip herself to and from the Bethlehem area. Even if they did not break the journey with stops at the homes of family/friends, there is no reason to suggest that it could not have been completed on foot.

The Birthplace

The Bible does not say that the Lord Jesus was born in a hotel stable, as "Inn" is the Greek word *kataluma*, and can mean guest chamber, lodging place, or inn: the only other time this word is used in the New Testament, it means a furnished, large, upper story room within a private house and it is translated "guest chamber" (KJV) or "guest room"/"room" (ESV), not "inn" (Mark 14:14–15). The Greek language has a word for a hotel or inn. In fact, Luke used it in Luke 10:34, when he wrote about the Good Samaritan who took the beaten man to the "inn" (*pandocheion,*) and paid the "innkeeper" (*pandochei*, vs. 35) to care for the man. Since Luke was quite familiar with the proper term for inn, why didn't he use it in the account of the birth of Jesus? The probable answer is that Joseph and Mary did not attempt to stay at an inn/hotel.

(In the KJV "inn" was first published in 1611 and based on Erasmus's Greek translation of 1516. After three hundred years of French from the time of the Norman Conquest, it was in 1362 that English became the official language of England. Twenty years later, in 1382, John Wycliffe published the first English Bible translation based on the Latin *Vulgate* Bible from 400 AD, and he translated the Latin of the same Greek word as "chamber.") Moreover, it remains quite uncertain as to whether Bethlehem would have had a commercial inn. Inns, then as now, were found on major roads. No major Roman road passed through Bethlehem and small villages on minor roads simply had no inns.

Palestinian custom dictated that relatives from other towns were welcomed by the head of the extended family/patriarch and brought under his protection during their stay in his village. The only real way to verify personal identity in the ancient world (outside of public officials and the elites) was through family and local witnesses, in conjunction with local records. For someone to "sign off" that Joseph was who he claimed to be, would require witnesses who were themselves already authenticated (i.e., known to the persons officially recording). Joseph would have taken a loyalty oath or registered as part of the taxation census, whichever purpose the enrollment was for, in the presence of his fellow Davidic descendants. Jews were profoundly attached to their village of family origin, which was an integral part of their identity. Even if Joseph had never been there before he could appear suddenly at the home of a distant cousin, recite his genealogy, and he is immediately among welcoming family. Joseph had only to say, "I am Joseph, son of Jacob, son of Matthan, son of Eleazar, the son of Eliud," and the immediate response must have been, "You are welcome our brother. Our home is your home." Indeed, a Jewish man returning to his home village insults his family or friends by going elsewhere for accommodation. So with relatives in Bethlehem, Joseph being of the direct line from David (the kingly line via Solomon that was later disqualified in Joconiah—Jer 22:30), Mary also being of the direct line from David (the actual lineage of Jesus, via David's son Nathan), plus with his wife obviously pregnant, it is very highly unlikely that Joseph would have been made unwelcome in every house in the village.

Moreover, given Zacharias's standing in the district as a priest, this makes it even more unlikely that no resident of Bethlehem gave Mary any accommodation. Besides all of this, the biblical text gives no hint whatsoever that anyone was displeased with the accommodation secured. Joseph and Mary most probably attempted to secure the use of the guest-room in one of their relative's homes. It is worth reflecting for a moment on the difference in perspective between the twenty-first century concept of home in the West and that in first-century Palestine. The following quote is from a former Syrian peasant:

> The assertion that the Syrian, both ancient and modern, lives for the most part out of doors is substantially correct. The long and rainless summers, the almost exclusively agricultural and pastoral life of the people, outside the few large cities, and the primitive modes of travel, enable the Syrian to live his life out in the open. His one-story house, consisting of one or two rooms very simply furnished, conveys the impression that it is only an emergency shelter. However, it should not be inferred from the foregoing that the Syrian thinks lightly of his humble home. No; he is a

passionate lover of it, and associates with it the deepest joys and sorrows of life. But he does not have for his abode the two designations "house" and "home," which prevail in the West. The Hebrew word bayith and the Arabic bait mean primarily a "shelter." The English equivalent is the word "house." The richer term, "home," has never been invented by the son of Palestine because he has always considered himself "a sojourner in the earth." His tent and his little house, therefore, were sufficient for a shelter for him and his dear ones during the earthly pilgrimage. The word which is translated "home" in about forty places in the English version of the Bible does not differ in the original from the word "house," which is found in about three thousand five hundred passages in the Bible. The terms "tent," "house," "place of residence," and the phrases, "to go to his kindred," "to return to his place," etc., are all translated "home," and "go home."[9]

The point to note is that the willingness to share one's house with others in first century Judea is quite alien to most in the West today. Simple village homes often had just two rooms. One was kept for guests, attached to the end of the house or on the roof (1 Kgs 17:19: "And he [Elijah] said to her, 'Give me your son.' And he took him from her arms and carried him up into the upper chamber where he lodged, and laid him on his own bed").

The main room was a family room where the family cooked, ate, slept, and lived. The end of the room next to the door was either a few feet lower than the rest of the floor or was blocked off with heavy timbers. This was where the family cow, donkey, and sheep/goat would be kept each night. This served the dual purpose of keeping the animals safe from harm and theft and providing heat to the house in the cooler seasons. Such homes still exist today in Bethlehem. (This may shed some light on why Jephthah vowed to sacrifice whatever came out of his house first on his return from victory in battle (Judg 11:29–40), possibly expecting an animal to come rushing out from the "stable" end of the house.) A house in a first century village was small, probably a square, flat-roofed building made of dried mud bricks with the exterior being white-washed, although many were one room caves built into the face of rock. In villages, houses were clustered around small courtyards where the women did the laundry, cooked over charcoal or wood fires, and the children played. The houses were clustered together for protection and efficient use of land, leaving the open fields for cultivation. In these courtyards were chicken coops, dove cotes, woodsheds, straw sheds, and other small storage buildings. Animals were kept in the courtyards:

---

9. Rihbany, *Syrian Christ*, 242–43.

sheep and goats were raised for meat, milk, and wool; chickens for meat and eggs; donkeys for carrying heavy burdens.

The roofs of the dwelling-houses were flat, and are often alluded to in Scripture (2 Sam 11:2; Isa 22:1; Matt 24:17). Sometimes tents or booths were erected on them (2 Sam 16:22). They were protected by parapets or low walls (Deut 22:8). On the house-tops grass sometimes grew (Ps 129:6–7; Isa 37:27). They were used, not only as places of recreation in the evening, but also sometimes as sleeping-places at night, in the summer-time especially (1 Sam 9:25–26; 2 Sam 11:2, 16:22; Prov 21:9) and as places of devotion (Jer 19:13; Acts 10:9). Beds in separate bedrooms were unknown. Instead cushion-mattresses were spread side by side in the living room, in a line as long as the members of the family required, sleeping close together. The man portrayed in Jesus' parable in Luke 11 was being completely truthful as to why he should not rise:

> And He said to them, "Which of you who has a friend will go to him at midnight and say to him, 'Friend, lend me three loaves, for a friend of mine has arrived on a journey, and I have nothing to set before him'; and he will answer from within, 'Do not bother me; the door is now shut, and my children are with me in bed. I cannot get up and give you anything'?" (v. 57).

The houses usually had only one room, but might have had a second floor where married children lived. In villages the doorway opened directly on the street. If there were windows, they were cut in the walls and veiled by curtains. The floor was hard-packed dirt mixed with clay and ash to make it as hard as cement and covered with a few straw or leather mats. Furniture was sparse, probably only a few wooden stools and a low wooden table.

Stables and mangers in our modern sense were in ancient times unknown in Palestine. The Greek word in Luke 2:7, *phatnē*, widely translated "manger" properly denotes a primitive feeding trough for the cattle around the walls. It was built of rough slabs of stone placed on edge and plastered up with mortar, often comprising a ledge or projection in the end of the family room, into which the hay or other food for the animals was placed when animals were present. When the animals were absent, the trough was useful for securely placing other items.[10] The animals, usually a few sheep and goats, several cows and sometimes a donkey, were never taken into the houses except at night and then only in the winter season![11] The Bible does not say that the Lord was born in a manger, rather that he was laid in

---

10. Thomson, *Land and the Book*, 2:503; Bailey, *Jesus through Middle Eastern Eyes*, 31.

11. www.bible-history.com.

a manger (i.e., a feeding trough) as a makeshift crib. This may have been portable and taken from the animal side of the family room, to the spot in the room where Mary held the Lord, or alternatively as we have mentioned previously, more likely it may have been a more permanent fixture forming a ledge separating the animal and human quarters.

Some may ponder how the shepherds could have found the Savior if he was born in an ordinary house—see Luke 2:16: "And they went with haste and found Mary and Joseph, and the baby lying in a manger."

However, it clearly was God's will to bring the shepherds to Jesus and he utilized the supernatural agency of angels to inform them of the birth.

We would not be surprised, therefore, to discover that the angels were also utilized to lead them to the precise birthplace. Even if there was no supernatural guidance, by the time the shepherds arrived in Bethlehem, news of the birth may already have spread, notwithstanding the sound of the Lord crying which may have filled the air.

Bethlehem is one of those biblical places referred to as a "city" (*polis*) but city in those days was very different to the area and population sizes of a city today. In the Bible, as a common rule, a city was so named because it had walls, whereas a village did not. Yet one of the most famous biblical cities—Jericho—covered an area measuring a mere ten acres, or 400 by 100 meters! John describes Bethlehem as a village (*kōmē*) in John 7:42, when Jesus' audience are debating his true status. In his commentary on Matthew, R. T. France notes that the various accounts of Bethlehem's population at the time of Jesus' birth, estimates it to be one thousand at the very most, and possibly as small as three hundred. Given Jewish domestic custom where married sons and daughters and their children often lived in the patriarchal family home, then if the latter figure of three hundred were correct, that could equate to as little as forty houses!

Luke 2:11 says that Jesus was born "this day," (a Jewish day being calculated as from sunset to sunset) meaning sometime after sunset (6:45 p.m. in the second week of September in Judea). Sunrise at the same time of year is 6:20 a.m., therefore the Savior could have been born in the early evening, early morning, or any time in-between, of that "night" of shepherding (Luke 2:8). Also, we know that Luke the Doctor habitually included more detail in his account than the other Gospel writers, and if the Savior was born in Bethlehem's inn or hotel, if such existed, it is strange that Luke did not state that the shepherds found him lying in *the* manger of *the* inn. We close this sub-section by quoting France:

> It is, however, becoming increasingly recognized that the "stable" owes more to Western misunderstanding than to Luke, who

speaks only of a "manger." . . . The point of Luke's mention of the manger is not therefore that Jesus' birth took place outside a normal house, but that in that particular house the "guest-room" was already occupied (by other census visitors?) so that the baby was placed in the most comfortable remaining area, a manger on the living-room floor. There is therefore no reason why they should not be in the same "house" when Matthew's magi arrive.[12]

The "Sign"

Others may highlight the "sign" given by the angels to the shepherds in Luke 2:12, respecting swaddling cloths and a manger and question what the significance of the sign was, if the place of the Savior's birth was so ordinary. Some have postulated that the swaddling cloths were a prophetic foreshadowing of Christ's burial cloth. They highlight a supposed custom of Palestine in the New Testament era when travellers prepared for the eventuality of injury or death on a journey, by wrapping around their waist under garments a 15 foot by 1 foot piece of thin linen cloth. If a death occurred, this cloth was used to temporarily bind the body. The Greek root word used by Luke is *sparganoo*, which means "to clothe with strips of cloth."

However, this word is never used in the New Testament to refer to burial cloth, including any of the references to Christ's death, so the link is linguistically weak (there is a stronger foreshadowing link with "Myrrh," gifted by the Magi in Matt 2:11 and given with vinegar to the Lord in Mark 15:23). Others have postulated that shepherds used swaddling cloth to protect lambs immediately after birth, if the lambs were deemed to be without external blemish and so suitable for Temple sacrifice, therefore this was the significance of the sign for them. Still others have highlighted the normal practice of washing a newborn in salt water prior to swaddling them (used metaphorically as lacking in the case of Jerusalem's pathetic, unwanted condition due to her sins—Ezek 16:25), thus signifying Jesus' legitimacy, and combining that with the covenantal references to salt in the Old Testament and those references to salt in the New Testament.

These suppositions are all very interesting, but perhaps the true significance of the sign to the shepherds lies squarely in the realm of the ordinary! The Lord Jesus was, at birth, wrapped in swaddling cloths according to the normal custom of the day, an action that showed the ordinary tender care and affection of a mother. He was then placed in a suitably safe location,

---

12. France, *Gospel of Matthew*, 74–75.

into a conveniently located manger in which he could not roll over. These humble circumstances were in keeping with the theological status of the eternal Son of God's state of humiliation. Shepherds were near the bottom of the social ladder and indeed, their profession was declared unclean by some of their rabbis; therefore, they were isolated from religious ordinances.[13] Many places would not welcome shepherds. In many homes they would feel their poverty and be ashamed of their low estate but . . . not on this occasion, not in this house. They faced no humiliation as they visited this child, for he was laid in a manger. That is, he was born in a simple peasant home with the mangers in the family room and to all there present (Luke 2:18) they recounted the angelic appearances, to the amazement of everyone, except Mary. Jesus was one of them and with that assurance, the shepherds left to return to their flocks with praise in their hearts, oblivious to the fact that they were a practical illustration of the future of God's kingdom, comprising predominantly of the *foolish, weak, low*, and *despised* (1 Cor 1:26–28).

What made this "sign" so significant for the shepherds, first of all when they heard it, then en route into the village as they pondered it, and finally when they saw the infant Lord Jesus for themselves, was the amazing contrast between the terrifying glory of God manifested in the solitary, then multitudinous angelic appearances to them in the hill fields and the angels' identification of the newborn as Jehovah, all on the one hand, and on the other hand, Jesus' entrance into this life in such humble and ordinary circumstances.

With respect to the angels' mode of announcement and declaration and the question of whether they sang or spoke it, there are approximately 310 references in the Bible to singing (*sang, sing, singing*, and *song*) and 282 to angels (*angel, angels*), allowing for minor numeric variation between the English translations. It is an interesting observation that *none* of these references join the two and attribute singing to angels! That is not to say that angels cannot or do not sing, rather that the Lord has chosen not to inform us that they do. The term used by Luke informing us that the angels collectively were "praising" God (*aineō* 2:13) is the identical term he uses a few verses later in 2:20, where he describes the shepherds leaving the Savior and heading back to their fields, praising God for his arrival. Their praise was not necessarily in the form of song.

The Lord Jesus was very probably born in the house of relatives, but outside (under) the normal guest quarters, a simple two-room village home such as the Middle East has known for at least three thousand years, surrounded not by a supernatural glow or light from angel or star but by helping

---

13. Bailey, *Poet and Peasant*, 147.

hands and encouraging women's voices. Joseph and Mary circumcised the Lord at eight days of age, then presented him in the Temple of Jerusalem after forty days (Mary's period of purification—Lev 12:16). They returned to the Bethlehem area and settled there, either moving upstairs when the guest room of the same house became available, or moving into another building, possibly outside Bethlehem altogether. Joseph no doubt pursued his trade until Jesus was a toddler, when the family fled into Egypt from Herod's imminent wholesale infanticide. Egypt was an unsurprising destination as it was relatively near at hand and very accessible, via what was unquestionably the most important highway in the biblical world—the Great Trunk Road or Way of the Sea, linking Egypt with Lebanon and Mesopotamia. The road would have been accessed from Bethlehem by heading south on the Central Ridge Road to Hebron, then Beersheba, thereafter heading southwest into Egypt. It was also a Roman province, outside Herod's jurisdiction yet home to a large Jewish community of one million, according to Philo writing around 40 AD.[14]

The Magi

Just prior to the family's evacuation, the special star that had indicated to the Magi the birth of a new national king and had subsequently led them to Judah, reappeared to them while they were en route from Jerusalem to Bethlehem.

The Magi were astronomers with an interest in prophecy, from the east (Arabia, Persia, or India), where centers of astronomy are known to have existed. The star was noticed by them from their homelands in the east and up to two years prior to their eventual arrival in Bethlehem. The Greek word *paidion*, is used to describe Jesus at the time that the magi arrived (Luke 2:27), instead of the description of babe, the Greek word *brephos* (Luke 2:16). *Brephos* specifically refers to a baby, whether born or unborn, while *paidion* refers to a young child.

The Magi may well have descended from those who in previous generations had been influenced by Daniel and Esther, and thus were acquainted with Old Testament revelation of God, or they could even have been Jews themselves (although their ignorance of Mic 5:2: "But you, O Bethlehem Ephrathah, who are too little to be among the clans of Judah, from you shall come forth for me one who is to be ruler in Israel, whose coming forth is from of old, from ancient days," would militate against this).

Were they familiar with Balaam's prophecy in Num 24:17, when he was constrained by God to make a declaration respecting the coming of

---

14. Beitzel, *New Moody Atlas*, 84; Philo, *Works of Philo Judaeus*, 4:70.

Christ, referring to him as "a Star of Judah"? Were they familiar with Daniel's "seventy weeks" prediction (Dan 9:24–25) that Messiah would come 483 years after the Persian emperor gave the commandment to rebuild Jerusalem? Very possibly. In other words, these men were not necessarily casual observers of the night sky who happened to notice a new star; rather, they may have been anticipating the appearance of such, so that they had no need of specific guidance from the star's position to take them to Judah, as they fully expected that the newborn King of the Jews would be found in Jerusalem. The Greek word used for "star"—*aster*—does not afford us much of a clue in determining what the light of it was like.

The word occurs twenty-four times in the New Testament, e.g., Matt 24:29, 1 Cor 15:41, and Rev 1:16 and 2:28, with four uses of a related word and they are used in both a literal and metaphorical sense. (It is also used in the LXX Greek translation of the Old Testament in Num 24:17, just referred to). Here in Matt 2, its use in a literal sense indicates that it was a real star. It was possibly a nova or supernova, i.e., an exploding star that burns brightly for a time before disappearing (the record of which exists in Chinese astronomical sources, recorded in 4 and 5 BC).[15] In 2015, a supernova was detected which emitted more energy per second than all the stars in the Milky Way and 100 billion times more energy than the sun—if the star was such a type

---

15. McIver, *Star of Bethlehem*.

as this, then it was a very fitting sign for the entrance in human nature of the One who created this and every other star himself![16]

Other experts postulate theories respecting planetary conjunctions and comets.

However, given the significance of the event—the arrival of Immanuel—why may God not have created a brand new star, used it and then dispensed with it, just for this purpose alone? Ignatius, who was the apostolic father closest in time to the New Testament writers (died c. 110 AD), wrote of the star in chapter 19 of a letter to the Ephesians as follows:

> [It was] a star which so shone in heaven beyond all the stars, its newness caused excitement.[17]

The Lord made all of the stars and named all ten trillion plus of them, every one (Ps 147:4; Isa 40:26). He, of course, made their positions or constellations, as "signs" (Gen 1:14), as well as guides to time periods. Some of the constellations are named, such as the Bear, Orion, and the Pleiades (Job 9:9) and clearly they have theological meanings and instruction for us, predating all of the corrupting influences of ancient and modern astrology. If the Lord's star appeared in one of those constellations, then this would have provided further assistance to the Magi in identifying whose star it was.

Those Magi who made the journey may have come from numerous different localities, may not have numbered several but rather an entourage of dozens, requiring considerable planning over a period of time. Even with a large caravan, Persia to Jerusalem on horseback would be accomplished with ease within a month. Moreover, the Magi came from the Parthian empire (247 BC–228 AD), an area not controlled by the Romans but by those who were a serious challenge to Rome's empire. Indeed, several decades earlier they had invaded Palestine and caused Herod to flee to Rome! There, he gained the Romans favor and returned with a Roman army to expel the Parthians in 37 BC. In Parthian fashion, these Magi may not have travelled on dromedaries but on strong, beautiful horses, which all Parthians were widely renowned to use. Little wonder that their arrival in Jerusalem was very disconcerting to Herod and caused a great commotion among the populace:

> When Herod the king heard this, he was troubled, and all Jerusalem with him. (Matt 2:3)

---

16. See articles on the Star of Bethlehem in the Research Portal of the American Association of Variable Star Observers on www.aavso.org.

17. Chevallier, *Translation of the Epistles*, 64.

This would have grown by the minute due to Herod's confusion and alarm, allied to his unpredictable and violent character.

The Magi, of course, also speak to us evangelistically, as the Lord sends providential difficulties, the testimony of his people, and the wonders of creation, among other things, all to act as "stars" pointing lost sinners to Christ. The Magi were mistaken in their choice of Jerusalem, just as lost sinners search in the wrong place for what is of worth to satisfy them in life, but these Magi listened to and acted upon Scripture—Mic 5:2. In so doing, they found him whom they were seeking and that, of course, is where lost sinners must seek to find Christ—in the depths of God's wisdom, the depths of God's will, the depths of God's Word, even when others better placed than themselves fail to search in the right place, just as Herod and his religious advisors failed to do.

The manner of Christ's star's reappearance and guidance led the Magi to the very house the family occupied. This may indicate that the house was isolated from others, perhaps outside the main village, but we can only make suppositions because we do not know the precise nature of the star's operation or its position/elevation relative to the Magi's approach to the area and the exact location of Joseph's house.

There is nothing that explicitly states that the family were in Bethlehem itself when the Magi visited their house. The Magi discovered from Herod and his counselors that Bethlehem was the location where the Scriptures prophesied the birth of the Christ, then Herod directed the Magi there. However, we are told nothing of where exactly the star led the Magi, other than to the house "where the young child was" (Matt 2:9).

Moreover, Herod's infanticide was not restricted to the main village of Bethlehem, but also included the region/vicinity (*horion*) around it. The term *horion* used in Matt 2:16 is used another ten times in the Greek New Testament, sometimes denoting the area of a town such as Antioch Pisidia (southern Asia Minor), from which Paul and Barnabas were expelled (Acts 13:50) and other times denoting a much larger area, such as the tribal areas of Zebulun, and Naphtali (Matt 4:13). In his efforts to destroy any perceived rival to his throne, Herod extended his murderous campaign to homes within a certain radius surrounding Bethlehem. Did this policy reflect intelligence received by Herod and his officers, which indicated that Joseph had set up home outside Bethlehem itself?

When these Magi are represented in nativity plays as kings and not astronomers, the treasure they brought is often represented as being huge in volume, in keeping with the usual resources kings would have. Surely such a massive financial windfall to Joseph is not in keeping with the poverty and humiliation of Christ. No numeric values are stated—were there large or small quantities, was there one of each gift type or ten of each gift type?

We are not informed. The gifts were undoubtedly a providential blessing so that Joseph could provide for his family in Egypt and thereafter, but their preciousness was not found in their volume so much as in their nature: precious entities (theologically symbolic) and an amount which the various astronomers could afford, tokens of the homage they felt in their hearts to a divine child. The Greek word used in the plural by Matthew in 2:11— *thēsaurós*—translated "treasures," occurs seventeen times in the New Testament and is often used figuratively to denote the preciousness of something, e.g., Paul speaks of a human being understanding the glory of Christ, as one who possesses "this treasure in jars of clay" (2 Cor 4:7).

All of these facts contradict the popular nativity scenes that so often depict the Lord Jesus as a baby, surrounded simultaneously by stabled cattle and donkeys, shepherds, a star, three kings and their camels with treasure galore, all lighting up the "dark streets" of the "little town of Bethlehem." Roman Catholic veneration of Mary has resulted in an exaggerated portrayal of her, departing Nazareth in the final week of her pregnancy, arriving in Bethlehem with the birth imminent, experiencing a callous refusal of accommodation in the village hotel, necessitating childbirth in an adjacent livestock shed!

Summary

Mary and Joseph were in Bethlehem for some time before the birth, possibly days, possibly weeks, probably months. Joseph secured accommodation for himself and Mary, in a home where the guest room was unavailable but where the living room (with standard fitted mangers) was available. The Bible does not indicate the presence of any livestock in the immediate vicinity of the birth room; indeed, such is unlikely given that the weather was still warm enough for shepherds to graze their sheep on hill pastures throughout the night (commonly from March to November). The birth could have occurred at sunset or the following sunrise, with nothing revealed of the timescale between the birth and the angelic appearance to the shepherds. The star had no significance in indicating to locals in Judea or in the Bethlehem district (the shepherds included) where the house containing the Lord Jesus was situated, until one to two years after his birth, when he was a toddler. The Magi were astronomers, not kings, and numbered at least two and probably many more.

These are just some examples of the many erroneous ideas and interpretive misconceptions that have become embedded in the minds of people, due to their exposure to mythological, imaginative, and sentimental songs, literature, and drama over two millennia, none of which reflect what the Bible actually states.

Significance for the Christian

THERE ARE TWO ASPECTS to this, a social one and a religious one.

Social Significance

Christmas is a special time of year, has its own musical and culinary genre and is the period when annual family reunion is most likely to occur. For those living in the northern hemisphere with long winter nights and a minimal amount of sunshine, there is no impropriety in having a period of vacation in the middle of winter. There are even medical conditions diagnosed today that recognize the particular difficulties some people can face in winter, including SAD (seasonal affective disorder) and Vitamin D deficiency where the body is unable to produce enough of it naturally through sunlight exposure.

Having lights and decorations to brighten up towns and homes cannot, of course, meet humanity's real need to have the Light of the World in their hearts, which is borne out by the fact that depression and suicide peak during this season! But at a superficial social level, families reuniting, gifts being exchanged, and extra lights set up are some of the many characteristics we have come to associate with this unique time of year, and they can be practiced without any religious foundation or element necessary to achieve them at all.

The Christian is in the world but not of the world—John 17:14-17:

> I have given them your word, and the world has hated them because they are not of the world, just as I am not of the world. I do not ask that you take them out of the world, but that you keep them from the evil one. They are not of the world, just as I am not of the world. Sanctify them in the truth; your word is truth.

On a few occasions Christ's church on earth have found themselves in the blessed position where the Gospel has had a profound effect on their society, its leaders, its legislators, and the vast majority of their peers, resulting in a society governed greatly by God's Word.

However, for most of the church in every era it occupies the position of a minority group in a secular society with its own customs and traditions that change over time and it is in such a world that the Christian usually lives. There always exists a tension in conforming or otherwise to social norms and expectations, between what is permissible in God's sight and good for that society, and what is not permissible and would be bad for society. Commenting on these verses in John 17, Matthew Henry stated:

> But he prayed that the Father would keep them from the evil, from being corrupted by the world, the remains of sin in their hearts, and from the power and craft of Satan. So that they might pass through the world as through an enemy's country, as he had done. They are not left here to pursue the same objects as the men around them, but to glorify God and to serve their generation. The Spirit of God in true Christians is opposed to the spirit of the world.

The aim for the Christian ought to be in abstaining from worldliness, which does not simply mean avoiding obvious immoral behavior but also includes avoiding myths and practices rooted in paganism. As noted above, we live in an increasingly post-Christian society and for the vast majority of the population, Christmas is *not* a religious occasion.

When most people use the greeting "Merry Christmas" or "Happy Christmas," it is simply a recognition of the time or season of the year, no different to wishing someone "Happy Birthday," "Have a good holiday," or even "Goodnight." It is an annual season of pleasure, as much a relief from the routine of life as the annual summer holiday is. For most it is a time of vacation, family reunion, nostalgia, fantasy, expenditure, and general hedonism, to which peer pressure compels all to embrace, not to mention the commercial pressure via all forms of media. Mixed with all of this is a pseudo-religious element and for those living in northern Europe and much of North America, there is the contrast between snow, frost, icy chills, and prolonged darkness outside, and warm stoves and light inside, all of which combine to make it a unique and most special time of year. Unquestionably, the convention of the "office party" reaches its pinnacle at Christmas and there exists more drunkenness and sexual promiscuity at this time of year than at any other. In that sense, the "spirit of Christmas" very much lives on and retains the qualities of its Roman prototype, as it clearly did also in Increase Mather's day.

In 2015, the UK public spent £76 billion on Christmas (gifts, decorations, food, and travel, the highest spend in Europe).[1] This compares with an estimated total cash amount donated to charity in the UK for the *whole* of 2015, of £9.6 billion.[2] In the USA, a staggering $630 billion was spent on Christmas in 2015 (more than the whole GDP of 131 nations).[3] This is at a time when 1.5 billion people have no full Bible in their first language and 160 million have no Scripture at all in their heart language.[4] The marriage of religion with financial profiteering is nothing new (as the Savior highlighted in the Gentile Courts of the Jerusalem Temple) and have been commonplace in predominantly Roman Catholic lands into the modern era. The modern Protestant recognition of Romish holy days such as Christmas, Easter, Valentine's Day, and Mothering Sunday has occurred in parallel with escalating, commercial profiteering.

The festive season of Christmas and New Year is inescapable and when it comes around each year, it is futile for any to pretend that it is not Christmas time. The Christian has a duty to witness in all societies and at all seasons without compromising God's expectations of them. The challenge for the Apostle Paul and for each generation of believers was and is, in finding

1. Centre for Retail Research, www.retailresearch.org/shoppingforxmas.php.

2. Charities Aid Foundation, www.cafonline.org/docs/default-source/personal-giving/caf_ukgiving2015.

3. Christina Lavingia, "From Spending to Celebrating: The 2015 Holiday Season in 25 States," AOL, November 28, 2015. www.aol.com/article/2015/11/28/from-spending-to-celebrating-the-2015-holiday-season-in-25-stat/21272137/.

4. Source: These figures are compiled within the Wycliffe Global Alliance. www.wycliffe.org.uk/about/our-impact/

"the marketplace" (Acts 17:17) in order to witness of Christ. In the short term at least, Christmas is here to stay in Europe and North America and it is as much a feature of winter-time as going to the beach, barbecues, ice-creams, and fresh strawberries are a part of summertime. As beach missions are a legitimate means of evangelism, it is by no means illegitimate to use the Christmas season as an opportunity to witness of Christ and him crucified. There is no need to run and hide at the sight of a Santa approaching. Rather, go ask him if he has the gift of eternal life!

Another example of using the occasion evangelically, is seen in what is for many, a quintessential part of the season—the Queen's Christmas broadcast to the nation. Elizabeth II, we have cause to hope, not only bears a social relationship to us as a monarch but also a spiritual relationship to us as our sister in Christ. The Queen inherited the tradition of an annual broadcast begun by her grandfather, George V and continued what had become an expected custom. In more recent decades, Her Majesty has not failed to use this custom to commend Christ.

Another feature of Christmas is the increased level of charitable philanthropy that occurs. Appeals to the public for material or financial help meet with more success and contributions than at any other time of year. Those who have a family to gather around, a roof over their heads, good health, good pet welfare etc. and all in an environment free from war, disaster, and disease, show their sympathy for those who do not have these blessings. Both secular and Christian organizations hold special Christmas appeals. Whatever term is used to advertise the appeal—"Christmas," "Winter," "Holiday Season," or "New Year"—is irrelevant. What *is* relevant, is the opportunity to do good to others:

> So then, as we have opportunity, let us do good to everyone, and especially to those who are of the household of faith. (Gal 6:10)

God anointed Jesus of Nazareth with the Holy Spirit and with power. He went about doing good. (Acts 10:38)

Turn away from evil and do good. (Ps 34:14)

Do not neglect to do good and to share what you have, for such sacrifices are pleasing to God. (Heb 13:16)

But love your enemies, and do good, and lend, expecting nothing in return, and your reward will be great, and you will be sons of the Most-High, for he is kind to the ungrateful and the evil. (Luke 6:36)

As for the rich in this present age, charge them not to be haughty, nor to set their hopes on the uncertainty of riches, but on God who richly provides us with everything to enjoy. They are to do good, to be rich in good works, to be generous and ready to share. (1 Tim 6:17–18)

What good is it, my brothers, if someone says he has faith but does not have works? Can that faith save him? If a brother or sister is poorly clothed and lacking in daily food, and one of you says to them, "Go in peace, be warmed and filled," without giving them the things needed for the body, what good is that? (James 2:14–16)

We should not reject the opportunity this season presents to do good, simply on the basis that we do not endorse the religious practice of Christmas. There exists a social significance which compels the Christian to do good to others whenever they can.

Christmas largely remains as the Victorians intended it to be, a time of great fun. This is illustrated in the nativity plays broadcast in the media and replicated in schools up and down the country, where Jesus' birth is used as an occasion to entertain with music, costume, and drama, often in a trite and frivolous fashion.

However, there is nothing whatsoever trite in the doctrines of sin, judgement, hell, and salvation, which are central to the incarnation. This fact leads us into our evaluation of the endorsement of Christmas in a religious sense, which is, in many parts of the visible church, quite in keeping with the light-hearted Christianity that characterizes many churches. We could quote so many respected Christian teachers of the twentieth century who identified this trend. We will close this section with a quote from one of them—A. W. Tozer, in 1950, from his less well-known book, *The Divine Conquest*, later retitled *The Pursuit of Man*:

> But if I see aright, the cross of popular evangelicalism is not the cross of the New Testament. It is, rather, a new bright ornament upon the bosom of self-assured and carnal Christianity whose hands are indeed the hands of Abel, but whose voice is the voice of Cain. The old cross slew men; the new cross entertains them.
>
> The old cross condemned; the new cross amuses. The old cross destroyed confidence in the flesh; the new cross encourages it. The old cross brought tears and blood; the new cross brings laughter.[5]

Religious Significance

As we noted in the Introduction above, up until the 1960s, December 25 was a normal working day in some countries such as Scotland. It is a quite striking fact, that in the worship of God, the practice of Christmas has reinvented itself in purportedly Calvinistic churches where, in times past, it was repudiated. The chief problems with the religious observance of Christmas are:

First, it has false, blasphemous, papist origins, the effect of which is to undermine justification by faith alone that Christ died for the individual believer and bolster the false doctrine that Christ died for the church, therefore salvation/justification is accomplished by coming into the church. As the morality of society becomes less Christian, the Lord's people often agree with conservative statements issued by the Roman Catholic Church. With the modern diversity within Catholicism and the collegial style in which many of its views are presented, it is easy to imagine that its doctrines have now changed. However, we must be clear that the Roman Catholic Church has *not changed* its basic doctrines at all. It is a good works religion like all false religions are, such as Judaism, Islam, Buddhism, and Mormonism to name but a few. The Roman Catholic Church's official *Catechism* makes it quite clear that historic councils such as Trent (held in northern Italy in three parts from 1545 to 1563), are infallible. Trent pronounces a curse (anathema) upon anyone who says that faith alone in God's promise is sufficient to obtain God's grace.[6] As converted Roman Catholic priest Richard Bennet explains:

> Rome's reason for such a curse . . . is because of what she refuses to concede. For her, justification is not an immediate one-time act of God received by faith alone. Rather, Rome teaches that grace is conferred continually through her sacraments. . . . The

---

5. Tozer, *Divine Conquest* [later entitled *The Pursuit of Man*], 53–54.
6. US Catholic Conference, *Catechism of the Catholic Church*, para. 891.

concept that the sacraments automatically convey the grace of the Holy Spirit to people, is pivotal to papal Rome.[7]

Linking this with what we noted earlier about Mithraism and the ancient pagan worship of the goddess mother and child, it was as recent as 1954 that Pope Pius XII officially declared Mary the "Queen of Heaven."

Typical of her veneration is this historic artwork, which is found within the Church of the Holy Sepulchre, in Jerusalem. The use of indulgences, worship of Mary, invocation of dead sinners (elevated to an unbiblical status of heavenly "Saints" by the church), purgatory, the confessional (with absolution of sins pronounced), penance (where the absolution pronounced is not complete forgiveness but requires the performance of some ritual as a punishment), use of the Rosary and other superstitious relics, all remain as much officially sanctioned and practiced, as they were in the days when our spiritual forefathers protested against them. (We will not detail the hundreds of direct connections between Roman Catholicism and ancient pagan symbolism, as found in the architecture of Roman Catholic churches from the Vatican and St. Peter's Square to every other part of the world, the artwork in churches and shrines and on the ceremonial garments, and accoutrements used by Popes.)

Overshadowing all such practices, however, is the distortion of the Lord's Supper known as "the mass," where Christ is sacrificed repeatedly to atone for the sins of both the living and the dead. The priest is said to have power to "transubstantiate" or change the wafer of bread and cup of wine into the actual real body and blood of Christ.

---

7. Bennet, *Catholicism*, 279–80.

In effect, it reduces Christ to a thing that can be moved from the Father's right hand in heaven to earth by a sinful man (a priest), and elevates a thing (a wafer of bread) to the status of God the Son! It is such a dishonor to the Savior's one sacrifice for sins forever (Heb 7:27; 10:12), that it is little wonder that it has long been designated by so many as "abominable" and "blasphemous." It also defies the teaching of Acts 15:29 that the Lord's people should "abstain from things sacrificed to idols, and from blood."

The Mass is the most important form of worship for Roman Catholics, the Catholic Catechism requiring them to observe it at least once a week in order to keep the Sabbath holy (in accordance with the Ten Commandments).

Illustrated is a Mass performed by Joseph Ratzinger (Pope Benedict XVI) prior to his shock resignation in 2013, in the face of allegations of complicity in institutional child abuse concealment. Apart from this "Ordinary Mass," there is a daily Mass for those who wish it and for traditionalists a "Tridentine Mass," more ceremonial in form and performed in Latin. Requiem Masses are held following a death and Requiem Memorial Masses are held throughout the year for different organizations (e.g., the Catholic Police Guild have an annual memorial Mass in Westminster Cathedral, London, for recently deceased officers) and then there are wedding Masses and no doubt other occasions where Mass is celebrated. With over seventy saint's days and over sixty feast days per year, Mass can lawfully be celebrated at any one of them.

In Europe apart from the Ordinary Mass, there exist ten holy days of the year when the observance of mass is obligatory: January 1, the Feast of Mary, the Mother of God; January 6, Epiphany; March 19, St. Joseph; forty days after Easter Sunday, Ascension Thursday; fifty days after Easter, Corpus Christi; June 29, the Solemnity of St. Peter and St. Paul; August 15, Assumption of Mary into Heaven; November 1, All Saints' Day; December 8, the Feast of the Immaculate Conception; and December 25, Christmas.

However, of all the masses celebrated, Christmas remains the most significant for most Roman Catholics, particularly the Christmas Eve midnight mass in conjunction with Nativity plays and on Christmas Day morning, priests are permitted to say three Masses!

Christmas Eve Baby Jesus Mass, St. Peter's, Rome

It is little wonder that in the past, the Lord's people wanted nothing in the slightest to do with a religious act that so dishonors Christ and his atonement. The fact that millions of Bible-believing Protestants are observing a Roman Catholic holy day, which has not been commanded anywhere in God's Word, is striking and would be the cause of dismay to many Protestants from previous generations, upon whose shoulders the church has stood and enjoyed its greatest usefulness in God's hands.

> We cannot conform, communicate, and symbolise with the idolatrous Papists, in the use of the same, without making ourselves idolaters by participation.[8]

Every year at Easter there are people who go to Jerusalem, place thorns on their heads and carry crosses along the *Via Dolorosa*, reenacting the final

---

8. Gillespie, *Dispute Against English-Popish Ceremonies*, pt. 3, 35.

act of Christ's life. Few of the Lord's people would condone such actions, viewing them as something demeaning to the Lord's vicarious suffering. Are nativity plays any different? A plastic baby doll depicting the now exalted King of Glory is no less demeaning. Christ was once properly worshipped as a baby when he was a baby (by Simeon if not also by the shepherds) but to do so again in a church service is verging on idolatry. The atmosphere created by the role of costumed children and melodic music such as "Away in a Manger" or "Holy Night" appear to charm the senses and delude.

Reflect for a moment on the effect on converted Roman Catholics who have left that church and in their new freedom in Christ, come into a Protestant church around Christmas. When they see the Christmas tree, the nativity play, and all of the other trappings, they could not be blamed for wondering what all of it has to do with justification by faith alone. We end this point with a quote from a converted Roman Catholic woman, which is unlikely to be uncommon among converted Roman Catholics:

> I am, however, an x catholic and I abhor the works righteousness teachings of the Roman Catholic Church. In other words, Christmas was just another millstone around my neck as a Roman Catholic. Don't forget that it is a holy day of obligation, under punishment of hell for not observing it by attending the sacrifice of the mass, according to the Roman Catholic Church. I am grateful that I do not HAVE TO reverence December 25th and I can ignore it if I wish. I find the incarnation of God in the form of a baby in a manger a wondrous, pivotal event in the history of man and the world, and worthy of meditation and indeed an invocation to prayerful worship. So do we have to observe it on December 25th? No, we can do it any day we choose, like say February 29th. Yeah, I like that idea.[9]

Second, it amounts to an overemphasis on one doctrine (the incarnation), when the New Testament emphasis lies in different doctrines, namely the Death and Resurrection of Christ. There are approximately two hundred and fifty verses in the New Testament referring to the Lord's death and resurrection (almost two hundred of them being in the teaching epistles and outside the historical accounts in the Gospels), compared to ninety-five verses on his birth (ninety of them being in the opening historical narratives of Matthew and Luke and only five in the teaching epistles). Do we preach Christ and him incarnated? No! We preach Christ and him crucified. Do we remember his incarnation until he comes? No! We remember his death until he comes. Every day when we read and pray, hold family worship, or

---

9. Posted by "Grinchette" on December 6, 2010, at www.hornes.org/theologia/.

participate in a church service, we implicitly acknowledge the wonderful fact that Christ Jesus came into the world to save sinners. We do not need an annual festival to acknowledge this wonderful fact and that is why God never instituted one.

The irony is that when God *has* given us a day on which to remember a very great event in the history of the universe and the story of the Savior—the Lord's Day marking the resurrection of Christ—the vast majority of the world's population ignore it completely.

Why take four New Testament chapters (two in Matthew and two in Luke) and make it the biggest Christian event annually? Why not take six chapters of the New Testament on, for example, Christ's miracles and invent an annual festival, culminating in Miracle Sunday? There would be as much biblical warrant for instigating this as there exists for doing Christmas.

Third, allied closely to all this is the practical spiritual effect of the misplaced emphasis. Those with no live church connection or nominal church attendees are liable to be lulled into/confirmed in a false sense of security, by imagining that if they acknowledge and practice Christmas (i.e., the religious side of it) then they are giving assent to Christianity and thereby are spiritually safe. They sincerely sing carols and acknowledge that Christ came into the world in the form of baby Jesus but does salvation exist in such an acknowledgment? No! Salvation lies through acknowledging that the man Christ Jesus died for your own sins—something requiring humility/contrition on the sinner's part. The baby Jesus does not audibly address anyone, causes no offence to man's pride, and so is acceptable to the masses. "Love came down at Christmas," is a sound-bite with much appeal to the masses but what type of love is in mind? Liberal churches (including those until quite recently regarded as evangelical and Reformed) have abandoned the doctrine of penal substitution and electing love, maintaining instead that God's love is so universal and elastic as to embrace all manner of people irrespective of their beliefs or lifestyles. There is no room for criticism or separation, as the love of God that has "come down" finds no fault in anyone or anything.

Does it never strike the Lord's people as odd and leave them uncomfortable that while the world around them are offended at and hate the doctrines of original sin, repentance, election, hell, and so on, they absolutely love Christmas?

> If the world hates you, know that it has hated me before it hated you. If you were of the world, the world would love you as its own; but because you are not of the world, but I chose you out of the world, therefore the world hates you. (John 15:18,19)

As A. W. Pink stated:

> And who is it that celebrates "Christmas?" The whole "civilised world." Millions who make no profession of faith in the blood of the Lamb, who "despise and reject him," and millions more who while claiming to be his followers yet in works deny him, join in merrymaking under the pretence of honoring the birth of the Lord Jesus.
>
> Putting it on its lowest ground, we would ask, is it fitting that his friends should unite with his enemies in a worldly round of fleshly gratification? Does any truly born-again soul really think that He whom the world cast out is either pleased or glorified by such participation in the world's joys? Verily, the customs of the people are vain; and it is written, "Thou shalt not follow a multitude to do evil" (Exod 23:2).[10]

By endorsing Christmas in a religious sense, the Lord's people are encouraging institutional Christianity, where Christian salvation is regarded as being attained by giving assent to outward means such as church attendance and holy days. This, of course, is quite in order from a Roman Catholic perspective, where salvation is attained not by personal attachment to Christ and his righteousness but by attachment to the church, the very dogma that inspired the original invention of Christmas and other holy days in the first place. As Bennet observes, respecting the relationship between the unconverted and Roman Catholicism:

> Generally speaking, the world and those inside Catholicism love the ways of Rome.
> The Papacy is an organization fully adapted to man. It corresponds with the whole scope of his hopes, fears, desires, passions, quirks and preferences.[11]

Fourth, it is intrinsically false. We imbibe in our children a spirit of honesty from their earliest days and repeatedly warn and punish them if they deliberately tell lies, yet it is Christian parents and other adults such as school teachers who, in this context, repeatedly deceive children! We all make imaginative false pretences to children, from *Little Red Riding-Hood* or *Bugs Bunny* to *The Gruffalo*, where we present an animal that speaks and thinks like us. However, even the youngest child soon realizes that this is not reality and that in point of fact animals do not speak. Parents do not earnestly and consistently refute the child's realization and seek to maintain that the child is wrong and that, in fact, animals do speak! The interaction between adult and child is very different, however, when it comes to

---

10. Pink, *Studies in the Scriptures*, vol. 9, no. 10.
11. Bennet, *Catholicism*, 288.

Christmas and Santa, with many going to great lengths to perpetuate the delusion. We may regard this as harmless fun but can we be sure that this is how the Lord regards it?

Children are deluded for years, some even into their young teens with presents being concealed and then placed under the tree for the morning, hanging stockings up empty and later filling them, or leaving milk and biscuits out for Santa and then later removing part of the drink and biscuits, all in order to give the impression that Santa was there and partook of the provision! Not to mention the hiring of reindeer and sleigh to which children are brought, under the impression that they are Santa's, etc. The eventual realization that Santa is not, in fact, true, can be quite a shock for some children and also confusing about the necessity for absolute honesty, while also raising the question about what else mum and dad have told them that is not, in fact, true! In Christian families where parents present both Jesus and Santa as being real, when the child eventually questions the reality of Santa, it is common for them to also question the reality of Jesus. In this context of making the Santa discovery, many a parent has been perturbed to hear their biblically well-versed child ask, "Mum, is Jesus real?" This is because the child has heard their parents over many years attributing marvelous and supernatural feats to both Jesus and Santa. This applies also to questioning other amazing events in the Bible apart from the life of the Savior, such as creation in six, 24-hour days; the global flood of Noah; the parting of the Red Sea; the sun standing still for Joshua; Balaam's donkey speaking; Elijah's ascent to heaven; and Jonah spending three days underwater, to name but a few.

We may not like the idea of labeling a child's request to Santa as a prayer, but that is indeed what it is. A child who is taught to believe in Santa, does just that. They believe in Santa. Divine attributes of omniscience and omnipresence are attributed to Santa Claus. They believe in him in the same way that we believe in God. They have the same hope of Santa fulfilling their request as adults have of God fulfilling their request. There can be no doubt that Santa is transformed into an idol in the mind of a believing child. The objection that "we know it's not true, therefore it's okay" is unscriptural. The Jews and Christians who were killed for not bowing the knee to idols, knew that the false gods were mythological. Consider the famous 1934 song about Santa Claus, broadcast repeatedly on airwaves and in shopping malls each December:

> You better watch out. You better not cry. You better not pout. I'm telling you why; Santa Claus is coming to town.
>
> He's making a list and he's checking it twice; gonna find out whose naughty and nice. Santa Claus is coming to town.
>
> He sees you when you're sleeping; he knows when you're awake. He knows if you've been bad or good, so be good for goodness sakes.
>
> You better watch out. You better not cry. You better not pout. I'm telling you why; Santa Claus is coming to town.

John MacArthur Jr. in a 1990 sermon, warns us that in the letters of "Santa" lies the name Satan, which is very appropriate as this poem presents a false theology. Santa is presented as being transcendent, with equal powers to God, omniscient and omnipresent. He is watching children's behavior—naughty or nice, bad or good—and bestows earned favors accordingly. However, he cannot be trusted, as gifts are deposited anyway, irrespective of goodness or badness and his threats/promises are not always fulfilled, with relatively good people getting nothing and relatively bad people getting lots. MacArthur astutely observes that if a child is brought up to believe in such a character, then in adulthood they may well have difficulty believing in a transcendent, omnipotent, omniscient, and omnipresent God, as he is presented in the Bible. One who is a gracious God, not bestowing gifts on the basis of merit once a year but One who gives the greatest gift possible on the basis of grace through faith, with promises and threats that are continuous and certain.[12]

Quite apart from the parent/child relationship in the family, it is not a good witness to the unconverted world. It is commonplace for those antagonistic to the Gospel, to reject it as a myth and invention of man from a primitive and unenlightened age. While the unconverted will always find some excuse or other to reject the Gospel anyway, it cannot be helpful for them to see the Lord's people endorsing (explicitly or implicitly) something like Christmas which has such a large degree of myth and falsehood attached to it. How many people in society view God as the 'jolly wee man up

---

12. MacArthur, "A Son to Make Many Sons."

there,' who threatens punishment for misbehavior but ultimately will always give good gifts in the end? The portrayal of biblical inaccuracies is also reflected in some Christmas hymns or 'carols.' For example:

> All is calm, all is bright . . . radiant beams from thy holy face . . . —"Silent Night"

> Jesus asleep in the hay . . . the cattle are lowing, the baby awakes, but little Lord Jesus no crying he makes—"Away in a Manger"

> Ding dong merrily on high, the bells in heav'n are ringing —"Ding Dong"

> Born the king of angels . . . born this happy morning—"O Come All Ye Faithful"

> Herald angels sing, "glory to the newborn king"—"Hark! The Herald Angels Sing"

We noted the controversy in a previous chapter about the opening line and here in this next line, neither Wesley's original "kings of kings," or the altered lyric, "the newborn king," accurately reflects what the angels said as recorded by Luke, which was, "glory to God in the highest." Are we being too fussy on this point, too critical and pedantic?

Every word of God is significant and if we are going to quote the Bible in song, particularly what people or angels were inspired by God to say, then it behooves us to quote them accurately and convey *what* the Bible says. The angels are God's messengers who deliver his message. There must be a reason why at the birth of Christ, he commanded them to proclaim to the shepherds that this event warrants the rendering by people of glory to "God in the highest," otherwise he would not have directed his angels to proclaim this. What is the difference between "holy, holy, holy, is the Lord God Almighty," and "holy, holy, holy, is the Lord Almighty," in Revelation 4:8? Some might say they are one and the same thing, but are they?

Also,

> Born is the king of Israel. . . . They [Shepherds] looked up and saw a star, shining in the East beyond them far, and to the earth it gave great light, and so it continued both day and night . . . where Jesus lay . . . those wise men three . . . with his blood mankind hath bought—"The First Noel."

> So God imparts to human hearts the blessings of his heaven. . . . O holy child of Bethlehem, descend to us we pray, cast out our sin and enter in—"O Little Town of Bethlehem."

Many of these carols and others like them, emanate from Unitarian, Oxford Movement, or Roman Catholic composers, and the songs misrepresent Scripture, present weak, misleading theology at best and unambiguous Roman Catholic tradition at worst.

Again, there exists a great irony in all of this. When the Lord's people give a place to the manufacture of the timing of our Lord's birth, the manufacture of Christ's Mass and the manufacture of Santa Claus with other Christmas artifacts, all things that are not based on the truth, they are claiming to do so in celebration of the birth of the One who declared of himself, "I am . . . the truth" (John 14:6). Moreover, the Holy Spirit is called "the Spirit of truth" (John 16:13); the Gospel is called "the word of truth" (Eph 1:13); the Lord commands, "You shall not bear false witness against your neighbor" (Exod 20:16); Paul tells us to put away lying and speak the truth to our neighbor in order not to grieve the Holy Spirit (Eph 4:25, 30); and the Lord tells us that "God is Spirit and those who worship him must worship in spirit and truth" (John 4:24).

Fifth, it undermines and displaces the only biblical holy day the Lord has given us—the Lord's Day, or first day of the week, Sunday. As we noted already and will do later, this has been a consistent concern of Christians, from the early church to the first and second generation Reformers, to their successors during the Victorian era on both sides of the Atlantic, and to the present day. The most relevant biblical metaphor for the Christian life is that which Paul draws from the Old Testament and the Roman Empire of his day, which is, the Christian soldier—militant, at war, engaged in a spiritual bloody battle against Satan. The Lord declared the war in Gen 3:15. The Lord's Day is a bit like a soldier's period of leave, a time to relax and refresh, so we go back into the battle knowing, having been to and tasted the end of all things, that we will one day dwell in the house of the Lord forever. Conversely, the more we use the day positively for spiritual rest, the more we battle, as it is our worship, our rest, our joy, and our peace that are the very weapons of our warfare. It need hardly be said that running our business, doing the main weekly shop, or attending professional sporting events, as some Christians do on the Lord's Day, is not conducive to such spiritual rest. The growing endorsement of Christmas and other holy days by the Reformed branch of the visible church, throughout the twentieth and twenty-first centuries, has run concurrently with the growing disregard of the Lord's Day and its purpose as just described. Is this a mere coincidence? The more a liturgical calendar is embraced by a church, the less importance is likely to be attached to the Lord's Day.

Reflection

Those Calvinistic Reformers and their immediate successors who sought to eliminate from society the influences of Roman Catholicism, including Christmas, did so with great effort and in order that their fellow citizens might have a clearer view of Christ.

Is it not a legitimate question to ask whether or not their efforts were in vain, given the many Reformed churches today that endorse in Christ's name, Christmas services, nativity plays, inaccurate worship songs, and Christmas trees, etc., as well as other holy days? During the first and second Reformations in Scotland, many of the Lord's people were willing to be persecuted rather than accept any of the Romanizing practices as manifested in Episcopalianism. They recognized that the Episcopal Church of England had retained many superstitions that were part of Roman Catholic worship and from 1660 to 1688, thousands died because they refused to acknowledge Episcopal Church government and worship practices.

Judgement begins with the house of God (1 Pet 4:17) and few would deny that the present overt ungodliness that pervades our societies is in itself a judgement of God upon his church. Inordinate pride and failure to discipline impartially are obvious factors in a time period that has seen no universally acknowledged revival of the church by the Holy Spirit for over 150 years. Does it grieve the Holy Spirit or please the Holy Spirit to have his people endorsing something as unbiblical, worldly, and false as Christmas so often is? If, however, churches feel compelled to hold a church worship service during the winter vacation, when family reunion is so commonplace and as an alternative to the worldliness of the whole festive season, then instead of holding Christmas Eve "watch night" and Christmas Day services, would the former practice of holding New Year's Day services not be much more profitable? The great American theologian Jonathan Edwards certainly thought so.[13] It can be a good thing for a fellowship of God's people to commence a new year by being together and worshipping the Lord. Moreover, it is an excellent opportunity to bring unconverted family and friends under the sound of the Gospel, as the occasion naturally lends itself to reflection on another year gone and opportunities lost, as well as looking forward into a future full of uncertainties and the contrast therein with the certainties found in Christ.

It is interesting to consider how those who are outside the Protestant church view the ever-increasing liturgy being embraced by it. The following quote is from a blog entitled *Standing on my Head*, posted by a Roman Catholic

---

13. Edwards, *Sermons and Discourses*, 264.

priest—Father Dwight Longenecker—in 2009. Longenecker, who has been a parish priest for twenty years in South Carolina, was raised a Protestant in a fundamentalist Independent congregation in Pennsylvania. He studied literature at Bob Jones University and was heavily influenced by the writings of C. S. Lewis. He subsequently studied theology at Oxford and became a Church of England curate, school chaplain, and Vicar at Cambridge and the Isle of Wight, before switching to Rome. Having spent half of his life in the UK, the perspective he writes from is not exclusively a North American one:

> I was talking to a very nice Baptist fellow the other day who was interested in my journey from Bob Jones University to the Catholic faith. He said, "We go to a very liturgical Baptist church." I'm not quite sure what he meant, but he assured me that they had had an Ash Wednesday Service and they were "very liturgical."
>
> I expect he means what my Presbyterian mother means when she tells me her church is "liturgical." She means they are starting to observe Advent and Lent. They have a candlelight service on Christmas Eve with classical music and a printed order of service. In fact, many Evangelical churches are beginning to go "high church." The preachers sometimes wear robes, maybe they chant the odd psalm, have some candles here and there and they pick and choose other liturgical stuff they like and put together their own mish mash of a "liturgical" service. Far be it from me to criticize them. I think it is rather nice that some of our separated brethren want to be "more liturgical," and I don't really mind if they shop in a sort of ecclesiastical thrift store to find some bargains and take them home.
>
> What interests me more is how American Protestant denominationalism is disintegrating. Can anybody really tell the difference anymore between a Baptist or a Methodist or a Presbyterian or an Episcopalian? What is happening is that all the mainstream Protestant denominations are being "Anglicanized." In other words, the same range of opinion and practice that used to be the "big tent" hallmark of Anglicanism is now commonplace in all denominations. So you have low church and high church Baptists, Presbyterians, Methodist, and Lutherans. You have radical liberals and radical conservatives in all the denominations. You have those who are "Catholic" in their beliefs and practices and those who are "Evangelical." Yes, a "high church" Baptist is still lower than a "high church" Lutheran or Episcopalian, and a "low church Evangelical" Episcopalian is not quite as low as an independent Baptist, but the fine distinctions are secondary to the overall trend that there is no longer a clearly

identified denominational style. If you say "I'm Baptist" we used to know pretty much what that meant. Now you have to say, "I'm a liturgical Baptist" or "I'm an Evangelical Lutheran." I suspect what is true of their practice is true of their beliefs as well. Do you have to be a Calvinist anymore to be a Presbyterian? I doubt it. Do you have to believe in consubstantiation if you want to join a low Lutheran Church? Probably not. If you are a Baptist do you still have to deny infant baptism? Probably not always. As a result, what identity do any of the denominations have? They are increasingly defined not by their historical, theological or liturgical or ecclesiological views, but by their stance on moral and theological debating points. So Presbyterian Church USA is liberal and Presbyterian Church of America is conservative. Consequently, each has more in common with other denominations (either liberal or conservative) than they do with each other as fellow Presbyterians. PCA members will be closer to Missouri Synod Lutherans and PCUSA members will be closer to the main Lutheran body.

The point of these observations is this: can a particular ecclesial body maintain itself once it loses its identity? I suspect we will see the disintegration of these large Protestant denominations as each congregation increasingly asserts its own identity—and that identity will be determined by the sincere, but individualistic choices of its leadership. Thus Protestantism will become a collection of independent local churches doing Christianity however they see fit.[14]

Few can refute Longenecker's assessment and we see it demonstrated ourselves. Doctrine regulates practice and when doctrine/theology becomes vaguer and less precise, practice will become increasingly inclusive.

---

14. Dwight Longenecker, "Liturgical Baptists," *Standing on My Head*, March 12, 2009, http://www.patheos.com/blogs/standingonmyhead/2009/03/liturgical-baptists.html.

The Regulative Principle

WHATEVER TERM ONE WISHES to apply, it is beyond dispute that there is a biblical principle at play when it comes to identifying what is, or is not, acceptable worship.

The doctrine of God, as he reveals himself in the Bible, has a bearing upon how he is worshipped, or in other words, it "regulates" how he is worshipped.

It is this principle that is most commonly cited as conclusive evidence, by those who oppose the religious endorsement of Christmas and other holy days in church practice. For this reason, in this chapter we are going to examine the evolution of the principle at the Reformation, the Scriptures commonly cited in support of it, and finally the principle in action in its most common use, namely in determining the acceptable regular public praise of God.

Reformer's Differences

It ought to be said, and not always is by those believers opposed to Christmas, that historically there has always existed a difference of opinion within the Reformed branch of Christ's church on the question of the religious endorsement of Christmas. As we noted previously, great champions of the Reformed faith such as Calvin, Bullinger, and Turretin, felt personally that recognizing special days to celebrate biblical events, such as the Nativity, was discretionary on the part of each church. We noted also that doctrinal standards such as Bullinger's Second Helvetic Confession (the most widely accepted Confession in continental Europe apart from the Heidelberg Catechism) regarded the issue as discretionary and for each congregation to decide.

How can we account for this difference in interpreting the Bible? Did it really matter? Does it really matter today? We are all familiar with the religious sound bite: "In essentials, unity; in nonessentials, liberty; in all things, charity."

Sounds nice does it not? But which are the essentials and which are the nonessentials? Is worship in a particular manner one of the essentials or is it not essential to worship God in a particular manner? By the same token we could ask, why did Luther differ from Zwingli and Calvin in his biblical interpretation? What if the latter pair had agreed with Luther and there had never been what we now term a Calvinistic interpretation of the Bible?

Taking a further step back we could ask, what if there had been no reformation in biblical interpretation? Would it have really mattered? After all, true salvation is quite possible within the bounds of the Roman Catholic Church! Wycliffe, Tyndale, Luther, Zwingli, Calvin, Wishart, Knox, and thousands like them were all born and bred Roman Catholic and indeed some were pursuing full-time religious vocations within the church when they were born-again by the operation of the Holy Spirit. By and large, of course, there was no other church. Today, there are undoubtedly brothers and sisters in Christ who are saved within the bounds of the Roman Catholic Church (who unwisely remain). Should we then cease our opposition to the modern ecumenical movement, no longer regard the Church of Rome as not being a true church of Jesus Christ and stop being protesters/Protestants and undo the Reformation? Does it really matter? The answer need hardly be stated! Why did Paul differ in his views from Peter? Why did Paul differ with the Judaisers in Galatia?

The Reformers believed the church had become corrupt, so change was needed, but it was a change in the interest of preservation and restoration of a more authentic faith and life—a church reformed and always to be reformed according to the Word of God. The cultural assumption of the Reformers' day was that what is older is better. This is strange to our contemporary ears. We do not share this assumption. If anything, we applaud the new and innovative. One of the serious charges the Roman Catholic Church authorities hurled at the Reformers was that they were "innovating." John Calvin responded to this and other charges in his treatise *The Necessity of Reforming the Church*. As he put it:

> We are accused of rash and impious innovation for having ventured to propose any change at all [in] the former state of the church.[1]

---

1. Calvin, *Necessity of Reforming the Church*, 13.

He then goes on to counter that they were not "innovating" but restoring the church to its true nature, purified from the "innovations" that riddled the church through centuries of inattention to the Bible and theological laxity. He asserted that the Reformation's stimulus was not to rid the church of numerous and grievous abuses but to restore a biblical perspective in two areas: the worship of the church and the doctrine of salvation. The appeal was to a more ancient source, Scripture—*sola Scriptura* (Scripture alone). By submitting themselves to the Bible, the churches of the Reformation movement were purging themselves of these unwanted "innovations" and returning to a more ancient and therefore purer form of church life. They recognized that we are the recipients of the activity of the Holy Spirit, who reforms the church in accordance with the Word of God.

Calvin was well aware of the need of striking a balance in formulating church practice: "There is . . . a great difference between establishing some exercise of piety which believers may use with a free conscience, or . . . abstain from it, and making a law to entrap consciences in bondage."[2] For example, there is no explicit command or divine imperative changing public worship from the seventh day (Saturday) to the first day (Sunday) of the week, recorded in Scripture. Yet in the New Testament, the change from the seventh day to the first day is strongly implied (Acts 20:7; 1 Cor 16:2; Rev 1:10). Not every divine command or prophetic word has been inscripturated (i.e., included in the Bible). The universal practice of the Apostolic church, such as Lord's Day public worship, is binding because of the unique authority given to the apostles, i.e., direct revelation. If we do not accept the view of some that we still live in the Apostolic era with its gifts, we are left with Scripture alone to determine worship, not Scripture plus church traditions. Scripture gives no explicit command to hold Sunday schools, yet the implication is extremely strong. There is explicit command to teach our children and as just mentioned, there is the binding practice of Lord's Day worship. Are we to imagine that when the Apostolic churches met, there was no specific explanation given to children before, during, or after the sermon?

The Wittenburg Reformers like Luther and Melancthon, those in the Southern German cities and the Swiss Reformers like Zwingli and Bullinger, sought to establish a unified Protestantism, holding various conferences to iron out their doctrinal differences. Numerous compromises were made as different confessional standards were drawn up and revised. Political pressure was constant, amidst fears of local and regional civil wars between Roman Catholic and Protestant Cantons, with the success of the Reformation (in strictly human terms) often relying on the support of the Dukes

---

2. Calvin, *Institutes*, 2:1199.

and secular councils. To add to the confusion, the empire was at war with France, Italy, and the Ottoman Empire. As Merle d'Aubigné reflects:

> The Reformation, by restoring liberty to the church, was destined also to restore its original diversity, and to people it with families united by the great features of resemblance they derive from their common parent; but different in their secondary features, and reminding us of the varieties inherent in human nature. Perhaps it would have been desirable for this diversity to exist in the universal church without leading to sectarian divisions. Nevertheless, we must not forget that these sects are but the expression of this diversity. Switzerland and Germany, which had till this time developed themselves independently of each other, began to come in contact . . . and realised the diversity of which we have been speaking, and which was to be one of the characteristics of Protestantism. We shall there behold men perfectly agreed on all the great doctrines of faith, and yet differing on certain secondary points.
>
> Passion, indeed, entered into these discussions; but while deploring such a melancholy intermixture, Protestantism, far from seeking to conceal her diversity, publishes and proclaims it. Its path to unity is long and difficult, but this unity is the real unity.[3]

The Reformed church in Germany and Switzerland faced two great movements—the first was an enemy, the Roman Catholic Church, which sought to regain areas where they had lost control, and the second was a rival, Lutheranism, which also sought to control the same areas. Ulrich Zwingli (1484–1531) strongly opposed Roman Catholic teaching because he considered it as infringement on individual freedom. He rejected music in worship and removed all artworks from the church. He destroyed organs and other musical instruments in the church because according to him, they promoted self-indulgence. The death of Zwingli in battle against Roman Catholics in 1531, was a great blow to the Reformed church and retarded its consolidation. Calvin (1509–1564) broke from the Roman Catholic Church in the previous year, moved east from France to Geneva and in the following thirty years developed his theology with amazing energy.

When Calvin appeared on the scene in Geneva in 1536, Luther had another ten years to live, Philip Melanchthon (Luther's colleague) and Bucer (in Strasbourg) were at the height of their influence, Zwingli had been dead for five years and Bullinger had taken his place in Zürich. There was animosity between the followers of Luther and Bullinger, the start of which was the

---

3. Merle d'Aubigné, *History of the Reformation*, 334.

bitter disagreement between Zwingli and Luther over the issue of Christ's presence in the Lord's Supper. It was in this environment that John Calvin, a second generation Reformer, launched his Reformation work in Geneva.

The difference between the Swiss and German Reformers is well described by Schaff:

> The Swiss and the German Reformers agreed in opposition to Romanism, but the Swiss departed further from it. The former were zealous for the sovereign glory of God, and, in strict interpretation of the first and second commandments, abolished the heathen elements of creature worship; while Luther, in the interest of free grace and the peace of conscience, aimed his strongest blows at the Jewish element of monkish legalism and self-righteousness.
>
> The Swiss theology proceeds from God's grace to man's needs; the Lutheran, from man's needs to God's grace.[4]

The tension between the Swiss Reformers and German Lutherans continued and toward the end of Calvin's life, began to drive a wedge between the Swiss themselves in Geneva and Zurich. It was also during this period that the Roman Catholic Church countered all of this by formulating its dogmas in the Council of Trent (1545–1563) in northern Italy. This was the context in which confessional standards were formulated in the sixteenth century. By the time the London Divines formulated their Baptist and Presbyterian confessional standards, these English and Scottish Calvinists had the advantage of one hundred years of Protestant trial and error, including the review of thirty European formal Confessions of Faith, to enhance their combined learning and wisdom.

In answer then to the question posed repeatedly at the head of this chapter, "Does it really matter?" we see the duty laid upon every generation of Christians to attain, as much as is possible, a church reflecting the ideal model represented in the New Testament church. The influence of twelve hundred years of Roman Catholicism is very significant in understanding the evolution of theology and practice that has characterized the Reformation. If the Gospel had gone East with Paul and not West, if in the periods following the Apostolic era the church had apostatized in a different direction, both theologically and geographically, this would have certainly resulted in a very different model of apostasy to that which we have come to recognize as the Roman Catholic Church.

---

4. Schaff, *History of the Christian Church*, 8:10.

When in God's gracious providence the light of the Gospel was recovered and reform of religion occurred, it would also have occurred in a different way to what we have come to know as the European Protestant Reformation. Social and political factors also influenced the Reformation. Moreover, the church models that resulted from the Reformation would have resulted in different ones to those we recognize today as Presbyterianism or Anglicanism. Covenant theology and the practical issues determined by it, such as the form of government (Independency vs. Presbyterianism vs. Synodicalism) or subjects of Baptism (paedo vs. credo (believing)) would have been reviewed differently. The same is true of an issue like Christmas. In other words, the context in which these men lived must be taken into account.

Which Principle?

One major legacy of the Reformation is that Martin Luther and John Calvin articulated incompatible approaches to Scripture, as it relates to and instructs the Christian worship of God. In summary, Luther advocated that it was appropriate to worship God in ways not specifically forbidden by Scripture, as long as the elements of worship remained consistent with biblical teaching. This philosophy, which has generally been followed by the Episcopal/Anglican Church and the Roman Catholic Church as well as Lutherans, opens a substantial area of "adiaphora" (indifferent things) that may be acceptable in worship. In contrast, Calvin limited the worship of God only to those ways that Scripture instituted, prescribed, or commanded:

> We may not adopt any device [in our worship] which seems fit to ourselves, but look to the injunctions of him who alone is entitled to prescribe.
>
> Therefore, if we would have him approve our worship, this rule, which he everywhere enforces with the utmost strictness, must be carefully observed. . . . God disapproves of all modes of worship not expressly sanctioned by his word.[5]

In 1539, Cardinal Jacob Sadolet wrote to the churches in Geneva, urging them to abandon Protestantism and return to the Church of Rome. In Calvin's letter of reply to Sadolet, dated September 1, 1539, and sent from Basel, Calvin writes:

> I will not press you so closely as to call you back to that form which the Apostles instituted, (though in it we have the only model of a true church, and whosoever deviates from it in the smallest degree is in error).[6]

English separatists—Presbyterians, Congregationalists, and Baptists tended to embrace this philosophy.

The contrast is unequivocal: one allows that which is not forbidden; the other prohibits that which is not directly authorized. Or to put it another way, is scriptural silence permissive or prohibitive? This contrast has become known as the Normative Principle and the Regulative Principle. As a general rule, Reformed Independents and Presbyterians followed the latter principle. Anglicans, Lutherans, and Methodists embraced the former, while in the modern era many Protestant churches have cast off their Reformed heritage and placed an emphasis upon church evangelism at the expense of church

---

5. Calvin, *Necessity of Reforming the Church*, 17–18.
6. Calvin, *Selected Works*, 1:25–30.

principles, embracing both Arminian doctrine and the Normative Principle. (As an aside, the Roman Catholic Church holds to a policy best described as the "Inventive Principle." It says that the church is free to establish the parameters of worship, hence the inventiveness of certain elements, like the mass, etc. The church may invent or create as it pleases, as authority resides in the church and the church, in conjunction with church tradition, are regarded as an equal authority with the Bible. This view cannot coexist with the Regulative Principle and is indeed antithetical to it.)

In seventeenth century England, the teachings of John Calvin shaped most of the century's religious discourse. Regardless of whether one examines the worship principles as expressed in the writings of small English separatist groups, or in the nonconformists that achieved more mainstream recognition such as the Baptists, or in the more formalized and organized Presbyterians, it cannot be denied that doctrinal positions held by John Calvin permeated these groups and held enormous sway over them. In Scotland, Calvin's influence upon John Knox is indisputable and is seen, for example, in Knox's *Book of Common Order*. In England, Calvin's influence had been felt early on in the Reformation and had only strengthened among groups that found the established church and its compromises unsatisfactory. Each group, of course, would claim that its doctrinal positions, especially if clarified in a formal confessional statement, were faithful expositions of biblical teaching (rather than something John Calvin wrote). Hardwick, speaking of the latter part of the Elizabethan period, admits that:

> during an interval of nearly thirty years the extreme opinions of the school of Calvin, not excluding his theory of irrespective reprobation, were predominant in almost every town and parish.[7]

Moreover, Calvin exercised an enormous influence on such groups, even after his death. His *Institutes of the Christian Religion*, first published in 1536 (and which he himself considered as an organizational point into the in-depth study of the Scriptures), provides a succinct base for his thinking. Calvin himself revisited this document several times over twenty-three years; he had enlarged it four-fold by 1559 and left for his theological descendants what would become a normative statement of the Reformed faith.

In the language of Richard Hooker (1554–1600, Church of England theologian), comparing him to the twelfth-century scholastic master Peter Lombard, Calvin acquired an authority over the leading divines and the universities almost as great:

---

7. Hardwick, *History of the Articles of Religion*, 162–80.

as that of the 'Master of Sentences" in the palmy days of scholasticism, so that the perfectest divines were judged they which were skillfullest in Calvin's writings.[8]

Some writers have suggested that the Regulative Principle was a Puritan innovation and not something adhered to by the Continental Reformers (as an explanation as to why the Puritans banned Christmas, while Calvin and others did not).[9] However, this is demonstrably not the case, as evidenced in some of the continental doctrinal Confessions.

Confessions

The fundamental statement of the Lutheran Church is the Augsburg Confession of 1530 (arising out of a diet called by the Holy Roman Emperor in Augsburg, Bavaria, Southwest Germany), and it delineates a permissive view toward scriptural silence in several places. In Article 15, "Ecclesiastical Rites," it states, in part:

> Our churches teach that those rites should be observed which can be observed without sin and which contribute to peace and good order in the church. Such are certain holy days, festivals, and the like. Nevertheless, men are admonished not to burden consciences with such things, as if observances of this kind were necessary for salvation.[10]

Also for the Lutheran Church, the Formula of Concord (1576–77) and convened in Torgau, Saxony, in Northwest Germany) stands as a document of articulated principles at the other end of the sixteenth century. The Lutheran Church struggled to define itself doctrinally after decades of internal controversies, and the Formula of Concord sought to give doctrinal unity and peace to it. However, the controversies did not effect a shift in the Lutheran Church's approach to scriptural silence, ceremonies, or traditions.

The Thirty-Nine Articles of the Church of England also follow the Lutheran tendency toward freedom. Article 20, "Authority of the Church," proclaims that the church has authority to decree rites or ceremonies as long as it does not ordain anything contrary to Scripture or interpret one passage in contradiction with another.

Article 34, "Of the Traditions of the Church," likewise states that traditions or ceremonies do not have to be alike in all places and can be altered

---

8. Hooker, *Works*, 1:139–40.
9. Packer, "Puritan Approach to Worship," 4–5.
10. www.bookofconcord.org/augsburgconfession, Article 15.

by man's needs as long as they do not contradict Scripture. Taken together, these articles indicate that the church should uphold liberty in matters indifferent.[11]

The French (or Gallican) Confession of Faith (1559 and drafted by Calvin), Article 33, rejects all human inventions and laws of men that bind the conscience under the guise of serving God.[12] The Belgic Confession (1561), in Article 7, on the sufficiency of Scripture as the only rule of faith, asserts that Scripture contains the "whole manner of worship which God requires of us,"[13] and in Article 32, states:

> In the mean time we believe though it is useful and beneficial that those who are rulers of the Church institute and establish certain ordinances among themselves, for maintaining the body of the Church; yet they ought studiously to take care that they do not depart from those things which Christ, our only master, hath instituted.
>
> And, therefore, we reject all human inventions, and all laws which man would introduce into the worship of God, thereby to bind and compel the conscience in any manner whatever.[14]

The Heidelberg Catechism (1563) specifically addresses the second commandment, echoing many of Calvin's own statements.[15] The Synod of the Reformed Churches of the Netherlands, meeting in Dort (Dordrecht) in 1574 and 1578 (not to be confused with the more famous Canons of the Synod of Dort in 1618–19), decreed that only Sunday be observed as a feast day. It was acknowledged, however, that this may present ministers with a difficulty, as other feast days such as Christmas and Easter were "maintained by the authority of the government."

The Irish Articles of Religion (1615), evidence a prevailing Calvinism in the Irish Episcopal Church, which was, technically, under the authority of the Thirty-Nine Articles. As with the Lambeth Articles, the Irish Articles also were an attempt at amending the Thirty-Nine Articles. In the section addressing "Of the Service of God," Article 52 of the Irish Articles reads:

> All worship devised by man's phantasy besides or contrary to the Scriptures (as wandering on pilgrimages, setting up of candles, stations, and jubilees, Pharisaical sects and feigned religions,

---

11. http://www.anglicansonline.org/basics/thirty-nine_articles.html.
12. Schaff, *Creeds of Christendom*, 3:378.
13. Ibid., 388.
14. Ibid., 423.
15. Ibid., 343.

praying upon beads, and such like superstition) hath not only no promise of reward in Scripture, but contrariwise.[16]

The burgeoning Baptist community likewise reflected the influence of Calvin and Reformed Protestantism. The True Confession (1596), states in Article 17:

> That the rule of this knowledge faith & obedience, Concerning the worship & service of God and 'all other Christian duties, is not the opinions, devices, laws, or constitutions of men, but the written word of the ever living God, contained in the canonical books of the old and new Testament.

The London Confession, (1644), Article 7 says:

> The Rule of this Knowledge, Faith, and Obedience, concerning the worship and service of God, and all other Christian duties, is not man's inventions, opinions, devices, laws, constitutions, or traditions unwritten whatsoever, but only the word of God contained in the Canonical Scriptures.

The London Confession of 1689 (originating in 1677), states in Chapter 22:1–7:

> But the acceptable way of worshipping the true God is instituted by himself, and so limited by his own revealed will, that he may not be worshipped according to the imaginations and devices of men, nor the suggestions of Satan, under any visible representations, or any other way not prescribed in the Holy Scriptures.

Throughout the seventeenth century, the norm of theological thinking among English Puritanism, and the Dissent that derived from it, was a "prevailing Calvinism," from which deviations have to be established and evidenced. Particular Baptists were especially concerned to show, through their published confessions, their substantial agreement with the prevailing forms of Calvinistic orthodoxy.[17] Those with a stricter view of worship and the authority for acceptable elements in worship, viewed contributions of man, such as hymns, as man-made inventions. Such additions were on a par with other "innovations" fought by Reformed Protestantism, such as images and idols, feast days, and maledictions.

---

16. Ibid., 536.
17. Briggs, "Influence of Calvinism."

Scriptural Proofs

On the basis of the principle of *sola Scriptura*, Calvin as we have noted, along with all who subsequently ascribed to Calvinism or the Reformed faith, adopted what has become known as the Regulative Principle.[18]

Which Scriptures were under consideration in their persuasion that the Regulative Principle was the correct and prevailing scriptural principle? The following is a sample of the Bible verses most commonly cited and the interpretations adopted in support of this principle:

> In the course of time Cain brought to the LORD an offering of the fruit of the ground and Abel also brought of the firstborn of his flock and of their fat portions. And the LORD had regard for Abel and his offering, but for Cain and his offering he had no regard. So Cain was very angry, and his face fell. The LORD said to Cain, "Why are you angry, and why has your face fallen? If you do well, will you not be accepted? And if you do not do well, sin is crouching at the door. Its desire is for you, but you must rule over it." (Gen 4:3–7)

A lot of commentaries say that the problem there was subjective. There was a wrong attitude—a lack of faith in the heart of Cain. Well, that is undoubtedly true but it is only half of the truth, because there was also an objective offence. The Lord had respect to Abel *and* his offering but he did not respect Cain *or* his offering. That is why the Book of Hebrews emphasizes the objective aspect when it says, "by faith, Abel offered a more acceptable sacrifice" (Heb 11:4).

So it is a mistake to throw the emphasis entirely upon the subjective. The fact is that Abel paid attention to the instruction of his parents, who instructed him fundamentally in what we have in the first three chapters of the Bible: the creation, the Fall, and the problem of bridging the gap that now existed between fallen man and God. It appears that he took to heart the fact that God covered the nakedness of Adam and Eve with the skins of sacrificed animals. Cain, on the other hand, did not take account of these things.

Even if you take the view that a special revelation was given to Abel about how he should approach God, it really makes no difference in the end because God made it clear to Cain what was and what was not acceptable. The reason why he was rejected and became reprobate was that he was not willing to submit himself wholeheartedly and totally to the prescribed way of approach to the living God or, as some would argue, to the Regulative Principle.

---

18. Calvin, *Institutes*, book 1, ch. 11, para. 4; ch. 12, paras. 1 and 3; book 2, ch. 8, paras. 5 and 17; and book 4, ch. 2, paras. 1 and 8–17. Also see his commentary on Jer 7:31 and sermon on 2 Sam 6:6–12.

Exod 20:4–6 (the Second Commandment):

> You shall not make for yourself any carved image, or any likeness of anything that is in heaven above, or that is in the earth beneath, or that is in the water under the earth; you shall not bow down to them nor serve them. For I, the Lord your God, am a jealous God, visiting the iniquity of the fathers on the children to the third and fourth generations of those who hate Me, but showing mercy to thousands, to those who love Me and keep My commandments.

On these verses, Calvin said, "Although Moses only speaks of idolatry [here], yet there is no doubt that by synecdoche, as in all the rest of the Law, he condemns all fictitious services which men in their ingenuity have invented."[19] Exod 25:40: "And see that you make them after the pattern for them, which is being shown you on the mountain." This is the account of the prescribed preparation, construction, and use of the Tabernacle in the wilderness. "See that you make them" (where the "them" refers to all the articles and aspects of the Tabernacle system). The things that went into the Tabernacle were produced as the Bible itself has been produced, by special divine revelation and inspiration. Exod 31:2–11 clearly shows this:

> See, I have called by name Bezalel the son of Uri, son of Hur, of the tribe of Judah, and I have filled him with the Spirit of God, with ability and intelligence, with knowledge and all craftsmanship ... And behold, I have appointed with him Oholiab, the son of Ahisamach, of the tribe of Dan. And I have given to all able men ability, that they may make all that I have commanded you ... According to all that I have commanded you, they shall do.

Lev 10:2: "Fire came out from before the Lord and consumed them," the two sons of Aaron, Nadab and Abihu, who were destroyed. Why did this happen? The same passage says it happened because they "offered unauthorized fire before the Lord, which he had not commanded" (vs. 1). The point made here is that it does not say that the two men lacked sincerity, or that they were devoid of good intentions, or that this happened to them because they did something God had expressly forbidden, rather that they did this without first making sure it was something God had commanded.

Num 16:8–40, where Moses and Aaron were appointed by the Lord to mediate between him, his people and Korah. Those who followed Korah, didn't like this exclusive arrangement. It appears that they wanted to break out of this narrow idea that there's only one right way, namely, the way God

---

19. Calvin, *Calvin's Commentaries*, vol. 2, on vs. 4.

set things up, so they rebelled against this restriction. The well-known result demonstrates, however, that this was exceedingly offensive to Jehovah.

Deut 4:2: "You shall not add to the word that I command you, nor take from it, that you may keep the commandments of the LORD your God that I command you." There is a sense in which this principle applies to all of life; however, some would argue that it does, with special intensity, apply to the pinnacle of all events in human life, which is the worship of the true and living God.

1 Sam 13:11–14 regarding King Saul: he was not authorized by God to partake in the priestly office but because of the pressure of circumstances, Saul felt compelled ("I forced myself") and offered a burnt offering because Samuel was late. It may well be, for all we know, that he acted with the best of intentions but we also know that God found it offensive. Samuel, the prophet, said, "You have done foolishly," because he did not limit himself to what God had authorized. It was because of this that God removed the kingdom from Saul and gave it to David (vs. 14). 2 Sam 6:7 and Uzzah:

> And the anger of the LORD was kindled against Uzzah, and God struck him down there because of his error, and he died there beside the ark of God.

When David first attempted to bring the long-neglected ark to Jerusalem, the oxen suddenly stumbled. At that moment Uzzah reached out his hand to steady the ark and God killed him. David was initially indignant and didn't understand it at the time but later David explained, "because we did not seek him according to the rule" (1 Chr 15:13), or as some would argue, 'we didn't observe the regulative principle—even in moving the ark." Contrast how different it was when, "So the priests and the Levites consecrated themselves to bring up the ark of the LORD, the God of Israel. And the Levites carried the ark of God on their shoulders with the poles, as Moses had commanded according to the word of the LORD" (1 Chr 15:14–15).

1 Kgs 12:32–33, regarding King Jeroboam: When he became king he wanted to consolidate his hold on the ten tribes that rebelled against the house of David. In order to do this, he "devised" or instituted a kind of worship which was "of his own heart." For this reason, a man of God from Judah was sent to denounce this unauthorized worship. Jeroboam, from that time forward, was always spoken of as the one who made Israel sin—corporately (1 Kgs 15:30). It appears that this act of innovation was the source out of which came Israel's ultimate downfall, when the worship that had been appointed by the Lord, was replaced by a new form of worship—not commanded by him and therefore accursed.

> Then David gave Solomon his son the plan of the vestibule of the temple, and of its houses, its treasuries, its upper rooms, and its inner chambers, and of the room for the mercy seat; and the plan of all that he had in mind for the courts of the house of the Lord, all the surrounding chambers, the treasuries of the house of God, and the treasuries for dedicated gifts; [And to his son he said] "All this he made clear to me in writing from the hand of the Lord, all the work to be done according to the plan." (1 Chr 28:11–12, 19 (Respecting the Temple))

The importance of this, it is argued, is that everything had to conform precisely to the pattern revealed first to Moses and then in a more elaborate form to David. The reason being that God would not be worshipped in any other way than how he had commanded.

> But he (King Ahaz) walked in the ways of the kings of Israel. He even made metal images for the Baals, and he made offerings in the Valley of the Son of Hinnom and burned his sons as an offering, according to the abominations of the nations whom the Lord drove out before the people of Israel. (2 Chr 28:2–3)

The prophet Jeremiah, commented on this (Jer 7:31): "And they have built the high places of Topheth, which is in the Valley of the Son of Hinnom, to burn their sons and their daughters in the fire, which I did not command, nor did it come into my mind." Worship that he had not commanded or authorized was therefore forbidden.

2 Chr 26:16: "... and entered the temple of the Lord to burn incense on the altar of incense," referring to King Uzziah. The high priest courageously intervened to oppose that act of unauthorized worship. He was vindicated by the intervention of God, for the king was instantly smitten with leprosy as a sign of God's judgment. Again, it is clear that what is not authorized by God's commandment is an abomination to him.

Matt 28:18–20: "And Jesus came and said to them, 'All authority in heaven and on earth has been given to me. Go therefore and make disciples of all nations, baptizing them in the name of the Father and of the Son and of the Holy Spirit, teaching them to observe all that I have commanded you. And behold, I am with you always, to the end of the age.'" This is exactly what the apostles did: they taught what Christ had commanded—not what he had commanded plus their own inventions. Knowing that all authority belonged to Christ, they knew there was no place for their own inventions. In the words of Calvin again, "He sends away the Apostles with this reservation, that they shall not bring forward their own inventions, but shall purely and faithfully deliver . . . what He has entrusted to them."[20]

Mark 7:6–7 (quoted from Isa 29:13): "And he said to them, 'Well did Isaiah prophesy of you hypocrites, as it is written, "This people honors me with their lips, but their heart is far from me; in vain do they worship me, teaching as doctrines the commandments of men."'" It is pointed out that the Lord Jesus spoke in this manner concerning Jewish traditionalism. You Scribes and Pharisees, he says, have worked out a fine way of setting aside the commands of God in order to observe your own traditions (vs. 9). No doubt what he said offended them but that's not what matters. What matters is that *God* was offended. According to the Lord Jesus, the cause of the offense was two-fold: (1) setting aside what God had commanded, and (2) diligently observing what was not commanded by God but only by man-made traditions.

> Our fathers worshiped on this mountain, but you say that in Jerusalem is the place where people ought to worship. Jesus said to her, "Woman, believe me, the hour is coming when neither on this mountain nor in Jerusalem will you worship the Father. You worship what you do not know; we worship what we know, for salvation is from the Jews. But the hour is coming, and is now here, when the true worshipers will worship the Father in spirit and truth, for the Father is seeking such people to worship him. God is spirit, and those who worship him must worship in spirit and truth. (John 4:20–24)

Consider Christ and the Samaritan woman, regarded by many as the clearest exposition of the Regulative Principle anyone has ever delivered. As Calvin points out on these verses, our Lord:

> divides the subject (that came up in that conversation) into two parts: First, he condemns the forms of worshiping God which the Samaritans used as superstitious and as false, and declares that the acceptable and lawful form was with the Jews. . . . He puts the reason for the difference, that the Jews received assurance from the Word of God about his worship, whereas the Samaritans had no certainly from God's lips; Secondly, He declares that the ceremonies observed by the Jews hitherto would soon be ended.

Concerning the first point, our Lord said, "You Samaritans worship what you do not know." Calvin drew this conclusion:

---

20. Ibid., vol. 16.

> All so-called good intentions are struck by this thunderbolt, which tells us that men can do nothing but err when they are guided by their own opinion without the Word or command of God.

He then goes on in dealing with the second point to say:

> We differ from the fathers only in the outward form because in their worship of God they were bound to ceremonies which were abolished by the coming of Christ.

So, if we ask what it means to worship God "in spirit and in truth" this is Calvin's answer: "It is to remove the coverings of the ancient ceremonies and retain simply what is spiritual in the worship." He continues by highlighting the trouble with this: "Since men are flesh . . . they delight in what corresponds to their natures. That is why they invent many things in the worship of God . . . (when) they should consider that they are dealing with God, who no more agrees with the flesh than fire does with water."[21] To worship God in spirit and in truth, then, is to worship God in the way that he commands—now that the Messiah has come and fulfilled all the promises of that ceremonial law. "It is simply unbearable," says Calvin, "that the rule laid down by Christ should be violated." Those who want to worship the true God, acceptably, *must* (that is the word Jesus used—*dei*—"necessary/must/duty") worship him in spirit and in truth. Any other way is useless.

> But now that you have come to know God, or rather to be known by God, how can you turn back again to the weak and worthless elementary principles of the world, whose slaves you want to be once more? You observe days and months and seasons, and years! I am afraid I may have laboured over you in vain. (Gal 4:9–11)

When Christ came, the Old Testament ceremonial system of worship was superseded. Included in this category of the obsolete were the annual sacred days and even the Jewish sabbaths. For the Galatians to go on celebrating those days was to act as if they were still waiting for the Messiah's advent. The argument that follows from this is, if the Apostle found it necessary to say this to people who observed days which had once been commanded by God, what would he say to people today who observe special holy days, like Christmas, that God never even mentioned in his Word, let alone commanded?

> All Scripture is breathed out by God and profitable for teaching, for reproof, for correction, and for training in righteousness, that the man of God may be complete, equipped for every good work. (2 Tim 3:16–17)

---

21. Ibid., vol. 17.

It is suggested that worship which is not clearly and fully revealed by God, is no legitimate part of his worship at all.

> Thus it was necessary for the copies of the heavenly things to be purified with these rites, but the heavenly things themselves with better sacrifices than these. For Christ has entered, not into holy places made with hands, which are copies of the true things, but into heaven itself, now to appear in the presence of God on our behalf. (Heb 9:23–24)

Some would maintain that the whole Book of Hebrews is an extended application of the regulative principle of worship. It argues that the whole system of worship commanded by God in the time of Moses is now obsolete because of the coming of Christ, the fulfiller of it. What do we have in its place? The answer is, we have the real thing. Not the old "patterns" (copies) of heavenly things, but "the heavenly things themselves." Whereas the people of God in the time of Moses came to an earthly mountain (12:18), we "come to Mount Zion . . . the city of the living God . . . the heavenly Jerusalem," and so on (12:22). The church today, in other words, is supposed to live in the realm of heavenly realities and not any longer in the realm of shadowy representational symbolism. The example is used of a mother who neglected her infant children, to go up to her bedroom and play hour after hour with the dolls of her childhood, to illustrate that this is exactly what we see in many once-Reformed churches. They go back to the "weak and worthless elementary" principles of worldly ceremonial and symbolic worship.

Believers under the New Covenant are supposed to worship in the realm of spirit and truth—not in the realm of the material and representational, as their Old Testament brothers and sisters did. The truth is that these "weak and worthless" symbols of Old Testament ceremonial worship have no legitimate place in the New Covenant church. The church does not need holy days, elaborate choirs/orchestras, purple robes, candles, incense, dancing, or dramatic performance. Why not? Because these shadowy representations only get in the way of reality which is the privilege of going each Lord's Day, in the Spirit like John, in the faithful observance of the commanded exercises of God's worship, right into the heavenly places and the presence of Jesus. The original purpose of the Regulative Principle was not to unnecessarily restrict public worship, but to liberate stricken consciences from practices within worship that were not expressly set forth in the Scriptures. Those Reformers and second Reformation Puritans that defined the principle insisted that no man, including ecclesiastical authorities, had the right to constrain a worshipper to participate in an activity of worship that had no scriptural warrant.

However, even within the Reformed community which adopted the Regulative Principle, there existed a great variation in the degree of strictness with which the principle was applied to church worship and life in general, a variation that remains today. As with any Christian principle, there exists the danger of adopting a legalistic position whereby we end up applying the principle in a Judaistic/Roman Catholic fashion. As John M. Frame says:

> The regulative principle itself warns us not to add to the Word of God. We need to remind ourselves that one way we are tempted to add to the Word is to try to make it more precise and specific than it is. That was one error of which Jesus accused the Pharisees. We might wish that God had given us more specific guidance as to what pleases him in public worship and in the rest of life.
>
> But we must be content with what He has actually revealed to us, turning neither to the right nor to the left. This reasoning pertains also to the attempt by some to make traditional Reformed worship practices, even those not mentioned in the Confessions, normative for the church. The regulative principle in Scripture is actually a guard against the absolutisation of human tradition. See Isa 29:13, Matt 15:8,9.[22]

Or, to use the metaphor of Reisinger and Allen, perhaps the Regulative Principle should be treated as:

> a hedge that acts as a boundary around broadly prescribed areas of worship that should not be overstepped, rather than a coat-rack upon which every aspect, circumstance, and mode of worship must be hung in order to be approved. Outside its boundaries we should not and cannot go. Yet within its boundaries, there is ample room for variation in worship style and practice.[23]

Praise

The Regulative Principle was applied to numerous aspects of church life by seventeenth century puritans, seeking to establish a scriptural ecclesiology, e.g., confirming some in their doctrine of Believers Baptism and the rebuttal

---

22. John M. Frame, "A Fresh Look at the Regulative Principle: A Broader View," June 4, 2012, www.frame-poythress.org/a-fresh-look-at-the-regulative-principle-a-broader-view/.

23. Reisinger and Allen, *Worship*, 11.

of paedo-baptism. However, the most common application of the Regulative Principle was (and remains today) in the realm of praise in the public worship of the church.

As mainstream dictionaries inform us, "worship" is a contraction from "worth-ship" i.e., to give worth or due honor to someone/something. This is what God is due from us—"Ascribe to the LORD the glory due his name; bring an offering, and come into his courts! Worship the LORD in the splendour of holiness; tremble before him, all the earth!"(Ps 96:8–9).

Here, the Hebrew word for worship is the one most commonly used in the Old Testament—*shachah*—meaning literally to bow down, depress, prostrate oneself in adoration. The most commonly used New Testament word—*proskyneo*—used, e.g., "And they worshiped him and returned to Jerusalem with great joy"(Luke 24:52), means literally to kiss toward (the hand or ground), to do homage. When we engage in public worship, we adore and honor God. Although all who ever adopted a strict application of the principle[24] would automatically reject the endorsement of Christmas, it may be helpful in our understanding of the application of the principle to Christmas, if we appreciate the struggle that occurred in seeking to apply the principle to praise.

The question of what was or was not legitimate praise was of course not new to the seventeenth century puritans, no more than it was to the Reformers. The same issue had to be addressed by the early church. As Nick Needham highlights, the early church deliberately did not use instrumental music in its worship, because they had a concern:

> for the distinctiveness of New Testament worship and for spirituality as its central feature.... In harmony with this, the situation in early church worship was one of "plain" or unaccompanied singing of psalms.... The use of musical instruments was rejected as contrary to the tradition of the Apostles—a feature of sensuous pagan or Old Testament Jewish worship, but not of the spiritual Christian worship.[25]

For the purpose of simplicity, we will restrict our focus largely to English Baptists.

---

24. Evident in the writings of the following: George Gillespie, William Ames, Samuel Rutherford, Jeremiah Burroughs, David Dickson, Thomas Watson, Matthew Henry, John Owen, James Begg, James Bannerman, William Cunningham, Thomas Ridgeley, Thomas Boston, John Cotton, Thomas Manton, William Romaine, R. L. Dabney, James H. Thornwell, John L. Girardeau, and John Murray.

25. Needham, "Musical Instruments," 25–26.

In seventeenth century England, congregational singing was a mark of distinction among Christian groups. Acceptable texts, musical forms, and participants all varied from one religious group to another. Puritans restricted congregational song to metrical psalmody, while the Anglican tradition embraced a rich heritage of cathedral music. This divergence was much more than a matter of differing tastes. Reformed influence in England rejected, in principle, elements of worship for which there was no scriptural warrant. The psalms were viewed as God's provision for song within the religious community and consequently, uninspired texts such as hymnody were disallowed. Metrical psalmody was only one step removed from Scripture, an accommodation of the psalms for musical purposes. Presbyterians used the Psalter but most separatists did not. Quakers excluded all singing. General Baptists rejected metrical psalmody on the basis that it introduced a set form into worship and quenched the Holy Spirit's activity in the worship service. They accepted only spontaneous, charismatic singing that was not limited to predetermined forms and applied this rationale to other set forms of worship as well, such as the *Book of Common Prayer*.

Calvin's pulpit, St. Piere, Geneva

Interestingly, Calvin himself did not practice exclusive psalmody. Although the Regulative Principle, as it came to be termed, evolved from Calvin's principle of *sola Scriptura* more than from any other single theologian, when applying the principle himself in his church he did not exclude manmade hymns based on Scripture.

Calvin himself composed hymns for his Genevan congregation to sing in their public worship services alongside the psalms, including a series he wrote on the Ten Commandments, the Song of Simeon (Luke 2:25–35), the Lord's Prayer, and the Apostles Creed, all of which appeared in the first songbook he prepared. In this he followed the example of his Strasbourg mentor, Martin Bucer (1491–1551).[26]

Calvin disapproved of musical instruments and of songs generally based upon Scripture, preferring instead those using the actual words of Scripture. He interpreted Eph 5:19, "addressing one another in psalms and hymns and spiritual songs, singing and making melody to the Lord with your heart," and Col 3:16, "teaching and admonishing one another in all wisdom, singing psalms and hymns and spiritual songs, with thankfulness in your hearts to God," as referring to all types of song, Old Testament Psalms and Christian hymns, not as different technical terms to describe different types of Old Testament Psalms. Unlike Zwingli who opposed any form of music in church, Calvin on the other hand encouraged congregational singing, preferably led by children in order to encourage humility and musical simplicity, while also holding that cheerfulness should characterize singing![27] Children learned the new musical settings of the psalms in school, then were used by Calvin to teach the congregation in church. When the Psalter was used for praise, song choice was dictated by a chart that hung in the rear of Genevan churches, which prescribed a disciplined pattern for singing through the entire Psalter over a period of several weeks. The first indication of Calvin's theology of sung prayer comes out in his lament on January 16, 1537, when he and Farel presented to the city council their "Articles for the Organization of the Church and its Worship in Geneva":

> We are not able to estimate the benefit and edification which will derive from the [congregational singing] until after having experienced it. Certainly at present the prayers of the faithful are so cold that we should be greatly ashamed and confused.[28]

He became convinced through experience that metrical structure was the most accessible form for the people of that day, with texts from Scripture but arranged in poetic meters. In the preface to the Genevan Psalter of 1565, Calvin stated, "The result of singing is like a spur to incite us to pray to and

---

26. Dyck, "Calvin and Worship," 7.
27. Garside, "Origins Calvin's Theology of Music," 16; Stipp, "Music Philosophies," 5.
28. De Greef, "Calvin's Writings," 50.

to praise God, to medi-tate on his works, that we may love, fear, honor, and glorify him."[29]

One of the early Baptist leaders was John Smyth (c. 1570–1612), ordained an Anglican priest in 1594 and from Nottinghamshire, who eventually became a Baptist pastor. Smyth left and joined a Separatist congregation in Gainsborough, Lincolnshire. These illegal congregations were comprised mostly of Puritans who had relinquished hope of reforming the Anglican church from within; they represented a multitude of different theological views. Numbering just a few in and around London in 1600, they mushroomed in number by 1625. The congregation moved in 1607 to Amsterdam in order to worship freely and there, was influenced by part of the Anabaptist movement, in particular by Mennonites, adopting a Baptist position in 1608. (Although the Calvinistic Protestant Dutch Reformed faith had been adopted as the state religion, the Netherlands nevertheless exhibited a tolerance rare in Europe toward others with divergent faiths, including Remonstrants (Dutch Arminians), Renaissance Humanists, Roman Catholics, Anabaptists, and Jews. The Puritan Pilgrim Fathers lived in Leiden, in the Netherlands for twelve years before sailing to settle Plymouth, Massachusetts.) A portion of Smyth's congregation, including Thomas Helwys, returned to Spitalfields in East London in 1611, thereby establishing one of the first Baptist churches in Britain.

Of course, there may well have been Baptist congregations in Britain in the early centuries after the New Testament era. That aside, later on, John Wycliff (c. 1330–1384) and his followers known as Lollards who preached anticlerical and biblically centered reforms, appear to have had Baptists among their ranks, such as William Sawtre who was burnt at the stake in 1400 for holding views deemed heretical, including opposition to paedo-baptism. In 1535 there were twenty-two Baptists martyred and in 1539 another thirty-five were pursued from England to Holland where they too were martyred. In 1535, the English Ambassador in Antwerp, Sir John Hackett (responsible in 1527 for arranging the arrest of the printer who had reprinted William Tyndale's English New Testament), wrote to Thomas Cromwell, Secretary of State, complaining that "divers places are affected by this new sect of 'rebaptizement,'" and he went on to highlight the danger to England perceived by some in the royal court in Brussels—"he marvelled that those whose eyesight was so sharp as to see over the seas could not see the fire that burns before their own doors, and the commotion of this new sect of rebaptizement, which numbers 6,000 now, and is daily increasing." He tells about the shiploads of

---

29. "John Calvin's Preface to the Genevan Psalter," Semper Reformanda. http://www.semperreformanda.com/men-of-god/john-calvin/john-calvin-index/john-calvins-preface-to-the-genevan-psalter/.

emigrants and says that they were so sympathized with that it was difficult to enlist soldiers to fight against them, that the Regent had sent ten thousand ducats to help the Bishop of Münster to crush them, and a wild report was current that Henry VIII had sent money to the Anabaptists of Münster in revenge for the Pope's refusing his divorce.[30] While of course we could also mention the Albigenses and Waldenses, who for a great many centuries prior to the Reformation contained groups that were clearly Baptist, for our purposes in this chapter we are focusing on Baptists in the post-Reformation period.[31]

In any event, although Smyth subsequently adopted erroneous views before his death (denying the doctrine of original sin), in a treatise written in 1609 that outlined the distinction of separatists from the official Church of England, Smyth's opening summary explicates three points that pertain to worship. In essence, Smyth opposed the use of books in singing and the singing of more than one person together, and he considered the use of meter and rhythm as constraints on the activity of the Holy Spirit.

The earliest record of a Baptist worship service is found in a 1609 letter from Hughe and Anne Bromheade, members of Smyth's congregation:

> The order of the worship and government of our church is, first, we begin with a prayer, after reading some one or two chapters of the Bible give the sense thereof, and confer upon the same, that done we lay aside our books, and after a solemn prayer made by the first speaker, he expounds some text out of the Scripture, and prophecies out of the same, by the space of one hour, or three-quarters of an hour.
>
> After him stands up a second speaker and prophecies out of the said text the like time and space, some time more, some time less. After him the third, the fourth, the fifth, &c as the time will give leave. Then the first speaker concludes with prayer as he began with prayer, with an exhortation to contribution to the poor, which collection being made is also concluded with prayer. This Morning exercise begins at eight of the clock and continues to twelve of the clock the like course of exercise is observed in the afternoon from two of the clock to five or six of the clock. Last of all the execution of the government of the church is handled.[32]

The Congregationalist minister Henry Ainsworth (1571–1622), a defender of psalmody, rejected Smyth's positions as contradictory. His entire

---

30. *Letters and Papers, Foreign and Domestic,* 7:136, 165–67.

31. Armitage, *History of the Baptists,* 302–3; Orchard, *Concise History Baptists,* 299–301.

32. Burrage, *Early English Dissenters,* 1:176–77.

book, *A Defence of the Holy Scriptures* (1609), directly challenged John Smyth's understanding of worship and Christian ministry. On the matter of singing, Ainsworth was dissatisfied that Smyth recognized singing as a gift of the Holy Spirit, yet led a congregation that remained song-less.

Nearer to the end of the seventeenth century, the General Baptists still largely maintained the views that Smyth had espoused regarding singing. The best source for views representative of the General Baptists after they had existed for the better part of a century is *Christianisimus Primitivus*, written in 1678 by the influential leader Thomas Grantham. This grouping of Baptists was termed "General" because they did not believe in a limited atonement, rather that Christ died for all people in general. Neither did they believe in the perseverance of the Christian in a state of grace; instead they believed that once saved, a person may still lapse and perish in hell. A long-time proponent of religious toleration, Grantham had signed "A Brief Confession or Declaration of Faith," presented to King Charles II in 1660, and also the "Second Humble Addresse" and the "Third Addresse," all of which petitioned the state that the Baptists were of peaceful intent and respected civil authority. He often found himself jailed during the era of persecution, however, and he frequented controversies that took the form of public debates. Grantham found no biblical support for the regular, congregational singing of the Psalms, especially in meter in the church and he was most bothered about the mixed singing of psalms and hymns, for which he found no scriptural authority. In particular, Grantham feared the consequences of introducing unwarranted singing into worship. Not even the Book of Psalms qualified in his opinion! While psalms provided a good guide, the failure of the New Testament (in his opinion) to present an example of their use in the primitive church, meant Grantham found it inconclusive that they would please God in worship. Grantham feared that metrical songs would introduce forms of prayer and the possibility that artful singing would lead to the introduction of musical instruments.

The Particular Baptists, with which Benjamin Keach maintained affiliation, took a more favorable stance toward singing than did the General Baptists. Certainly, their stance was more flexible. Throughout the seventeenth century, the Particular Baptists' position on singing vacillated from opposition to acceptance. The General Baptists were formed first and as we have seen, split off from a Separatist church and had ties to the Anabaptists of Holland; the Particular Baptists (termed such because they believed in a limited atonement, or that Christ died for his elect people in particular) split off from an early Independent church in London under John Spilsbury (1593–1668). Unlike Separatists, Independents tended to operate autonomously without formally breaking away from the Anglican Church. It was between 1633 and 1638 that this first Particular Baptist church was constituted in Wapping, East London, and by 1644 a group of seven congregations in and around London all adopted the First London Confession of Particular Baptists, affirming Particular Atonement, believers' baptism by immersion, and perseverance of the saints (preceding the *Westminster Confession of Faith* by two years). Hercules Collins (d. 1702) was the third pastor of the church founded by Spilsbury in Wapping. In 1680 he penned his *Orthodox Catechism* as a theological summary. This document was essentially the Heidelberg Catechism of 1562 adjusted to the Particular Baptist tenets. Its comprehensive nature was similar to *Christianisimus Primitivus*, which the General Baptist, Thomas Grantham, had written two years earlier.

At the end of the *Orthodox Catechism*, Collins attached an appendix focused solely on the ordinance of singing. Though only twelve pages long, it provided a succinct yet effective statement of position in acceptance of congregational singing.

He advanced two main points, both of which Keach echoed a decade later. First, vocal singing is an ordinance that Scripture instituted, and second, man has a moral obligation to praise God, the creator of the universe. Like Grantham, Collins appealed to religious leaders of the past, including Justin Martyr, Augustine, and Beza. At the end of his short essay, Collins also addressed the primary objections typically advanced by those who opposed singing—concerns such as a mixed congregation (converted and unconverted), the mode of singing, and the role of spiritual worship of the heart. In these responses, Collins approved of singing metrical psalms but he also embraced hymns of human composition.

In 1646, another General Baptist, Francis Cornwell, who suffered imprisonment under Archbishop William Laud for failing to conform to Laudian Ceremonies, published a book against stinted or shortened forms of psalms. Once a Church of England vicar, Cornwell's efforts to justify infant baptism as scripturally authorized, led him to abandon his support for the practice and to accept adult baptism as a correct understanding of Scripture. In his treatise against shortened forms of psalms, which was actually a historical account of a conference between John Cotton and church leaders in Boston, New England, on the same subject, Cornwell set forth twelve reasons of opposition. Much of Cornwell's aversion is familiar, as the rationale presented is identical to arguments presented by Grantham. The above evidence indicates that the matter of singing must have been a brewing controversy, long before its public debate among Particular Baptists in the 1690s.

Benjamin Keach was pastor at Horsleydown, South London (this same congregation would later become known as New Park Street and called as their pastor, C. H. Spurgeon). Under his leadership, hymns were originally sung after the Lord's Supper, the first occasion being in 1668 and it was the first known occasion when a modern hymn was sung in England.[33] Keach composed the hymn himself, based on the sermon he had just preached. He later justified the innovation by arguing that the Lord sung a hymn after inaugurating the Lord's Supper in the upper room, while others remonstrated that this hymn was surely a psalm. Hercules Collins, among others, supported Keach and gradually hymns were used on special days of thanksgiving and then by 1682 on a weekly basis after the Sunday sermon (which had the practical advantage of allowing any of the congregation to leave before the singing, if their conscience provoked them not to participate). Keach's implementation of singing infringed on Particular Baptist worship practice in two ways: first, it broke with the separatist/independent tradition, which

---

33. Curwen, *Studies in Worship Music*, 97.

generally prohibited all singing; second, it involved the use of hymns of human composition rather than the psalms.

As James Brooks suggests, Keach sought to correct the church from what he perceived to be the error of a lost ordinance—congregational singing. He appears to have adopted a logical approach, carefully analyzing several facets of the practice including its antiquity, whether or not it was a moral duty, singing as an ordinance of Christ, the testimony of Old Testament saints, prophets, and early Christians, and the form singing should take—all in an effort to affirm the validity of singing as a required ordinance of the Christian church.

How to determine this truth in regards to ordinances of worship and valid biblical patterns to follow, was also one of his major frustrations. He believed the example of Christ singing with his apostles at the Last Supper sufficient as a pattern to be followed, yet he was greatly troubled that his opponents claimed Christ left an insufficient directive. Not everyone in Keach's congregation supported this new worship style, as the congregation previously had prohibited all singing. An open controversy, first in the congregation and then extending to Baptists at large, erupted around 1690 and evolved into a virulent printed debate. Isaac Marlow, Keach's chief antagonist (a wealthy jeweller and member of the congregation at Horsleydown), published *A Brief Discourse Concerning Singing* in 1690. Keach responded in 1691 with *The Breach Repaired in God's Worship*, his most extensive apology of congregational singing as an ordinance from God. Keach's introduction of singing led his detractors, a minority of his congregation, to challenge him on "will-worship"—the introduction of a man-made element into the worship service. Twenty-six members left the Horsleydown congregation, including the wife of Isaac Marlow. A respected layman as well as a delegate to the General Assemblies and the treasurer of the assembly's fund, Marlow launched a pamphlet war on the matter.

The tension between Keach and Marlow reached its apex in a representative assembly of Particular Baptist churches in 1692. The assembly focused its attention on the dispute and thus assured its public nature. However, the assembly never addressed the actual details of the fracas, concentrating instead on cultivating unity in the fragile association of churches. In 1692, representative leaders from most (if not all) of the Particular Baptist churches met in a national General Assembly in London.

The narrative of the assembly never reflects any discussion on the merits or demerits of the argument concerning singing, whether it was right or wrong, helpful or harmful, required or voluntary. The committee's concern was one of process—the character of the discussions, the inflammatory remarks therein, their public nature, and the consequent reflections on individuals, congregations, and God. In effect, they ordered both men to drop the subject! Keach abided by the committee decision inasmuch as he did not publicly write any more pamphlets on the subject of the debate on singing. Marlow, on the other hand, was most aggrieved and felt the committee had not even bothered to look at the evidence. He continued to publish pamphlets and was ostracized as a consequence. Ultimately, Marlow viewed Scripture as lacking any positive instruction to authorize regular, ordinary singing. He viewed the Scriptures as silent on the matter and to him, such silence equalled prohibition. Keach, on the other hand, sought to introduce regular, vocal congregational singing into the Sunday worship. He believed God ordained the practice for the Christian church and that pre-composed forms were an acceptable method of accomplishing this ordinance. Like Marlow, he supported patterns, examples, and commands as authoritative. He differed, however, in his definition of singing and on how to relate scriptural passages on singing to these criteria.

Brooks shows that at the end of the seventeenth century, both the General Baptists and the Particular Baptists had a history of addressing the propriety of congregational singing in worship. Their views differed from each other and for the Particular Baptists, differed within the movement itself. In the century's final three decades, a representative of each group produced a small, summative theological statement: Thomas Grantham for the General Baptists, and Hercules Collins for the Particular Baptists. On the matter of singing, Grantham's *Christianisimus Primitivus* echoed John Smyth's views and foreshadowed the position of Isaac Marlow. Hercules Collins's views reflected opposite conclusions and pointed in the direction that Benjamin Keach would take. Hymns composed by people, rather than the strict use of the psalms composed by people but inspired by the Holy Spirit, broached a series of uncomfortable questions. From Marlow's viewpoint, congregational singing and hymns written by men weakened the Regulative Principle of worship and destabilized its theoretical foundation for determining worship practices. In their writings, Keach and Marlow both affirmed the supreme authority of Scripture. They also both believed that the Reformation had not been completed. Even after 150 years, they both argued that the nonconformist churches in England were still struggling to become more perfectly reformed. They both believed that the necessary reformation and purification would be achieved by a faithful replication of scriptural teachings.

For worship, this assumption translated to reproducing patterns of activities described in Scripture; instructions prescribing Christian worship activity and therefore limiting the capacity of the Christian church to embrace activity not explicitly commanded. As Brooks summarizes, Benjamin Keach challenged fundamental worship practices of the Particular and General

Baptists and on the issue of congregational singing, promoted interpretive principles generally embraced by those of a Lutheran heritage, in a fellowship that had strictly adhered to principles derived from Calvin. Keach uniquely blended the opposing interpretations of these historical forces.[34] He argued that he more faithfully replicated the biblical pattern by implementing man-made congregational song. From the perspective of Christian liberty, he argued that singing was not prohibited by the Bible and was consistent with a type of praise known to have been offered at some point in the past.

What these sixteenth and seventeenth century protagonists would have made of today's concert style church services using 200-person choirs, 100-piece orchestras, synthesizers, and elaborate lighting effects, is an intriguing speculation!

What Do We Learn from All of This Respecting Christmas?

First, as we can see from our synopsis on the implementation of the Regulative Principle in praise, there existed a great variety of views respecting what was deemed legitimate or otherwise in the light of Scripture. Zwingli and Marlow differed from Calvin and Keach. In similar fashion, the Reformed community in Geneva and elsewhere held different views on the endorsement of Christmas and other holy days, than those of other communities.

Second, the debate over the acceptability of different forms of praise would, over time, become delineated as the distinction between the *elements* and the *circumstances* of worship. The former is regarded as that which is mandatory, such as reading the Scriptures, prayer, ordinances of Baptism and Lord's Supper, praise and preaching, as these elements are all explicitly stated in Scripture. Whereas the circumstances relate to how, where, and when these elements are performed, such as the venue, the type of seating, the physical mode of standing or sitting, the time and frequency of services, the types of praise and music utilized, etc. As we have seen, some men believed congregational praise to be one of the elements of worship, therefore permissible, while others believed it was not part of the elements and therefore never permissible (the General Baptist Assembly of 1689 endorsed soloists in public worship and pronounced congregational singing "foreign to evangelical worship").[35] All of the men in question were seeking to implement the Regulative Principle, seeking to identify how far it went. To use the hedge analogy of Reisinger and Allen again, was singing, was a

---

34. Brooks, *Benjamin Keach*, 200.
35. Whitley, *Minutes of the General Assembly*, Vol. 1, *1654–1728*, 27.

musical instrument, was a man-made hymn, when used in public worship, inside or outside the hedge border?

Third, the pertinent question is, are annual holy days commemorating scriptural events merely circumstantial to worship or are they elements of worship? If they are part of the elements of worship, explicitly stated in Scripture and mandatory, then each congregation has liberty to decide the circumstances by which the days will be utilized. If they are not part of the elements, the logical conclusion is that no congregation has any liberty to introduce them in any circumstance, as worship should consist only of what God commands.

Fourth, obviously the birth of the Savior is a historical and scriptural fact and requires, as is true for all scriptural truths, to be a subject expressed in all of the elements of worship. While no one would question the legitimacy of expressing such a truth on any or on every day of the year, is it legitimate to generally confine the expression of that truth to a special/consecrated/hallowed or holy day once a year?

If it is legitimate, then there can be no objection raised to an Anglican, Lutheran or even Roman Catholic liturgical calendar. How were the truths of God expressed by the apostles led by the Holy Spirit, in Jerusalem, Antioch, Galatia, Colossae, Ephesus, Philippi, Corinth, Thessalonica, or Rome? Were the churches instructed to appoint annual holy days to express these truths? The answer of course is, no, they were not instructed to do so, therefore this was reflected practically in the absence of Apostolic endorsement of all such days during the Apostolic era.

Fifth, as the principle has implications for praise which simply cannot be avoided, so it has implications for the religious endorsement of Christmas, or otherwise.

Many argue that God's Regulative Principle is too strict and legalistic. They argue that it confines the human spirit and that it stifles human creativity. They teach that it is an overreaction to the abuses of Roman Catholicism. As we have just seen, there has always been a variety in the degree of implementing the Regulative Principle, yet as a general rule, a church that does not accept and obey God's Regulative Principle at all, has no legitimate basis to object to new ideas and innovations in worship, whatever type that might be. Christians who do not endorse Christmas in a religious sense are sometimes labeled as being "legalistic," at the expense of the preeminence of love, by those Christians who do embrace it. However, many who embrace Christmas reject some twenty-first-century contemporary worship music, regarding it as unacceptable and dishonoring to God. This is because they feel that it places too much emphasis upon the music at the expense of meaningful doctrinal lyrics, also that in some cases it is indistinguishable from a secular concert. In other words, they believe such practice to be outside "the hedge"! Those with such reservations refuse to implement this style into their churches, neither will they worship in churches where it is prevalent. The reason they reject the worship style is because their view of worship is regulated by their doctrine of God. Might not the proponents of such contemporary worship accuse *them* of being legalistic and failing to show them the preeminent love of Christ?

While some Christians who do not endorse Christmas may indeed act "legalistically" in this or other areas of their lives, many others who do not endorse Christmas are simply applying the very same principle, believing that God's honor demands it.

As Samuel Waldron highlights, the Regulative Principle of worship has implications for the whole of a biblical and faithful ecclesiology. If you give sinful man the autonomy of choosing how he will worship, the historical pattern is clear. Man will choose a worship style that is man-centered, with a leaning either toward entertainment (thus the popularity of gospel concerts, church musical directors, large bands, drama groups, choirs, music soloists, etc.), or to ritual and pomp (cathedrals, incense, candles, bells, mandatory prayer books, holy days, popish robes, and vestments), with all manner of liturgy based upon human and church tradition.[36] G. I. Williamson summarizes the Regulative Principle in this way:

> Are we at liberty to do as we please, to fashion our own "style" of worship, whereas the people of God in Old Testament times had to be sure that they worshipped God only as He commanded? No, the truth lies in the opposite direction: we—above all—should abhor and shun all these innovations. Is this not what underlies the following warning? "See that you do not refuse him who speaks. For if they did not escape who refused him who spoke on earth, much more shall we not escape if we turn away from him who speaks from heaven. . . . Therefore, since we are receiving a kingdom which cannot be shaken, let us have grace, by which we may serve God acceptably with reverence and godly fear. For our God is a consuming fire." (Heb 12:25, 28, 29). If we dare to invent our own way of worship, when God has told us from heaven what He requires, our sin will be much greater than that of Israelites under the old covenant. The way of worship under the new covenant has now been instituted by the Lord Jesus. Unlike the shadowy worship of old, this worship will never be superseded until our Lord's second coming. How

---

36. Waldron, *Regulative Principle*.

audacious and daring for any of us, then, to presume to change what He has commanded![37]

Problems with the Regulative Principle

Does then the Regulative Principle, applied to the subject of Christmas, amount to an open and shut case? Has a question like the propriety of holy days been answered conclusively and beyond doubt by this principle? Well, it would be nice to think so; however, the reality is somewhat different, as the Regulative Principle is not without its problems, another truth that some opponents of holy days are reluctant to admit. The reality is that God could have given the New Testament church a new version of Leviticus for the purpose of directing new covenant worship with a hundred explicit do's and don'ts, but he did not. Even the Old Testament is not in essence a rule book; rather, it is a narrative. This fact must have at least some bearing on the way we attempt to formulate what it means to regulate church worship and church government according to the Bible.

There does exist a basic problem of hermeneutics, or interpretation of the Bible, if we approach it as something which it is not. The Bible is very clearly not a rule book for worship. By the application of the principle rigorously, as some apply it, the fact is that we are bound to accuse our Lord Christ himself of not complying with the same principle! We refer in the next chapter under "Reason 5" to the Feast of Purim in some detail but consider, for the moment, several other New Testament era practices, none of which was prescribed by the Mosaic law: the Feast of the Dedication of Jerusalem, the worship performed in Synagogues, and the Temple worship.

The Feast of the Dedication of Jerusalem (John 10:22), also known as Hanukkah, or the Feast of Lights, celebrated the cleansing and rededication of the temple after three years of desecration by Antiochus Epiphanes, king of Syria, in 164 BC, the time of the Maccabees. Respecting the origin of the Synagogue, Alfred Edersheim opines:

> In point of fact, the attentive reader of the books of Ezra and Nehemiah will discover in the period after the return from Babylon the beginnings of the synagogue. Only quite rudimentary as yet, and chiefly for the purposes of instructing those who had come back ignorant and semi-heathenish-still, they formed a starting-point.

In describing the worship of the Synagogue, Edersheim continues:

37. Williamson, "Regulative Principle of Worship."

> The symbolical and typical elements which constituted the life and center of Temple worship had lost their spiritual meaning and attraction to the majority of that generation, and their place was becoming occupied by so-called teaching and outward performances.
>
> Thus the worship of the letter took the place of that of the spirit, and Israel was preparing to reject Christ for Pharisaism. The synagogue was substituted for the Temple, and overshadowed it, even within its walls, by an incongruous mixture of man-devised worship with the God-ordained typical rites of the sanctuary.[38]

Both Hannukah and Synagogue worship were a part of first century Jewish worship and both could be characterized as practices that were established "according to the imaginations and devices of men," as ways of worship "not prescribed in Holy Scripture," to quote the *Westminster Confession of Faith*, chapter XXI:1.

No respected New Testament commentator would suggest that the Lord Jesus did not attend the synagogue, or the feast mentioned by John. With regard to the temple in Jerusalem, many Jews in Jesus' day regarded the temple as defunct (no Ark of the Covenant, no "shekinah" glory of God's presence, a complex built without Divine command by a quite ungodly man in Herod, and having a corrupt priesthood). As a consequence, some Jews such as the Essenes, moved home out of Jerusalem in disgust, adopting a rural monastic lifestyle. On that basis they wanted nothing to do with the temple, yet our Savior acknowledged (at least implicitly) the legitimacy of the temple during his public ministry. When Jesus healed the leper (Mark 1:40–45), he instructed him to go to the priest and offer for his cleansing what Moses commanded (Lev 14:1–32). The declaration that a leper was cleansed involved sacrifices in the temple. Then there is the matter of the temple tax (Matt 17:24–27), where the tax collectors seek out Jesus and his disciples in Capernaum. Jesus instructs Peter to do a bit of solitary fishing and when he does, he catches a fish that had swallowed a coin worth enough to pay the annual temple tax for both of them. The temple tax was used for the upkeep of the temple which included the sacrifices. Finally, consider the disciples' preparation for the Last Supper (Mark 14:12–25), which involved the offering of a Passover lamb in the temple.

Notwithstanding the uniqueness of the God-man, born and raised a Jew and the embodiment of all of the Old Testament types, the question these issues obviously raise is, if the Lord Jesus did not strictly follow the Regulative Principle in this regard, then why should we?

---

38. Edersheim, *Sketches Jewish Social Life*, chs. 16, 17.

Another problem with it, or rather not with the principle itself but with the interpretation and application of it, is that too much emphasis is placed by some upon Old Testament texts. The Old Testament is as relevant to us as the New Testament and God is unchangeable in himself. Paul reminds Timothy that the inspired Scriptures (Old Testament) are "profitable for teaching, for reproof, for correction, and for training in righteousness"(1 Tim 3:16). To quote the ancient maxim: "The New is in the Old concealed, the Old is by the New revealed." However, we no longer live under Law but under Grace/Gospel, for God's promised covenant of grace, revealed obscurely under the types and shadows of the Old Covenant, has been fully established and completed in the New Covenant in the sacrifice of Christ. Clearly, while the Lord does not change his character, his expectation of how his visible church is to function has certainly changed. If that were not the case, then church leaders finding, for example, a sister in Christ who had acted foolishly and was guilty of adultery, would not seek her repentance and restoration to active membership of the fellowship, but would simply execute her! Many of the Old Testament applications of the Regulative Principle relate to Scriptures where specific commands and requirements for acceptable worship are broken and ignored.

We lack a list of specific commands and requirements for acceptable worship in the New Testament; therefore, we have to seek to determine what is acceptable to God or otherwise, in a similar way to how we have to seek to determine what the will of God is for our lives.

It is unreasonable for some to dogmatically assert that a certain church practice today is clearly sinful and contrary to God's wishes, on the premise that an Old Testament Scripture rendered a certain practice as sinful. As an example, does Nadab and Abihu's failure to approach God reverently and worship in a manner commanded, render any and all public worship led by children sinful, due to the fact it is neither commanded nor explicitly suggested in the New Testament?

So much for the Regulative Principle, but do we really need to be convinced of a doctrinal principle of whatever name, to decide what practice performed in Jesus' name is worthy of him or otherwise? After gathering up all the information we can about the person of God, can a little bit of sanctified common sense not just inform us conclusively, what is likely to please or displease God?

Twelve Reasons Justifying the Endorsement of Christmas

THERE CONTINUES TO BE an increase in the number of Reformed churches endorsing Christmas today. These are churches whose Calvinistic doctrinal basis remains largely unaltered from the days of their forefathers who refused to endorse Christmas.

In light of this fact it is necessary to examine some of the chief reasons given to justify this growing practice. People speak of "The Twelve Days of Christmas," so here are twelve reasons for Christmas! Some of the following answers given to the reasons have already been stated either explicitly or implicitly in previous chapters. The reasons are not exhaustive but are representative of common views held by conservative, evangelical Christians with a high view of the Bible, not liberals whose views we might expect to be very different to a Reformed/Calvinistic viewpoint.

Reason 1

Probably the most common reason cited, historically and presently, is based upon the principle of "liberty of conscience." Scriptures are cited such as Col 2:16: "Therefore let no one pass judgment on you in questions of food and drink, or with regard to a festival or a new moon or a Sabbath," and Rom 14:5–6: "One person esteems one day as better than another, while another esteems all days alike. Each one should be fully convinced in his own mind. The one who observes the day, observes it in honor of the Lord. The one who eats, eats in honor of the Lord, since he gives thanks to God, while the one who abstains, abstains in honor of the Lord and gives thanks to God." One writer states on these verses in Romans:

> It would be difficult to be much clearer than this. Believers have freedom to esteem one day over another or to view all days the same. In other words, Christians can choose to worship God in certain ways on December 25, or they can choose to treat every day the same and we have no business telling a fellow believer what he or she must do on this point. . . . In the so-called "grey areas" of the faith, we have the freedom to make decisions for ourselves based on the guidance of the Holy Spirit and our own conscience.[1]

Answer

The principle of Christian liberty is a very precious one and we need to distinguish between the exercise of it personally, in private, and the exercise of it collectively, in public worship. We consider the private aspect further under Reason 4.

The conscience dictates differently to different Christians, depending on their different interpretation of the Bible. What is regarded as a sin to one is regarded as no sin to another and in the same vein, what is a grey area to one is black and white to someone else. Liberty of conscience has always been applied to numerous aspects of public worship. In this book we have already touched on some of those aspects. Are musical instruments acceptable or do they lack New Testament warrant? Are congregational singing or man-made hymns acceptable or not? Is the Lord's Day a continuation of the Sabbath or not? Are ladies head coverings a binding principle everywhere or is the lack of explicit teaching outside of First Corinthians indicative of a local cultural issue? For many churches, these issues are all matters of liberty of conscience. Is the religious endorsement of Christmas in public worship another such matter?

Let us consider the passages in Romans, Colossians, and Galatians.

Paul, in his epistle to the Romans, was addressing a situation unique to the early church. There were Jewish believers who regarded the holy days of the ceremonial economy as having abiding sanctity. The "days" spoken of in Romans were days commanded by God in the old economy. Paul is referring to the ceremonial holy days of the Levitical institution and virtually all commentators concur with this interpretation (over twenty standard Reformed commentaries take this view).[2] Paul allows for diversity in the church over the issue of Jewish holy days because of the unique historical circumstances.

---

1. Chaffey, "Christians Celebrating Christmas."
2. Schwertley, *Regulative Principle*, 43.

As Schwertley reasons, when the Savior died on the cross, the ceremonial aspects of the law (e.g., animal sacrifices, Jewish holy days, circumcision, etc.) were done away with. Prior to the destruction of Jerusalem and the temple in AD 70, the apostles allowed certain practices by Jewish Christians as long as no works-righteousness was attributed to these practices. In Acts 21:26 we even encounter the Apostle Paul going to the Temple to announce the expiration of the days of purification. Jewish believers who were already accustomed to keeping certain holy days of the Mosaic economy were allowed to continue doing so for a time. Once the Temple was destroyed, the canon of Scripture completed and the church had existed for a whole generation, these unique historical circumstances ceased. It would have been wrong for the weak Jewish believers to force the church to have a worship service in honor of Mosaic ceremonial holy days because the strong Gentile believers would feel compelled to attend the public worship of God. Therefore, those who did celebrate Jewish holy days had to do it privately to the Lord. Those who use this passage to justify celebrating Christmas would likewise be forced by Paul's injunction to keep the day a private affair. Thus, public Christmas worship services and church Christmas events would have to cease as, under this argument, they would violate the freedom of Christians not to celebrate such a day. Here the apostle instructed the strong to be patient with the weak, because the weak did not yet understand the liberty they had in Christ. The truth is that they were no longer under any obligation at all to observe even the special days that God had once appointed, neither were they obligated to observe some of the clean and unclean rules about food. The problem was that some members of the church in Rome did not yet understand these things. As long as it was only a particular member of the congregation that had this problem of weakness, Paul was willing to patiently bear with that person. He was willing to have the church tolerate membership for a person who felt constrained, by a misinformed conscience, to observe those days.

In Gal 4:10–11 and Col 2:16–17 the observance of days is condemned by Paul because in these instances the celebration of days was connected with heresy. The situation at Rome was different. The days were kept because of a genuine misunderstanding. Heresy and ideas of works-righteousness were not involved. So in Gal 4, the apostle had a different concern and we always need to compare Scripture with Scripture. The great twentieth century theologian John Murray used to say, "the difference between right and wrong, between truth and falsehood, is not a chasm but a razor's edge."[3] In Gal 4, the apostle is speaking of something done by the church, as a corporate

---

3. Murray, "Sanctity of Truth."

body. This is very clear from the plural pronouns. The Galatian church had yielded to the demands of the weak by instituting an observance of these days in a corporate manner. When this was imposed upon the church body, the apostle was quite uncompromising in his opposition.

In Col 2:16–17, the point that Paul is making is that the food and festival days had become idols to some in the church there and unhelpful in facilitating their relationship to Christ, whereas their original intention was as a means of relating to God.

The reference to Sabbath day points clearly to the Jewish calendar, for only Jews kept the Sabbath. That being the case, holy day/religious festival and new moon celebration must also point primarily to the ritual calendar of the Jews. Paul's thought is that the Christian is freed from obligations of this kind (Gal 4:9–11). No one, therefore, should be permitted to make such things a test of piety or fellowship (Rom 14).

The false teachers were telling the Colossians the lie that Christ is not enough but that they also needed to keep the Jewish ceremonial rituals and legalism, as commanded in the Mosaic Law. As Barnes on Col 2:16 argues, Paul counters with the argument that Paul has here in mind the ascetic regulations and practices of one wing of the Gnostics (possibly Essenic or even Pharisaic influence). He makes a plea for freedom in such matters on a par with that in 1 Cor 8:9 and Rom 14:15. The Essenes went far beyond the Mosaic regulations:

> Since you have thus been delivered by Christ from the evils which surrounded you and since you have been freed from the observances of the law, let no one sit in judgment on you, or claim the right to decide for you in those matters. You are not responsible to man for your conduct, but to Christ; and no man has a right to impose that on you as a burden from which He has made you free.[4]

A. T. Robertson on Gal 4:10 states:

> The meticulous observance of the Pharisees Paul knew to a nicety. It hurt him to the quick after his own merciful deliverance to see these Gentile Christians drawn into this spider-web of Judaizing Christians, once set free, now enslaved again. Paul does not itemise the "days" (Sabbaths, fast-days, feast-days, new moons) nor the "months" (Isa 66:23) which were particularly observed in the exile nor the "seasons" (Passover, Pentecost, Tabernacles, etc.) nor the "years" (sabbatical years every seventh year and the Year of Jubilee). Paul does not object to these

---

4. Barnes, *Notes on the New Testament*.

observances for he kept them himself as a Jew. He objected to Gentiles taking to them as a means of salvation.⁵

Clearly, this is a very different circumstance to the invention and adoption of Christmas into the life of a church, then facing criticism from fellow believers for endorsing it. Those who are unhappy with such criticism cannot use Gal 4 or Col 2 in their defense. Indeed, if anything, the latter passage tends to actually condemn the adoption of Christmas.

R. P. Nevin's analysis applies:

> If the Apostle Paul were permitted to revisit earth, we might imagine him addressing them somewhat after the following manner: "Ye men of a half-reformed church, ye observe days and times. Ye have a whole calendar of so-called saints' days. Ye observe a Holy Thursday and a Good Friday. Ye have a time called Easter, and a season called Lent, about which some of you make no small stir. Ye have a day regarded especially holy, named Christmas, observed at a manifestly wrong season of the year, and notoriously grafted on an old Pagan festival. . . . I am afraid of you, lest the instruction contained in my epistle, as well as in other parts of Scripture, has been bestowed upon you in vain."⁶

Notice the Lord's instructions in Exod 20:1–6:

> And God spoke all these words, saying, "I am the LORD your God, who brought you out of the land of Egypt, out of the house of slavery. You shall have no other gods before me. You shall not make for yourself a carved image, or any likeness of anything that is in heaven above, or that is in the earth beneath, or that is in the water under the earth. You shall not bow down to them or serve them, for I the LORD your God am a jealous God, visiting the iniquity of the fathers on the children to the third and the fourth generation of those who hate me, but showing steadfast love to thousands of those who love me and keep my commandments."

Here in these verses we have the first two of the Ten Commandments. The Roman Catholic Church and the Lutheran Church misrepresent the commandments and treat the second commandment as if it were a part of the first. To retain ten commandments, they divide the tenth into two parts, which gives us two commandments forbidding the same sin—covetousness. The practical result of this is the removal of any specific command as to *how*

---

5. Robertson, *Word Pictures*.
6. Nevin, *Misunderstood Scriptures*.

God ought to be worshipped, which is what the Lord has given us in verses 4-6. As we noticed above in the preceding chapter, the difference between the two schools of thought, in the past at least, has been that Reformed churches imbibed worship which was very simple and spiritual—reading, preaching, prayer, singing psalms/hymns, and administration of Baptism and the Lord's Supper, i.e., only what has been commanded in the Bible. In contrast, Roman Catholicism and Lutheranism follow what is commanded in the Bible *and* things not expressly commanded or forbidden—so Rome has seven sacraments and a place for icons, images, articles such as crucifixes, candles, rosary beads, clerical vestments etc., all deemed to be useful symbolic reminders of spiritual truth. There are many things, Christmas trees included, which affect our senses and the atmosphere of a worship service, but these outward things affect the unbeliever just as much as the believer. In and of themselves these things cannot do what only the Holy Spirit can do, in conveying God's truth to man's heart and drawing forth worship to God (which is in reality nothing else but the Spirit of God returning to the source from which he first came).

Do we not hear so often, people saying that Christmas "is really for the children"? In verse 6 of Exod 20, God tells us about the benefit of keeping worship pure and that when it is not, it is the children who suffer! When we bring into worship things that God has not commanded, it is our children who learn these things and do not understand that they are worshipping God in a wrong way and are being influenced by things which have a human origin rather than a divine one. The danger is that the worship offered and subsequently transmitted to their own children, may be grieving to the Spirit and spiritual blessing lost, because they have not learned to think of him as he has shown himself actually to be, rather as men have imagined him to be. Some people exercise liberty of conscience to reject Christ and worship false gods, while also encouraging others to do so. Is this alright? If it is not alright, upon what basis do we criticize them? There is only one basis, which is God's revealed will in his Word, whereby we see that all men have a duty to worship him alone. A Christian may exercise liberty of conscience respecting which Bible version to use and legitimately choose one version over another, as God's revealed will does not stipulate any particular version. Does the Christian have liberty of conscience to organize the celebration of Christ's birthday in annual public worship services, to which God's people are expected to attend and to which the unconverted are invited? We would suggest that as the Savior and apostles did not instruct this, then we do not have the right or liberty to do it, notwithstanding the inclusion in some services of drama (nativity plays) and artifacts of questionable merit.

Liberty of conscience cuts both ways! If it is wrong for a fellow believer to tell others that they are wrong to organize Christmas services, then it is also wrong for a fellow believer to tell others that they are wrong to abstain from the organizing of Christmas services. Whether or not we are for or against the religious endorsement of Christmas, we have no liberty to absolutize for others, on the basis of our own personal convictions. For a believer to accept or decline an invitation to a brother's home, where Christmas is celebrated, is a legitimate exercise of liberty of conscience, both in the invitation and in the response. However, if the leadership of a church organizes and sanctions public services of worship such as Christmas, Good Friday, Easter, Ascension, Pentecost, the Assumption of Mary, or All Souls Day, they are, unwittingly or otherwise, binding the conscience of the believers over whom they rule, to engage in something for which there exists no biblical warrant whatsoever. What liberty is there for the ("weaker" some might say) brother in sanctioned public worship, except in exercising absence? At the outset of this answer, we noted that the application of liberty of conscience occurs with respect to many aspects of public worship, such as music styles, dress code, the sabbath, and so on. What makes Christmas different to these other aspects is the *root* of the practice. These other aspects *all* arise out of references in the New Testament to the practices. We read about the Lord's Day, praise, head coverings, and so on, in the New Testament after Pentecost and since the Apostolic era the church has attempted to work out their appropriate application. In contrast, Christmas, the specific and annual celebration of Christ's birth, has *no* New Testament reference. It originated in the context of the loss of Apostolic doctrine. It grew by synchronizing with pagan practices. It is embedded with myths and falsehood and its nineteenth century resurrection was a secular movement, not a spiritual one.

Let us illustrate by hypothesis. Liberal churches commonly believe in a universal salvation and that Hell, if it exists at all, is but a temporary affair. It is therefore understandable for them to focus most of their energies on alleviating social ills and caring for the environment, not on evangelism and biblical theology. Let us suppose that they become so concerned for God's creation and the use of it by humanity that they decide to invent an annual celebration of creation on July 25. It is, of course, a biblical fact that God created, as it is a biblical injunction for people to exercise care over his creation. They initially call it Green Day or Greengod Day. Rome lends its support, a special mass is incorporated and it becomes known as Greenmas Day! Support grows and it becomes an ecumenical success, with a syncretizing of non-Christian views. Several weeks of church activity characterise the run-up to Greenmas Day. However, with the passage of time, perhaps centuries, the festival loses its original meaning, and concern for the environment is reawakened. Then some "green" politicians and environmentalists decide that it would help their cause to reinvent Greenmas and great effort is expended on it. The public find it charming, the liberal churches are delighted and the world of commerce spots a bonanza! As Greenmas develops its own musical and culinary genre, blossoms beyond anything its original inventors could ever have imagined, more and more churches then begin incorporating it into their church life. With the passage of time, the question among churches is no longer, "Who is doing Greenmas?" but "Who is still *not* doing Greenmas?" Then a Reformed church discovers that it is the *only* church left in its community not endorsing the religious celebration of Greenmas. Pressure is mounting from the bottom up, for the church to no longer remain the odd one out. Now the question is this—when the leadership of the Reformed church formally meet to discuss the matter and whether or not to adopt Greenmas into worship in Christ's name, is the practice under discussion merely one to which liberty of conscience applies? We would suggest that it is definitely not and that biblical, Christian liberty of conscience must be bounded by revelation concerning the instituted elements of Christian worship, seen especially from Pentecost onwards. *Unless*, of course, the church's interpretation is changing from reformed to something else, such as a Roman Catholic inventive style or a Lutheran/Anglican normative style, with anything acceptable so long as it is not expressly forbidden in Scripture. As creation is clearly scriptural, an annual Greenmas Day may be viewed as very helpful to faith. However, if a church believes that we have in the New Testament a template and pattern to guide us in our practice and since there exists no record of the apostles appointing a specific, annual day for the remembrance of God's creation or humanity's responsibility toward it, then the principle of liberty of conscience is extraneous to the issue.

In other words, a church is not free to devise its own ways of worship, no matter how strong the cultural consensus may be. A church finds liberty in Christ and liberty in worship is to be found in worshipping according to the New Testament template as laid down by Christ, through his apostles. Consequently, Christian love is exercised toward fellow believers when we do not institute patterns in worship that offend their consciences, or require that they participate in worship that is not in accordance with Scripture.

We would humbly suggest that the passages quoted above in Romans, Galatians, and Colossians, to highlight liberty of conscience, appear to fall short as a convincing reproof against those who criticize the religious endorsement of Christmas.

Reason 2

The Puritans observed that if a pagan practice or name had lost its original meaning, then it was permissible to use it. For example, the uses of the terms "Sunday" or "Monday" were originally related to mythologies about sun and moon gods, originating in the Roman culture and then transposed into northern European equivalents. The same is true of the names of the months of the year we use. As sun and moon worship was largely unheard of in seventeenth century Britain, the use of the terms in the common weekly calendar was deemed quite acceptable. Using the same argument, some Christians today maintain that it is permissible to have Christmas trees in their churches and homes, as they have lost the original idolatrous meaning that they held in the days of Jeremiah/Middle Ages, or that it is permissible to hold Christmas services as in doing so they are not observing a Roman Catholic mass.

Answer

The practice of cutting down trees to worship them in homes had long ceased before the era of the Puritans, yet the use of trees in the home at Christmas was condemned by the Reformed church in that era! This in itself should give us a large hint that the argument is a hollow one. The fact of the matter is that our use of the names of weekdays is in a nonreligious context, whereas when the Lord's people use church Christmas trees and hold religious services, it is *precisely* in a religious context. Trees are not brought into homes or churches at any other time of year but solely in preparation for December 25 and the twelve or so days thereafter.

There are very few educated Roman Catholics who believe that Christ was born on December 25, most accepting the majority view of experts that it was possibly Spring and probably Autumn. (September 11 being favored by most and based upon numerous different strands of evidence, including data regarding John the Baptist's birth, the twenty-four priestly courses and especially the course of Abijah, Quirinius who was a senior Roman official in Syria/Judea who conducted the census (Luke 2:2) and Herod's death at a moon eclipse, etc.) Moreover, as we noted previously, Palestinian shepherds did not graze their sheep overnight in fields in December, due to the rainy season (two feet of rain can fall from December to February), lack of pasturage, and the degree of cold. The hill fields were used from March to November. If the flock was small it would be stabled in the shepherd's own peasant house (with the family sleeping on a temporary mezzanine type of raised floor; if larger, then it would be stabled in a stone sheepfold, comprising an outer walled enclosure and adjoined to part of that wall, a secure low building with roof and walls. Yet Roman Catholics insist on celebrating Christ's birth on December 25 and the reason they do so is because their church has, for over a millennium, formally decreed this day as a holy day that is obligatory to celebrate. So when the Lord's people endorse Christmas in a religious sense, they are endorsing a religious season invented and decreed by Rome!

Besides, why would the Lord's people want to associate themselves with objects, symbols, and practices, harmless in themselves yet so similar to those utilized in paganism, Roman Catholicism, Old Testament idolatry, and thus offensive to God?

There is nothing intrinsically harmful in the symbol of the gammadion cross or swastika—a square shaped mark on a contrasting background and revered symbol of Hindi and other eastern religions for millennia, indicating auspiciousness and prosperity. However, in the modern era with its Nazi associations, I suspect that most Christians would consider it an indiscretion for a Christian family to use the symbol in their home, or on their bodies. Similarly, Buddha or Krishna idols are only metal or plastic ornaments but are they appropriate for display in a Christian home, given their association with idolatry?

Another example is Ankh jewelry now widely sold as Christian jewelry—it resembles the crucifix but with a loop above the transverse bar. It is an ancient Egyptian hieroglyph, symbolizing eternal life and was depicted being carried by virtually every pagan deity the Egyptians believed in. There are many ancient pagan artifacts, copies of which can be purchased today for home decoration. In and of themselves, these items are harmless but the problem lies in their associations. Framed photographs, jewelry, anniversary dates on a calendar, and mementos are harmless in themselves but if they relate to your spouse's former boyfriend/girlfriend, would you be offended if your spouse cherished and displayed them in the family home? Unquestionably!

There is then a legitimate question over the propriety of endorsing all of the paraphernalia associated with Christmas and there exists a responsibility to investigate what the Lord's mind-set may be on such things. God has such a strong hatred of idolatry that Israel was not just commanded to avoid the worship of idols; Israel was also specifically ordered to destroy everything associated with idolatry:

> You shall surely destroy all the places where the nations whom you shall dispossess served their gods, on the high mountains and on the hills and under every green tree. You shall tear down their altars and dash in pieces their pillars and burn their Asherim with fire. You shall chop down the carved images of their gods and destroy their name out of that place. You shall not worship the LORD your God in that way.
> . . . take care that you be not ensnared to follow them, after they have been destroyed before you, and that you do not inquire about their gods, saying, "How did these nations serve their gods?"—that I also may do the same. (Deut 12:2–4, 30)

When Jacob set out to purify the camp (i.e., his household and attendants) the earrings were removed as well as their foreign gods (Gen 35:2–4) because their earrings were associated with their false gods. They were signs of superstition. When Elijah went to offer his sacrifice in his contest with the prophets of Baal on Mt. Carmel, he did not use the pagan altar, even though it was objectively just wood and stones. He did not take something made for idols (e.g., Saturnalia) and attempt to sanctify it for holy use (e.g., Christmas) but instead he rebuilt the Lord's altar (1 Kgs 18:32). Christians should not take the pagan festival of Yule or Saturnalia and dress it with Christian clothing but rather sanctify the Lord's Day, as did the apostles. When Jehu went up against the worshipers of Baal and their temple, he did not save the temple and sanctify it for holy use. Instead, he slaughtered the worshipers of Baal and then "they demolished the pillar of Baal, and demolished the house of Baal, and made it a latrine to this day" (2 Kgs 10:27).

Moreover, we have the example of Josiah (2 Kgs 23), for he not only destroyed the houses and the high places of Baal but also his vessels, his grove, and his altars, even the horses and chariots that had been given to the sun. There is also the example of penitent Manasseh, who not only overthrew the strange gods but their altars too (2 Chr 33:15). Moses, the man of God, was not content to execute vengeance on the idolatrous Israelites, without also utterly destroying the monument of their idolatry. In 1 Cor 10:6–7, we read, "Now these things took place as examples for us, that we might not desire evil as they did. Do not be idolaters as some of them were; as it is written, 'The people sat down to eat and drink and rose up to play.'" The Israelites fell into idolatry at Sinai during the absence of Moses (Exod 32:6). The people sat down to eat and drink at a feast in honor of the golden calf. They rose up to play and to dance religiously around their idol. Paul says that their behavior, and God's view of their behavior, is an example and was a pertinent warning to Corinthian brethren to shun the banquets in idol temples and their accompanying festivities. Three thousand Israelites fell on the occasion referred to (Exod 32:28).

In Corinth, there were temples dedicated to Aphrodite, Poseidon, Hermes, Venus-Fortuna, Isis, Demeter, and Asklepios, to name but a few. What would Paul's likely attitude have been to a converted Corinthian partaking of the Lord's Supper while wearing a pagan symbol—although they would no longer be idolizing or worshipping as in the past, e.g., a "shield of Zeus" necklace or a "golden-fleece" ring or one of the numerous symbols representing virility, or a hand-held ornamental trident? Or what about Stephanas, preaching while wearing something like this? Would Paul have been indifferent and would the Lord have been indifferent?

While believers today may not idolize the Christmas season or Christmas tree as the Israelites or secular Corinthians idolized various objects and artifacts of the gods/forces they symbolized, it is difficult to conceive the Lord's approval of the use of a tree in his worship. The scriptural evidence suggests that God does not want his church to take pagan days, and those pagan and popish rites and paraphernalia that go with them and adapt them to Christian use. He simply commands us to abolish them altogether. You may not be offended by the Christmas tree, the mistletoe, the holly berries, and the selection of a pagan day to celebrate Christ's birth but is God offended? God commands us to get rid of the monuments and paraphernalia of paganism. The Lord is infinitely more zealous of his honor than we are. He is a jealous God. Could Israel take festival days to Baal, Ashteroth, Dagon, and Molech, alter them, integrate them into the Lord's covenant worship and make them pleasing to him? Surely God wants his bride to eliminate forever the monuments, the days, the paraphernalia, and the mementos of idolatry.

> Thus says the LORD: "Learn not the way of the nations, nor be dismayed at the signs of the heavens because the nations are dismayed at them, for the customs of the peoples are vanity. A tree from the forest is cut down and worked with an axe by the hands of a craftsman." (Jer 10:2–3)

In Rom 14 and 1 Cor 10, Paul addressed the case of Christian conscience over the eating of meat offered to idols. Should they eat this meat or otherwise? The Lord guides Paul to point out that the meat is not pagan in itself. The meat is meat! The original use of the meat in pagan worship does not affect the intrinsic nature of the meat itself. The meat is meat so eat it as food for your bodies, says Paul. Likewise, a tree is a tree! The fact that trees were at one time used in pagan worship does not affect the intrinsic nature of a tree; therefore, there is nothing wrong in a Christian taking a tree inside their home for purposes of decoration. The problem arises around the *use* of the tree. Is it for a religious purpose? Is the celebration of Christ's birth a religious purpose?

Reason 3

The birth of the Savior is a true, historical, and biblical fact and event, therefore it cannot be wrong to remember his incarnation.

Answer

The incarnation was a stupendous event, the culmination of a plan promised to our first parents thousands of years earlier, yet also a plan with an eternal dimension, that the infinite God of all would take to himself the nature of his creature and take it forevermore: "the mystery of godliness: He was manifested in the flesh" (1 Tim 3:16). So it is indeed a true event and one most worthy of our recognition, remembrance, and celebration every day of the year, not just on a few days in December.

The baptism, temptation in the wilderness, transfiguration, resurrection, and ascension into heaven of the Lord Jesus (to name but a few important events in his earthly life) are also true, historical, and biblical events. The Lord's people who are Protestants and Reformed in their doctrine do not, however, celebrate those events with annual festivals, as they do not find any biblical warrant for doing so. It is inconsistent to adhere to one holy or feast day, commemorating one biblical event as prescribed by the Roman Catholic Church and not to adhere to all of the other holy days decreed by Rome, from January through November! Moreover, the birth of Christ without a life lived in sinless purity, without a death as the substitute in the Father's execution room and without a resurrection defeating Satan and sin's power, would have been a birth of no meaning to sinful humanity:

> Since therefore the children share in flesh and blood, he himself likewise partook of the same things, that through death he might destroy the one who has the power of death, that is, the devil. (Heb 2:14)

Herein lies the greatest wonder of all—that God would be forsaken of God and that God, in the person of the Son, would suffer cruelty at the hands of his creatures. The incarnation was but *a part* of the means to save his people. As John Owen states in his famous treatise, *The Death of Death in the Death of Christ*:

> The end of any thing is that which the agent intends to accomplish in and by the operation which is proper to its nature, and which it applies itself to.... So the end which Noah proposed to himself in the building of the ark was the preservation of himself and others.... The end is the first, principal, moving cause of the whole. It is that for whose sake the whole work is.[7]

Owen highlights how the incarnation of the Lord was part of the means to accomplish the end, which was his death and the greater end thereafter, the

---

7. Owen, *Works of John Owen*, 10:160.

recovery and redemption of his elect people from the state of alienation, misery, and wrath, into a state of grace, peace, and eternal communion with him.

Reason 4

Even if it is wrong to have Christmas celebrations in a church service, it surely cannot be wrong for Christians to observe Christmas privately in their homes.

Answer

As we stated previously, there is a distinction to be made between the private and public religious endorsement of Christmas. To come back to the point of Christian liberty, we certainly need to avoid being unbiblically judgmental. If Christians in good conscience sincerely practice certain things in their own home, as to the Lord, it is not for others to censor them for it, even although the distinction between private and public is not as great as some may imagine.

There is no biblical evidence to support the idea that the manner in which one worships God, as gleaned from the Bible, is applicable only to public worship. In fact, the biblical evidence supports the opposite view. Cain was condemned for an innovation in private worship (Gen 4:5). Noah, in family worship, offered clean animals to God (Gen 8:20–21), with which God was pleased and so accepted Noah's offering on behalf of himself and his family. Abraham, Jacob, and Job offered sacrifices to God in private or family worship, according to God's Word. God accepted these lawful offerings. The idea that innovations in worship in the context of family and private worship are of no concern to God is void of biblical warrant. If not, would it be permissible to have little shrines in our homes where we burn incense, wear religious vestments and such, as long as we keep such things out of public meetings? "For where two or three are gathered in my name, there am I among them" (Matt 18:20). At the outset of the Reformation in Scotland, John Knox issued the following charge to the heads of households:

> You are ordained of God to rule your own houses in his true fear, and according to his Word. Within your own houses, I say, in some cases, you are bishops and kings; your wife, children, servants, and family are your bishopric and charge; of you it shall be required how carefully and diligently you have always instructed them in God's true knowledge, how that you have studied in them to plant virtue and repress vice.[8]

---

8. Knox, *Works*, 4:137.

To endorse Christmas in the family worship of a Christian home is not drastically different to doing so in church. The fact is that the Christmas tree retains a religious significance. Some Christians, sensitive to the false and mythological aspects of Christmas, seek to dereligionize it by omitting from the tree nativity scenes, angels, the star, and Santas. They use the tree merely as a tinsel-lit decorative shape to brighten up the home. However, the tree's use began as a religious artifact in Germany and although the Victorian reinvention of Christmas was largely a secular movement, the tree positively retained a religious significance, evident by its widespread adoption in Protestant church services. This use has continued to the present day. It is a Roman Catholic decree that is foundational to the common understanding in the calendar month of December, that it is now the first week of Advent, then the second week of Advent, and so on, thus signaling the arrival of the appropriate time to exhibit the Christmas tree. Likewise, the expiration of the twelve days of Christmas signals the appropriate time to remove it, and Protestant churches duly oblige. This practice is then mirrored at home. Disassociating the tree from religion is a delusion. Even the unconverted who hold no firm religious convictions understand that the Christmas tree they erect each year in their homes has a religious association. Indeed, the story of baby Jesus that imbibes the feel-good factor through a general sentimental atmosphere of peace and goodwill, void of any particular and personal implications for their own relationship with God, is an aspect of the tree which they *want* to retain. If believers wish to engage in the decorous practice of brightening up the home in the depths of winter, there exists no need to use a real or artificial tree to achieve this.

Nevertheless, to reiterate, if believers want to embrace Christmas in their own home as religious acts of worship, then they must be allowed the liberty of their integrity, with no condemnation.

Reason 5

When it is pointed out that the Lord has given us no biblical warrant for observing the birth of Christ with an annual festival, some of the Lord's people cite the Old Testament example of the Feast of Purim. Esther was elevated to Queen of Persia (Esth 1:1—2:17) in the days of Ahasuerus (Xerxes I) in Susa, one of the three rotating royal capitals of the Persians covering the southern regions of the empire (Susa being the winter one).

The background to the feast was the age-old enmity between the Amalekites and Israel and behind that, the perpetual attempt by Satan to thwart the fulfillment of the promise of a Redeemer from the seed of the woman, given in the hour of the Fall.

Pictured is Susa or Shushan (modern day Shush in Iran), 1935, showing the outline of the ancient city prior to modern over-building. It is correctly pointed out that Purim was an annual festival instigated by Esther and Mordecai, firstly in Susa and then under Ezra and Nehemiah in reestablished Jerusalem, which had no express authority or direction from God. It remained a part of Jewish life and calendar during the four hundred silent years that followed the return from captivity and was undoubtedly recognized by the Lord Jesus and his apostles.

Answer

There exists a vast difference between Purim and Christmas. Purim was based on a historically accurate recollection of an event, not subject to mystical embellishments and innuendo as was true of the birth date of the Savior and the evolution of Christmas. It correctly reflected true biblical doctrine—God's sovereignty and providence—not altering biblical doctrine as an incentive to pagans to join the church, or with the invention of the Mass, which attacks the biblical doctrines of justification by faith and the atonement. Unlike Christmas services, constituted in Christ's name, Purim was not a special religious holy day but rather was a time of collective social thanksgiving.

The events of Purim are gladness and joy among the Jews, a feast, and a holiday.

> That they should make them days of feasting and gladness, days for sending gifts of food to one another and gifts to the poor. (Esth 9:22; see also 8:16–17)

It was a day of joy, marked by loud raucous celebration, feasting, drinking, and costume wearing. To this day it is known as the Jewish Mardi-Gras or Jewish Halloween. There is no mention of any religious observance connected with the day, such as special worship services, ceremonies, or Levitical/priestly activities. It had more of a communal rather than a religious character (very similar to Hanukkah or the Feast of Lights, invented to mark the victory of the Maccabean revolt and the rededication of the Temple in 165 BC). Unlike the ordained feasts found in the Pentateuch, it was permissible and commonplace for the Jews during Purim to labor and conduct business transactions. Neither did it have the status of a national feast day, and therefore did not require attendance at Jerusalem. That is not to say that it was exclusively secular with no religious element at all. Undoubtedly, the day of celebration and thanksgiving was inextricable from the memorial of God's grace and goodness in delivering the Jews. To the mind and heart of the godly Jew, the day was full of worship, but not in any formal, ceremonial way. Indeed, this is surely also true of Purim's original institution by Mordecai and Esther. Although the Lord is not explicitly mentioned in the Book of Esther, he is unmistakably and constantly revealing himself in his providence. Similarly, although he gave no explicit command to institute the feast of Purim, it is extremely likely that the Holy Spirit laid it upon the hearts of Mordecai and Esther to mark his deliverance and that when they did so, it met with his approval. This again sets Purim apart from the likes of Christmas, as the latter is completely of human invention and by human authority.

Interestingly, the *Westminster Confession of Faith* cites Esther as a proof text in its section on festivals. In chapter 21 entitled "Of Religious Worship and the Sabbath Day," we read:

> In addition to ordinary religious worship of God on the Lord's Day, there are also solemn fastings and thanksgivings upon special occasions, which are, in their several times and seasons, to be used in a holy and religious manner.

One of the proof texts for this statement is Esth 9:22:

> As the days on which the Jews got relief from their enemies, and as the month that had been turned for them from sorrow into gladness and from mourning into a holiday; that they should

make them days of feasting and gladness, days for sending gifts of food to one another and gifts to the poor.

The part of chapter 21 copied above is the second part of the chapter and is clearly distinct from ordinary weekly worship, referred to in the first part. This highlights the fact that in citing Esther here, it is not worship services that the divines had in mind, as the feast of Purim was not a worship service. Besides, even if Purim had been appointed by the Lord, to seek a warrant for days of religious commemoration under the New Covenant Gospel era of the church, from the Jewish festivals, is not only to overlook the distinction between the old and new dispensations, it also forgets that the Jews were never allowed to institute such religious memorials for themselves. Rather, they were only to keep those which infinite Wisdom had expressly and by name set apart and sanctified. Christmas, or the Feast of the Nativity, lack any such scriptural warrant.

We close our answer with a quote from Thomas McCrie (1772–1835), the Scottish Presbyterian divine from Edinburgh. In his commentary on Esther he states:

> From what has been said, we may infer that this passage of Scripture gives no countenance to religious festivals, or holidays of human appointment, especially under the New Testament. Feasts appear to have been connected with sacrifices from the most ancient times; but the observance of them was not brought under any fixed rules until the establishment of the Mosaic law. Religious festivals formed a noted and splendid part of the ritual of that law; but they were only designed to be temporary; and having served their end in commemorating certain great events connected with the Jewish commonwealth, and in typifying certain mysteries now clearly revealed by the gospel, they ceased, and, along with other figures, vanished away. To retain these, or to return to them after the promulgation of the Christian law, or to imitate them by instituting festivals of a similar kind, is to dote on shadows—to choose weak and beggarly elements—to bring ourselves under a yoke of bondage which the Jews were unable to bear, and interpretatively to fall from grace and the truth of the gospel.
>
> "Ye observe days and months, and times and years. I am afraid of you, lest I have bestowed upon you labour in vain." "Let no man therefore judge you in meat, or in drink, or in respect of a holiday, or of the new moon, or of the Sabbath days, which are a shadow of things to come." Shall we suppose that Christ and his apostles, in abrogating those days which God himself

had appointed to be observed, without instituting others in their room, intended that either churches or individuals should be allowed to substitute whatever they pleased in their room? Yet the Christian church soon degenerated so far as to bring herself under a severer bondage than that from which Christ had redeemed her, and instituted a greater number of festivals than were observed under the Mosaic law, or even among pagans.

There are times when God calls, on the one hand, to religious fasting, or, on the other, to thanksgiving and religious joy; and it is our duty to comply with these calls, and to set apart time for the respective exercises. But this is quite a different thing from recurrent or anniversary holidays. In the former case the day is chosen for the duty, in the latter the duty is performed for the day; in the former case there is no holiness on the day but what arises from the service which is performed on it, and when the same day afterwards recurs, it is as common as any other day; in the latter case the day is set apart on all following times, and may not be employed for common or secular purposes.

Stated and recurring festivals countenance the false principle, that some days have a peculiar sanctity, either inherent or impressed by the works which occurred on them; they proceed on an undue assumption of human authority; interfere with the free use of that time which the Creator hath granted to man; detract from the honor due to the day of sacred rest which He hath appointed; lead to impositions over conscience; have been the fruitful source of superstition and idolatry; and have been productive of the worst effects upon morals, in every age, and among every people, barbarous and civilised, pagan and Christian, popish and protestant, among whom they have been observed.[9]

Reason 6

Some maintain that the use of Christmas trees in the home or church service is fine because the tree, as an evergreen, is a *symbol* of life and appropriate for the celebration of the commencement of Jesus' life, also of the eternal life that would be brought to us through his life. In similar fashion others regard the tree as a very useful *reminder* of God coming into the world in the person of his Son and also the method of his vicarious death on a cross of wood, or as they highlight, on a "tree" (as it is termed in Acts 5:30; 10:39;

---

9. McCrie, *Lectures on the Book of Esther*, 279–86.

13:29; 1 Pet 2:24). Citing the example of the twelve stones erected by Joshua as a memorial on the banks of the Jordan River, one writer states:

> Sadly, Israel eventually forgot, and they embraced worldly ideas. This is one of the main reasons that Christians should celebrate Christmas: that we will never forget what God has done for us. Our focus should be on why we celebrate Christ's birth and how the symbols remind us of the truth.[10]

Answer

If a Christmas tree (assuming its appearance as a tree has not been totally obscured by the addition of Santas, angels, baubles, lights, and tinsel), whether it is real or plastic, is indeed a useful and necessary reminder of Christ and his work, to the believer and the unbeliever, then why is it not used 365 days a year? Why only use it once a year?

Christ rose from the dead on only one specific day, yet his resurrection is not symbolically remembered during only a few weeks every year, but every week throughout the year, as his people gather together on the first day of the week.

Christ died on only one specific day, yet his death is not symbolically remembered during only a few weeks every year, but every week throughout the year somewhere in the visible church in the breaking of bread. Christ was born on only one specific day, yet his birth is symbolically remembered only for three weeks once a year! If a tree is a necessary reminder of a great biblical truth, why is it not used every week, as are the symbols of bread and wine as a reminder of Christ's death and Lord's Day gatherings as a reminder of his resurrection?

Besides, where do we find from the example of the Lord Jesus or his apostles that they routinely used materials, natural or man-made, to symbolically emphasize their preaching, teaching, or worship? With the exceptions of baptism and the Lord's Supper, we do not. As Jesus is the Light of the World, should we hold candles during our times of worship or should pulpits be encircled with lit candles when Christ is preached? When we evangelize on the streets and preach Christ and him crucified, should we all carry crosses and crucifixes? If seeking to highlight the eternal life found in the union a sinner can have in Christ, ought we to adopt the Ankh symbol, referred to above in a previous Reason/Answer?

---

10. Chaffey and Ham, "4 Misconceptions."

Is it biblical and appropriate to use icons and images in the worship of God on certain occasions? If we believe that it is, then let us be consistent and renounce Reformed dogma and embrace Lutheranism, Roman Catholicism, or Orthodoxy.

As an aside, recent decades have not only seen more Protestant churches endorsing Christmas but also using children's literature depicting drawings of Christ, on the basis that such is a useful reminder of him and means of instruction. They are usually modeled on the idealistic representations of antiquity that coincided with the loss of sound doctrine. Numerous characters in the Bible are physically described for us, e.g., Job's daughters, Sarah, Rachel, Rebekah, Joseph, Samson, Eglon, Saul, David, Eliab, Goliath, Absalom, Solomon's 'Shulammite,' Vashti, Esther, Elisha or Zacchaeus. Why do Matthew, John, Peter, and Jesus' half-brothers, James and Jude, not deem it necessary to relate the details of his physical appearance to us? Surely the answer is that in his attributes, profusely described metaphorically in his Word by his Spirit, he is portrayed to the eye of faith in such a glorious manner and to such an inestimable extent, that any physical image can only be a detraction. See Rev 1:13–16 for a good physical description!

Both Calvin and the Second Helvetic Confession condemned the making or displaying of such pictures.[11] The problem is not idolatry and breaching the second commandment, although that is commonly cited in this regard. The problem is that he is God and that cannot be conveyed by a drawing, as the person of other Bible characters can be. The holy Scriptures are the sole means of instruction given us by the Holy Spirit and require no supplement:

---

11. Schaff, *Creeds*, 1:358, ch. 4, "Second Helvetic Confession"; Calvin, *Institutes*, book 1, ch. 11, sec. 2–15.

And how from childhood you have been acquainted with the sacred writings, which are able to make you wise for salvation through faith in Christ Jesus. (2 Tim 3:15)

When we endorse pictures of Christ we are in danger of dishonoring the Holy Spirit, for it is his glory to show us the Savior.

Reason 7

A different argument seeks to distance the original idea for Christmas from paganism. The argument is that there was no pagan festival kept on December 25 and the choice of that date by the church was completely independent of influence from paganism. Christmas, it is argued, is not pagan in its institution, and is therefore quite permissible for the Christian.

Answer

Strictly speaking, the religious festival of Saturnalia was from December 17 to 23, then the festival of the Sol Invictus or Invincible Sun was on the 25th. From what we have noted above in the chapter "Down the Centuries," it is indeed the case that the suggestion of December 25 as being Christ's likely birthday (c. 221) did precede the inauguration of the Sol Invictus (c. 273). Moreover, it is quite possible that the date for the latter was deliberately selected in order to compete with Christ's chosen birthday and reinvigorate worship of the pagan deity.

However, as we also noted, worship of the sun had been slowly spreading westward from the Indian subcontinent for a millennia and was prevalent in the Roman Empire since Pompey's era (c. 70 BC) and was practiced in the city of Rome during the Apostolic era. In the third week of December, around the winter solstice, much prominence was given to sun worship and the sun's supposed rebirth after the solstice. The early church fathers were clearly perturbed by the growth in Mithraism around the Roman Empire. It was well established in the areas of the New Testament church, *before* anyone suggested December 25 as the Savior's birthday! The Kalends or celebration of the New Year commenced on January 1; however, in the practice of many there was no hiatus in the festivities—it was very much a three-week festive season commencing in the third week of December. As we have also already noted, many of the traditions of Kalends migrated into those of Saturnalia and as the centuries passed, into Christmas as well. The late historian Clement Miles (referred to earlier and an acclaimed expert on the origins of Christmas) states:

> The real reason for the choice of the day [December 25] most probably was, that upon it fell the pagan festival just mentioned. . . . What more natural than that the church should choose this day to celebrate the rising of her Sun of Righteousness with healing in his wings, that she should strive thus to draw away to his worship some adorers of the god whose symbol and representative was the earthly sun! There is no direct evidence of deliberate substitution, but at all events ecclesiastical writers soon after the foundation of Christmas made good use of the idea that the birthday of the Savior had replaced the birthday of the sun.[12]

From the inception of Christmas to the present day, in Protestant as well as Roman Catholic countries and regions, there exists an enormous amount of myth and superstition surrounding Christmas. This is especially true respecting Christmas Eve, all associated with the supernatural—from animals talking, to the appearance of the dead, or appearances of Christ or the Virgin Mary or the apostles, plus elements introducing the sun, moon, or stars, the vast majority of which are obviously pagan in origin. Even if it could be conclusively proven that December 25 was a date originally selected by the church, or even by born-again Christians within the church and without any thought or reference whatsoever to pagan festivals, what biblical warrant was there for selecting any birthday? There was none, a fact clearly not lost on Origen, hence his denouncement (which we noted previously) of the idea in 245 AD! We recognize the value of the early church believers whose writings are extant, living as they did so much closer than us to the Savior and the apostles. We learn from them that as early as 221 AD, they were discussing the idea of recognizing an annual birthday commemoration for the Lord; however, that idea in itself does not render it a good thing to do. There were plenty of errors perpetrated in the second and third century church!

Excursus on Mithraism's Similarity to Christianity

Similarities between ancient religions and the New Testament account of the Savior are not surprising. Quite apart from the activity of Satan and demons to confuse and subvert the promise of salvation as given in the Garden of Eden, from a human perspective, the knowledge of a Savior to

---

12. Miles, *Christmas*, 23.

come was known in the post-Flood era. Moreover, about a century after the Flood, that knowledge was dispersed with the sons and grandsons of Noah all over the earth. Central to that knowledge were the notions of a blood sacrifice to atone for sins and a future promised messiah. By 2000 to 1900 BC, another three centuries after the Flood, that knowledge was so diluted that it required fresh revelation from God, creating a repository of truth through Abraham/Israel.

Given the further and more detailed written revelation about the Savior given in the Old Testament from 1500 BC (commencing with Moses) to 400 BC, it is little wonder that pagan religions and myths would borrow some of that knowledge, ancient and more recent, oral and written, to formulate their own religious beliefs. The Old Testament reveals many truths about Christ subsequently found in the New Testament: incarnation of God, eternal sonship, virgin birth, God among his people, only begotten Son, substitutionary atonement, crucifixion, atonement by blood, resurrection of the Christ, ascension to the right hand of God, and return of Christ, to name but a few.

Other New Testament motifs, such as the Good Shepherd, were common and popular beliefs from earlier centuries and formed a part of Greek mythology, respecting benevolence. Moreover, with the explosion of Christianity in the second half of the first century, it is very likely that false cults adopted some of the teachings of what they realized to be a very successful religion! There is, therefore, no cause for alarm to discover that various motifs and features of authentic salvation, as revealed in the New Testament, were prevalent in some earlier pagan religions. As we noted in an earlier chapter, claims that Christianity copied Mithraism are false and lack any credible or substantive evidence.

Reason 8

It is acknowledged that Christmas had been banned by our Protestant forefathers, both in Britain and North America, but it is argued that this ban was not because the religious endorsement of Christmas was viewed by them as being wrong in principle, rather because it had lost its religious meaning and become so secular and ungodly that it verged on being blasphemous.

Answer

This view is demonstrably incorrect. While those who banned Christmas certainly were not slow to condemn the social sinfulness that characterized the whole "festive" period, they banned it first and foremost on religious/biblical grounds. Seeking to reform the visible church and to bring it as close as possible to the idealistic model of the first century church revealed in Scripture, they found no warrant to retain Christmas in the life of the church. We have noted earlier the fact that it was banned in Scotland, England, and New England, so we will look more closely at the bans in this order.

Scotland

In Scotland, John Knox (1514–1572) was born and bred Roman Catholic (as all then were) and went on to become a deacon and then a priest, before being converted under the ministry of George Wishart. Knox, therefore, was very acquainted with Christmas.

From the outset of the Scottish Reformation, the discussion focused upon the nature of true worship. John Knox repeatedly confronted his papal adversaries by contending that true worship must be instituted by God. True worship is not derived from the innovations of men. Knox condemned the false worship of Roman Catholicism. In a public debate against the Papists, Knox declared:

> That God's word damns your ceremonies, it is evident; for the plain and straight commandment of God is, "Not that thing which appears good in thy eyes, shalt thou do to the Lord thy God, but what the Lord thy God has commanded thee, that do thou: add nothing to it; diminish nothing from it." Now unless that ye are able to prove that God has commanded your ceremonies, this his former commandment will damn both you and them.[13]

In 1560, Knox and several others drew up the *First Book of Discipline*. After an opening explanation of the nature of the Gospel, it states:

> By contrary Doctrine, we understand whatsoever men, by Laws, Councils, or Constitutions have imposed upon the consciences of men, without the expressed commandment of God's word: such as be vows of chastity, foreswearing of marriage, binding of men and women to several and disguised apparels, to the superstitious observation of fasting days, difference of meat for conscience sake, prayer for the dead; and keeping of holy days of certain Saints commanded by men, such as be all those that the Papists have invented, as the Feasts (as they term them) of Apostles, Martyrs, Virgins, of Christmas, Circumcision, Epiphany, Purification, and other fond feasts of our Lady. Which things,

---

13. Knox, *Works*, 1:69.

because in God's Scriptures they neither have commandment nor assurance, we judge them utterly to be abolished from this Realm; affirming further, that the obstinate maintainers and teachers of such abominations ought not to escape the punishment of the Civil Magistrate.[14]

England

In England in the early seventeenth century the Puritans saw Christmas as an unwelcome survival of the Roman Catholic faith, as a ceremony particularly encouraged by the Roman Catholic Church and also by the Roman Catholic community in England and Wales who refused to attend the Church of England as required by law. The Puritans saw it as basically a popish festival with no biblical justification. What the Puritans wanted was a much stricter observance of the Lord's Day, plus the abolition of the popish celebration of Christmas, as well as of Easter, Whitsun, and assorted other festivals, and saints' days.

In 1643, Parliament (the Long Parliament) called and appointed an assembly of divines to discuss the reform of the Church of England. The assembly met in Westminster Abbey and was comprised of one hundred and twenty ministers, twenty members of the House of Commons, and ten members of the House of Lords (plus five ministers and three elders from the Church of Scotland, although they had no voting rights). This Westminster Assembly reported back to parliament at various times until its main work was completed in 1648. In early 1645 the English Parliament approved by ordinance a document of the assembly's work entitled, *A Directory for Public Worship of God throughout the Three Kingdoms of England, Scotland, and Ireland. Together with an Ordinance of Parliament for the Taking Away of the Book of Common Prayer, and the Establishing and Observing of this Present Directory throughout the Kingdom of England and the Dominion of Wales*. This Directory rejected the propriety of Christmas in the life of the church. The motives for instigating the Directory can be seen in the preface:

> In the beginning of the blessed Reformation, our wise and pious ancestors took care to set forth an order for redress of many things, which they then, by the word, discovered to be vain, erroneous, superstitious, and idolatrous, in the publick worship of God. This occasioned many godly and learned men to rejoice much in the Book of Common Prayer, at that time set forth;

---

14. Ibid., 2:185–86; see also 2:534.

> because the mass, and the rest of the Latin service being removed, the publick worship was celebrated in our own tongue: many of the common people also receive benefit by hearing the Scriptures read in their own language, which formerly were unto them as a book that is sealed.
>
> Howbeit, long and sad experience hath made it manifest, that the Liturgy used in the Church of England, (notwithstanding all the pains and religious intentions of the Compilers of it), hath proved an offence, not only to many of the godly at home, but also to the reformed churches abroad. For, not to speak of urging the reading of all the prayers, which very greatly increased the burden of it, the many unprofitable and burdensome ceremonies contained in it have occasioned much mischief, as well by disquieting the consciences of many godly ministers and people, who could not yield unto them, as by depriving them of the ordinances of God, which they might not enjoy without conforming or subscribing to those ceremonies.... We have, after earnest and frequent calling upon the name of God, and after much consultation, not with flesh and blood, but with his holy word, resolved to lay aside the former Liturgy, with the many rites and ceremonies formerly used in the worship of God; and have agreed upon this following Directory for all the parts of publick worship, at ordinary and extraordinary times. Wherein our care hath been to hold forth such things as are of divine institution in every ordinance; and other things we have endeavoured to set forth according to the rules of Christian prudence, agreeable to the general rules of the word of God.

Under a Section entitled "Touching Days and Places for Publick Worship," the following is stated:

> THERE is no day commanded in Scripture to be kept holy under the gospel but the Lord's day, which is the Christian Sabbath. Festival days, vulgarly called Holy-days, having no warrant in the word of God, are not to be continued. Nevertheless, it is lawful and necessary, upon special emergent occasions, to separate a day or days for publick fasting or thanksgiving, as the several eminent and extraordinary dispensations of God's providence shall administer cause and opportunity to his people. As no place is capable of any holiness, under pretence of whatsoever dedication or consecration; so neither is it subject to such pollution by any superstition formerly used, and now laid aside, as may render it unlawful or inconvenient for Christians to meet together therein for the publick worship of God. And therefore we hold it requisite,

that the places of publick assembling for worship among us should be continued and employed to that use.

In June 1647, Parliament reiterated this by passing an Ordinance confirming the abolition of the feasts of Christmas, Easter, and Whitsun. During the 1650s, parliamentary legislation was passed to reinforce the structure that had been put in place by the end of the 1640s. Specific penalties were to be imposed on anyone found holding or attending a special Christmas church service. It was ordered that shops and markets were to stay open on December 25, the Lord Mayor being repeatedly ordered to ensure that London stayed open for business on December 25. When it met on December 25, 1656, the second Protectorate Parliament discussed the virtues of passing further legislation clamping down on the celebration of Christmas (though no bill was, in fact, produced).

New England

As intimated earlier in the chapter on Christmas development in modern Britain, we will now give similar, lengthy attention to its development in North America.

In New England, most Baptists, Quakers, and Congregational and Presbyterian Puritans regarded the day as an abomination, while Anglicans, Lutherans, the Dutch Reformed, and other denominations celebrated the day as did Roman Catholics. When the Church of England promoted the Feast of the Nativity as a major religious holiday, the Puritans attacked it as residual Papist idolatry. The Plymouth Pilgrims put their loathing for the day into practice in 1620 when they spent their first December 25 in the New World, physically constructing their first building there.

The Old State House, Boston, (previous page) was built in 1712, as the government offices of the Massachusetts Bay Colony. Massachusetts and Connecticut followed the Plymouth colony in refusing to condone any observance of the day. Following the 1647 ban on Christmas in England, New England followed suit passing a series of laws making any observance of Christmas illegal. A law passed by the General Court of Massachusetts Bay Colony in 1659, punished anyone "found observing, by abstinence from labor, feasting, or any other way, any such days as Christmas day, shall pay for every such with offense five shillings" (the equivalent today of £500 in wages).[15]

Laws suppressing the celebration of Christmas were repealed in 1681, following pressure from the British Government, but Puritans continued to regard the day as an abomination. With such an onus placed upon Christmas, non-Puritans in colonial New England made no attempt to celebrate the day and many spent the day quietly at home.

We noted earlier in the chapter entitled "Down the Centuries" how in 1687, in Boston, Massachusetts, Increase Mather opposed Christmas.

He wrote that December 25 was observed as the birth date of Christ, not because

> Christ was born in that Month, but because the Heathens Saturnalia was at the time kept in Rome, and they were willing to have those Pagan Holidays metamorphosed into Christian

---

15. Dow, *Every Day Life*, 111.

[ones]. . . . It is not a work but a word makes one day more holy than another. There is no day of the week, but some eminent work of God has been done therein; but it does not therefore follow that every day must be kept as a Sabbath. The Lord Christ has appointed the first day of the week to be perpetually observed in remembrance of his resurrection and redemption. If more days than that had been needful, He would have appointed more. It is a deep reflection on the wisdom of Christ, to say, He has not appointed days enough forh his own honor, but He must be beholding to men for their additions. The Apostle condemns the observation of Jewish festivals in these days of the New Testament, Gal 4:10; Col 2:16. Much less may Christians state other days in their room. . . . All stated holidays of man's inventing, are breaches of the Second and of the Fourth Commandment. A stated religious festival is a part of instituted worship. Therefore, it is not in the power of men, but God only, to make a day holy.[16]

Jonathan Edwards (1703-1758) widely acknowledged to be America's most important and original philosophical theologian and one of America's greatest intellectuals, was a Congregationalist in Massachusetts. In God's providence, he played a critical role in the Great Awakening. Edwards did not observe Christmas in his church.[17]

Samuel Davies, (1723-1761), Presbyterian minister in Hanover County, Virginia (subsequently becoming president of the College of New Jersey, later called Princeton), and with Edwards, one of the leaders of the First Great Awakening, stated in a sermon on December 25, 1758:

> To remember and religiously improve the incarnation of our divine Redeemer, to join the concert of angels, and dwell in ecstatic meditation upon their song; this is lawful, this is a seasonable duty every day; and consequently upon this day.
>
> And as Jesus improved the feast of dedication, though not of divine institution, as a proper opportunity to exercise his ministry, when crowds of the Jews were gathered from all parts; so I would improve this day for your instruction, since it is the custom of our country to spend it religiously, or idly, or wickedly, as different persons are differently disposed. But as the seed of superstition which have some times grown up to a prodigious height, have been frequently sown and cherished by very inconsiderable incidents, I think it proper to inform you, that I may guard against this danger, that I do not set apart this

---

16. Mather, *Testimony against Several Profane*, 35.
17. Edwards, *Sermons and Discourses*, 264, n. 8.

day for public worship, as though it had any peculiar sanctity, or we were under any obligations to keep it religiously. I know no human authority, that has power to make one day more holy than another, or that can bind the conscience in such cases. And as for divine authority, to which alone the sanctifying of days and things belongs, it has thought it sufficient to consecrate one day in seven to a religious use, for the commemoration both of the birth of this world, and the resurrection of its great Author, or of the works of creation and redemption. This I would religiously observe; and inculcate the religious observance of it upon all. But as to other days, consecrated by the mistaken piety or superstition of men, and conveyed down to us as holy, through the corrupt medium of human tradition, I think myself free to observe them or not, according to convenience, and the prospect of usefulness; like other common days, on which I may lawfully carry on public worship or not, as circumstances require. . . .

The commandments of God have often been made void by the traditions of men; and human inventions more religiously observed than divine institutions; and when this was the case, St. Paul was warm in opposing even ceremonial mistakes.

Having premised this, which I look upon as much more important than the decision of the question, I proceed to show you the reasons why I would not religiously observe days of human appointment, in commemoration of Christ and the saints. What I have to say shall be particularly pointed at what is called Christmas Day: but may be easily applied to all other holy-days instituted by men:

1) The first reason I shall offer is, that I would take my religion just as I find it in my Bible, without any imaginary improvements or supplements of human invention.

All the ordinances which God has been pleased to appoint, and particularly that one day in seven, which he has set apart for his more immediate service, and the commemoration of the works of creation and redemption, I would honestly endeavour to observe in the most sacred manner. But when ignorant presuming mortals take upon them to refine upon Divine institutions, to make that a part of religion, which God has left indifferent, and consecrate more days than he has thought necessary; in short, when they would mingle something of their own with the pure religion of the Bible: then I must be excused from obedience, and beg leave to content myself with the old, plain, simple religion of the Bible. Now that there is not the least appearance in all the Bible of the Divine appointment of Christmas, to celebrate the birth of Christ, is granted by all parties; and the Divine authority is not so much as pretended for it. Therefore, a Bible-Christian is not at all bound to observe it.

2) Secondly, the Christian church, for at least three hundred years, did not observe any day in commemoration of the birth of Christ. For this we have the testimony of the primitive fathers themselves. Thus Clemens Alexandrinus, who lived about the year one hundred and ninety-four, "We are commanded to worship and honor him, who, we are persuaded, is the Word, and our Savior and Ruler, and through him, the Father; not upon certain particular or select days, as some others do, but constantly practicing this all our life, and in every proper way." Chrysostom, who lived in the fourth century, has these words, "It is not yet ten years, since this day, that is, Christmas, was plainly known to us;" and he observes, the custom was brought to Constantinople from Rome. Now since this day was not religiously observed in the church in the first and purest ages, but was introduced as superstitions increased, and Christianity began to degenerate very fast into popery; ought not we to imitate the purity of these primitive times, and retain none of the superstitious observances of more corrupt ages?

3) Thirdly, if a day should be religiously observed in memory of the birth of Christ, it ought to be that day on which He was born. But that day, and even the month and the year, are

altogether uncertain. The Scriptures do not determine this point of chronology. And perhaps they are silent on purpose, to prevent all temptation to the superstitious observance of it; just as the body of Moses was secretly buried, and his grave concealed, to guard the Israelites from the danger of idolizing it. Chronologers are also divided upon the point: and even the ancients are not agreed. The learned generally suppose that Christ was born two or three years before the vulgar reckoning. And as to the month, some suppose it was in September, and some in June.

And they imagine it was very unlikely, that he was born in the cold wintry months of December, because we read, that at the time of his birth, shepherds were out in the field, watching their flocks by night; which is not probable at that season of the year. The Christian epocha, or reckoning time from the birth of Christ, was not introduced till about the year five hundred; and it was not generally used till the reign of Charles the Great, about the year eight hundred, or a little above nine hundred years ago.

And this must occasion a great uncertainty, both as to the year, month, and day. But why do I dwell so long upon this? It must be universally confessed, that the day of his birth is quite uncertain: nay, it is certain that it is not that which has been kept in commemoration of it. To convince you of this, I need only put you in mind of the late parliamentary correction of our computation of time by introducing the new-style; by which Christmas is eleven days' sooner than it was wont to be. And yet this chronological blunder still continues in the public prayers of some, who give thanks to God, that Christ was born as upon this day.

And while this prayer was offered up in England and Virginia on the twenty-fifth of December old-style, other countries that followed the new-style, were solemnly declaring in their thanksgivings to God, that Christ was born eleven days' sooner; that is, on the fourteenth of December. I therefore conclude, that neither this day nor any other was ever intended to be observed for this purpose.

4) Finally, superstition is a very growing evil; and therefore the first beginnings of it ought to be prevented. Many things that were at first introduced with a pious design have grown up gradually into the most enormous superstition and idolatry in after ages. The ancient Christians, for example, had such a veneration for the pious martyrs, that they preserved a lock of hair, or some little memorial of them; and this laid the foundation for the expensive sale and stupid idolizing of the relics of the saints in popish countries.

They also celebrated their memory, by observing the days of their martyrdom. But as the number of the martyrs and saints real or imaginary, increased, the saints' days also multiplied to an extravagant degree, and hardly left any days in the year for any other purpose. And as they had more saints than days in the year, they dedicated the first of November for them all, under the title of All-saints-day. But if the saints must be thus honored, then certainly much more ought Jesus Christ. This seemed a natural inference: and accordingly, these superstitious devotees appointed one day to celebrate his birth, another his baptism, another his death, another the day of Pentecost, and an endless list that I have not time now to mention. The Apostles also must be put into the Calendar: and thus almost all the days in the year were consecrated by superstition, and hardly any left for the ordinary labours of life. Thus the people are taught to be idle the greatest part of their time, and so indisposed to labour on the few days that are still allowed them for that purpose.

This has almost ruined some popish countries, particularly the Pope's dominions in the fine country of Italy, once the richest and best improved in the world. Mr. Addison, Bishop Burnet, and other travellers, inform us, that everything bears the appearance of poverty, notwithstanding all the advantages of soil and climate: and that this is chiefly owing to the superstition of the people, who spend the most of their time as holy-days. And if you look over the Calendar of the Church of England, you will find that the festivals in one year, amount to thirty-one. The fasts to no less than ninety-five, to which add the fifty-two Sundays in every year, and the whole will make one hundred and seventy-eight: so that only one hundred and eighty-seven days will be left in the whole year, for the common purposes of life. And whether the poor could procure a subsistence for themselves and their families by the labour of so few days, and whether it be not a yoke that neither we nor our fathers are able to bear, I leave you to judge. It is true, that but very few of these feasts and fasts are now observed, even by the members of the established church. But then they are still in their Calendar and Canons, and binding upon them by the authority of the church; and as far as they do not comply with them, so far they are dissenters: and in this, and in many other respects, they are generally dissenters, though they do not share with us in the infamy of the name. Now, since the beginnings of superstitious inventions in the worship of God are so dangerous in their issue, and may grow up into such enormous extravagance, we ought to shun the danger, by adhering to the simplicity of the Bible-religion, and not presume to make more days or things holy, than the all-wise God has been pleased to sanctify. He will be satisfied with the religious observance of his own institutions; and why should not we? It is certainly enough, that we be as religious as He requires us. And all our will-worship is liable to that confounding rejection, "Who hath required this at your hands?" (Isaiah 1:12)[18]

With the exception of three years, the United States Congress sat every year on Christmas Day from 1789 to 1855. Dr. Samuel Miller, professor of ecclesiastical history and church government at Princeton Seminary, wrote confidently in 1835: "Presbyterians do not observe Holy days."[19] By the 1840s many states began to make Christmas a legal holiday, Alabama being the first in 1836. Massachusetts followed in 1856. The success of this measure was largely due to the growing number of Irish Catholics in the electorate. In the aftermath of the American Civil War (1861–65) Christmas became the festival high point of the American calendar. The day became a federal holiday in 1870 under President Ulysses S. Grant in an attempt to unite north and south. In the early nineteenth century, fear that excessive drinking, aggressive begging, and riotous processions associated with Christmas posed a threat to public order, moved middle-class and upper-class Americans to remake Christmas as a family holiday. As we noted this above in the chapter "The Origins of Victorian Christmas Customs," in a British context, so in like manner, the social and business elite in North America collaborated with the press to reshape Christmas into a well-regulated domestic celebration. The chief beneficiaries of this kind of Christmas were children. In 1885 the United States declared Christmas Day a federal holiday.

However, opposition to ecclesiastical holidays remained in American Presbyterianism. This is a significant fact given the make-up of North America.

America after the Revolution was a very different place than Europe and even from the mother country she had painfully broken away from. Unlike most European countries, which had one established state church, America was simply awash in different forms of Christianity. Immigrants seeking freedom from the religious persecution of Europe had flooded into the New World and by the 1800s America was a nation unlike any other. A large town might have Lutheran, Roman Catholic, and Presbyterian churches and while these churches were initially strongly associated with the immigrant populations they served (German Lutherans, French Catholics, Scottish Presbyterians), the strong American desire for novelty

---

18. Davies, "Christmas-Day Sermon," 362–86.
19. Miller, *Presbyterianis*, 74.

and experimentation gradually began to overcome the initial distaste for worshiping outside of one's own tradition.

Opposition also remained among Congregationalists. One of their prominent preachers, Henry Ward Beecher, stated in 1865, "To me Christmas is a foreign day."[20]

Speaking of the South after the Civil War, one historian opined that there existed no recognition of either Christmas or Easter in any of the Protestant churches, except the Episcopal and Lutheran. For a full generation after the Civil War the religious journals of the South mentioned Christmas, only to observe that there was no reason to believe that Jesus was actually born on December 25; it was not recognized as a day of any religious significance in the Presbyterian Church.

In 1870, one journal comments:

> If the exact date were known, or if some day (as December 25) had been agreed upon by common consent in the absence of any certain knowledge, we would still object to the observance of Christmas as a holy day. We object for many reasons, but at present mention only this one: that experience has shown that the institution of holy days by human authority, however pure the intention, has invariably led to the disregard of the Holy Day, the Sabbath instituted by God.

In the following decade [the 1880s] this same journal sorrowed to see

> a growing tendency [to introduce church festivals into Protestant denominations], even in our own branch of the church. True, it is by no means general, and has not been carried very far, but it is enough to awaken our concern and to call for that least a word of warning that the observance of Easter and Christmas is increasing amongst us.[21]

In 1899, the General Assembly of the PCUS (Presbyterian Church of the United States) was overtured to give a "pronounced and explicit deliverance" against the recognition of "Christmas and Easter as religious days." It was on the eve of the twentieth century but the response was unequivocal:

> There is no warrant in Scripture for the observance of Christmas and Easter as holydays, rather the contrary (see Gal. 4:9–11; Col. 2:16–21), and such observance is contrary to the principles of

---

20. *Supreme Court Reporter*, 104:1385.
21. *Southern Presbyterian Review*, vol. 21.

> the Reformed faith, conducive to will-worship, and not in harmony with the simplicity of the Gospel of Jesus Christ.[22]

This response would be reiterated in similar fashion in future General Assemblies of 1903, 1913, and 1916. A similar pattern occurred in Independent Baptist churches. Samuel Jones, a Baptist student at Isaac Eaton's Hopewell Academy, New Jersey (the first Baptist educational institution in America), wrote the following diary entry on December 25, 1757:

> Christmas Day! But our school goes on as usual. The only difference was that we had two big turkeys for dinner. Mr. E[aton] told us that he did not observe Christmas as he was certain that our Savior was not born on the twenty-fifth or any other day in December.

In Rhode Island in the 1770s there was a growing ecumenical spirit among Lutheran, Anglican, Baptist, and Congregationalist churches, more often than not manifested most obviously at Christmas, where members and office-bearers in churches traditionally against Christmas on doctrinal reasons would attend Lutheran and Anglican Christmas services. However, nineteenth-century newspaper and local church records indicate that probably few Baptist congregations formally celebrated Christmas prior to the 1880s. By the 1890s, however, Christmas celebrations were common among Baptist congregations. Rather quickly, Christmas evolved into a time of special music and events within many Baptist churches, and about the turn of the century, various Christmas customs began appearing. These came through the introduction of frivolities like St. Nicholas in children's Sunday School, the use of Christmas trees, and other festive elements. The observance appears to have come from the lower levels of the church from sentiments of people in the congregations and worked its way into sermons and more general acceptance.[23] Katherine Richards concluded:

> A résumé of the development of Christmas observance in the Protestant Sunday-schools of the United States makes one thing clear; Christmas returned to Protestant church life because the rank and file of the membership wanted it.
>
> It made its way against official opposition in many denominations until there were so many local groups celebrating December twenty-fifth as the birthday of Jesus that opposition was futile and indifference impossible. Even when the denomination accepted Christmas as part of the church year, its position was magnified

---

22. Smith, *How is the Gold Become Dim*, 98.
23. Thompson, *Presbyterians in the South*, 434–35.

and its celebration increased in response to popular desire. As time went on, Sunday-school and other denominational leaders played a larger part in the promotion of certain types of Christmas observances but as a rule the local schools have remained the chief experiment stations. Christmas preceded other church festivals in general recognition and has continued to overshadow them in popular esteem.[24]

Like the Congregationalists, the Baptists and Presbyterians repudiated "all the saints' days" and observed "the Lord's day as the Sabbath and the only season of holy time commanded to Christians." It was 1851 before the Presbyterians produced a Sunday-school magazine, *The Sabbath School Visitor*. Its first approach to a Christmas reference came in the number for December 1, 1853, where, in a serial history of the Presbyterian Church, the action of the Scottish Assembly of 1618 at Perth in assenting to the observance of holidays was disapproved. December fifteenth of the following year brought an article on the birth of Christ which urged the careful instruction of children in the scriptural accounts of the nativity and the correction of all impressions received from tradition only. Although this procedure was expected to convince the children that Christmas was a most unlikely date for Jesus' birth no objection was made to its observance; indeed, the author used the occasion to urge the worship of the risen and exalted Savior. The December numbers from 1855 to 1858 contained poems, pictures and articles, on the nativity of Jesus but from 1859 to 1865 the subject of Christmas was dropped from the pages of the Sabbath School Visitor. Apparently the fires of the Christmas controversy were burning low. Though not yet accepted by the denomination as a whole, it could be mentioned and its religious as well as holiday, character could be recognized.[25]

Richards then cites the letters of J. W. Alexander of Princeton:

The drift of the Presbyterian attitude toward Christmas is further described in the letters of James W. Alexander, son of a Presbyterian minister and himself, teacher at Princeton Seminary, pastor of the Fifth Avenue Presbyterian Church in New York City and prolific writer for the American Sunday-school Union. On December 25, 1838, Dr. Alexander ventured to wish his correspondent a Merry Christmas; on Christmas Day of

---

24. Richards, *How Christmas Came to the Sunday-Schools*, 220.
25. Ibid., 90–92.

1843, he made one of a family reunion at his father's house in Princeton. In 1845 he speaks of Christmas meetings as common in New York City on Christmas. In 1851 Christmas saw Dr. Alexander in nine churches—five Roman Catholic, one Unitarian, and three Episcopal. His own longing for "anniversary festivals" was openly expressed next year, only to be set aside in obedience to Presbyterian tenets, as "against the second commandment."[26]

Another three years and "three hundred and fifty urchins and urchinesses" assembled on Christmas Day for a cake and candy fête in the Mission Chapel of the Fifth Avenue Church. Christmas, as a holiday, seemed to hold fewer dangers than Christmas as a religious festival. At all events it enabled Presbyterians to join in the pleasures of the season without a complete rejection of the historical attitude of the denomination on the matter of "set days." With the twentieth century the Southern Presbyterian, or the Presbyterian Church in the United States, to use its official title, joined the ranks of Christmas-keeping denominations. The process followed the familiar lines of official disapproval and ignoring of the day, of an increasing number of local celebrations, (many of which were of the holiday, Santa Claus, party type) and finally, of official recognition and attempts to change the character of the local observance.[27]

In 1889, Robert L. Dabney believed that the development of instruments in public worship, such as organs, would encourage a more ritualistic style of worship in the Southern Presbyterian Church, that would inevitably also incorporate holy days:

> That a denomination, professing like ours to be anti-prelatic and anti-ritualistic, should throw down the bulwarks of their argument against these errors by this recent innovation appears little short of lunacy. Prelatists undertake every step of the argument which these Presbyterians use for their organ, and advance them in a parallel manner to defend the re-introduction of the Passover or Easter, of Whitsuntide, of human priests and priestly vestments, and of chrism [anointing oil], into the gospel church.[28]

Oklahoma was the last state to make Christmas a legal holiday, doing so in 1907.

26. Ibid.
27. Ibid., 186.
28. Dabney, "Review of Dr Girardeau's Instrumental Music."

In 1950, the General Assembly of the PCUS formally sanctioned the religious observance of Christmas. This process in churches took time. The late Morton Smith (American historian and Presbyterian) notes that the appearance of Easter and Christmas into the official calendar of the Southern Presbyterian Church, did not actually occur until the late 1940s and 1950s. Smith cites the acceptance of the liturgical calendar as a mark of the growing apostasy in the church and that the change in attitude came with the growth of theological liberalism.[29] Many Christians in America by the late twentieth century routinely expressed resentment that Christmas was becoming increasingly secularized, unaware that for much of the prior century, many Christians refused to celebrate the holiday because of its pagan and Roman Catholic origins.

In conclusion, it is obvious that the objection to Christmas held by Puritans and their varied successors during the subsequent three centuries, on both sides of the Atlantic, was not based on the secularization of the season but on religious grounds, as a practice which dishonored Christ and found no warrant in his Word.

Reason 10

Some Reformers saw little harm in Christmas celebration by the church, e.g., Ulrich Zwingli and Heinrich Bullinger in Zurich and Calvin, Beza, and Turretin in Geneva.

Bullinger's view is reflected in his Second Helvetic Confession of 1566, which states regarding Christian feast days:

> Moreover, if in Christian Liberty the churches religiously celebrate the memory of the Lord's nativity, circumcision, passion, resurrection, and of his ascension into heaven, and the sending of the Holy Spirit upon his disciples, we approve of it highly.

Similarly, The Synod of Dordt (1618–19), famous for its excellent refutation of Arminianism, concurs. Article 53, "Days of Commemoration," reads:

> Each year the churches shall, in the manner decided upon by the consistory, commemorate the birth, death, resurrection, and ascension of the Lord Jesus Christ, as well as his outpouring of the Holy Spirit.

---

29. Smith, *How is the Gold Become Dim*, 97–105.

Answer

In our admiration for the first Reformers, there is a danger that we place too high an expectation on their opinions and practices. We have the luxury of looking back (2017 to 1517) on half a millennia of reformation, whereas the first and second generation Reformers faced a unique situation. The term "Reformer" is what we now use to identify these men, but in reality the term is a bit of a misnomer, as they were more revolutionaries than reformers, God having opened their eyes to the reality that the Papacy was beyond the possibility of reform and ought to be displaced.

No Reformer got it right on every point of doctrine or practice, as is reflected in the great variety of sixteenth- and seventeenth-century Confessions. The decision respecting what to do with the holy days, which were commemorating real biblical events, was not the most pressing concern of most Reformers. They were acutely aware that the general populace favored the retention of these days, as they were public holidays. Besides, after twelve hundred years of Roman Catholicism, it would be very surprising if every aspect of religious life were abolished perpetually, with no vestiges remaining. One of the particular gifts of the Reformation is the delineation of the doctrine of total depravity, where there is a recognition that there is no aspect of our lives that is unaffected by our estrangement from God. Even our best endeavors and highest aspirations are prone to sin and error, and confessions of faith and life in the church are no exception. This is why Reformed confessions tend to have their own built-in disclaimers. The preface to the *Scots Confession* invites all readers to offer correction from Scripture if they find the confession to be in error. The *Westminster Confession of Faith* asserts, "Councils may err and many have erred."

The Reformers knew that they held "this treasure in jars of clay" (2 Cor 4:7).

We would not agree with Luther's attitude toward the Jews in the latter part of his life, where in his book, *On The Jews and Their Lies*, he suggests that their synagogues, schools, and homes be burned down, their property and finances confiscated, their leaders executed or maimed if found teaching, then if all else fails, that they be deported en masse from Germany.[30] We would not agree with Zwingli respecting his attitude to Baptists, some of whom were executed in Zurich for holding steadfastly to their belief as being scriptural. The council of Zurich, having decreed rebaptism to be a capital offense warranting drowning, arrested Felix Mantz. On January 5, 1527, he was forcibly lowered beneath the icy waters of the Limmat River,

---

30. Luther, "On the Jews and Their Lies," 268–93.

with Zwingli and other pastors looking on, as he cried, "Into your hands O Lord, I commend my spirit."[31]

We would not agree with Calvin, instituting the Mosaic penal code of death for adultery, parental assault, and blasphemy, or for advocating torture of his theological opponents, or threatening to kill them if the opportunity presented itself.[32] We would not agree with Bullinger respecting his belief in the "Assumption" of Mary, based upon the glorious translation of Elijah into heaven:

> We believe that the Virgin Mary, Begetter of God, the most pure bed and temple of the Holy Spirit, that is, her most holy body, was carried to heaven by angels.[33]

While times have changed and they lived in a different day to ours, nevertheless they were obliged to follow the example of Christ and his apostles and the fact is, their views that we have just reviewed struggle to find a warrant from the New Testament.

It is very easy to criticise these great men, however. Would we have acted any differently had we been in their shoes? We may like to think that we would have but particular circumstances affect particular judgements. Hindsight is a wonderful thing and no doubt they would have said and done many things differently, were it possible to have gone back in time and relived them again.

The point we are seeking to stress here is that their views on holy days must be viewed in the light of the context of the day in which they lived and the circumstances they found themselves in, when called upon to make judgements on the issues. Although there were many very fine Christians among the ranks of the Anabaptists (Calvin married the widow of an Anabaptist pastor) and although the majority were unfairly judged by the extreme minority, nevertheless even the mildest of the Reformers felt that their extermination was necessary for the salvation of the churchly Reformation and social order.[34] Few of a Reformed persuasion would argue against the fact that Scripture is self-interpreting.[35] However, it is not at all

---

31. Williams, *Radical Reformation*, 146.

32. Harkness, *John Calvin*, 131; Kingdom, *Adultery and Divorce*, 21, 117, 179; Calvin, *Commentaries*, Deut 21:21 and 22:21; Schaff, *History of the Christian Church*, vol. 8, ch. 107, 436–38, and ch. 109, 444–53 (Schaff has extensive notes in these chapters, much of which is based upon Jean Picot's *History of Geneva*, Genève: Manget et Cherbuliez, 1811); Cottret, *Calvin: A Biography*, 208.

33. Bullinger, *On the Origin of Error*, ch. 16.

34. Schaff, *Creeds of Christendom*, 1:842.

35. What is obscure in one Bible passage may be illuminated by another; no single statement or obscure passage from one section of the Bible sets aside a doctrine which is clearly established by many other passages; and the obscure texts must be interpreted

clear that tradition, along with the connection of church and state, did not adversely affect the ability of the Reformers to objectively allow Scripture to interpret itself, without them imposing preconceived ideas on it. This appears to have happened with covenant theology in order to justify the continuance of the non-Apostolic models of the church/state connection, as well as infant-baptism resulting in the astounding view that God's everlasting covenant of grace applied to both the elect and the non-elect.[36] It also appears to have happened with the retention by some of holy days.

Excursus on Zurich and Geneva

On a more general note, there did exist social and political factors which influenced all of the Reformers. They had all been born and bred Roman Catholic and lived in a sacral world, where church and state were completely intertwined. The connection was so great that it would take earth shattering events of the magnitude of the French and American Revolutions to terminate this connection! This connection is demonstrably absent from the Apostolic Church from Pentecost onwards and it undoubtedly influenced the hermeneutics (theory and methodology of interpretation) used on the Scriptures. Another influence which affected the Reformers doctrinal emphases was Protestant groups that appeared to oppose a reformed theology. For example, the Socinians (anti-trinitarian and claiming in modern ultra-dispensational style, that God's saving purpose and people in the Old Testament was completely unconnected to those of the New Testament), the Arminians (rejecting election as based solely upon the free, sovereign grace and choice of God, advocating that it was based in part upon his foreknowledge of merit/faith in the person elected) and the Anabaptists (who not only repudiated their infant baptism as the Socinians did also, but repudiated the church-state connection and were largely pacifist). The doctrines of such groups were condemned in Lutheran and Reformed confessions.

The Holy Roman Empire, as we noticed earlier, now comprised of an area controlled by a large number of locally autonomous Dukes. At the Reformation there was a practical division along religious lines, with the north, the east, and many of the major cities—Strasbourg, Frankfurt, and Nuremberg—becoming Protestant while the southern and western regions largely remained Roman Catholic. In Switzerland only four out of the twelve Cantons adopted Protestantism, however, they were the largest cities: Bern, Zurich, Basel, and Schaffhausen. In Zurich, Henreich Bullinger succeeded

---

by obvious ones.

36. Denault, *Distinctiveness of Baptist Covenant Theology*, 155–56.

Zwingli several months after the latter's death in 1531. Bullinger distinctly recognizes, in the spirit of Christian liberty and progress, the constant growth in the knowledge of the Word of God and the consequent right of improvement in symbolical statements of the Christian faith. While he strongly defended Zwingli's life and teaching and was influenced by Luther and Melanchthon, Bullinger was an independent reformer. Bullinger's *First Decade* fixates upon the Theodosian Code as a set of legal documents that garnered considerable success in their execution. The Theodosian Code was first set forward by decree in 429 AD and had undergone its first edition by 437 AD. Contained within the first edition were 2,500 different decrees that covered all facets of life, including matters of society, cultural expression, and religious observance. The code was first decreed in the Eastern portion of the Roman Empire in Constantinople.

In the *Second Decade*, Bullinger (1504–1575) seems to suggest that the strengths of the Theodosian Code and later the Justinian, proved to be beneficial in sixteenth century Zurich (pictured), as it highlights Bullinger's commitment to his faithfulness to his understanding of providential history. A plausible suggestion for Bullinger's affinity for the code was that he, like those who composed it, believed that they lived in a Christian territory where the state had a proactive role in enforcing religious conformity. Bullinger resonated with this idea as he felt that their challenges of governance were identifiably similar. Of chief importance for Bullinger was how a Christian territory could protect and promote true expressions of faith among the people. He feared radical behavior, and any inclinations toward a challenge to the existing structures were often put on the same level as Thomas Muntzer's Peasant's War of 1524/1525.

Unlike the Baptists who became labeled as part of the Radical Reformation, Munzter was unbiblically radical and represented a real threat to the mainstream Protestant movement. Like Zwingli before him, Bullinger realized that the success of the Reformation in Zurich was dependent upon the support of the magistrates.

Since Christmas Day and the day after Christmas, as well as the days following Easter and Pentecost and in some places also New Year's Day and Ascension Day, were all statutory holidays in continental Europe, the pastors were therefore advised to preach on subjects appropriate to the occasion. The governments were reluctant to do away with these Christian festivals because they were very popular, especially with government officials and employees who hated to give up the holidays connected with them. We noted earlier the uproar in Geneva when Christmas was abolished.

Geneva is estimated to have had a population of 13,000 to 20,000 during Calvin's time there. Following Calvin's arrival in Geneva, he and Farel restructured the church. Where there had been seven or eight congregations within the city, they made them into three parishes or congregations. Calvin was one of five pastors of the Reformed Church of Geneva, which was divided into these three congregations. They were all French speaking, as the French refugees to Geneva far outnumbered the original Protestant congregation there. In addition to this main congregation, there were three refugee congregations—Italian, Spanish and English. Unlike the Italian and Spanish, the members of the English one were able to return to Britain after several years, so the congregation was disbanded. The Spanish subsequently joined with the Italians in the Italian congregation. They also restructured the more difficult and insecure congregations outside the city, in the countryside controlled by the city authority, reducing those twenty-five to thirty Roman Catholic parishes to twelve Reformed churches all with their own pastor. All of the pastors formed the Company of Pastors, dealing exclusively with church matters. A more influential body was the Genevan Consistory, composed of pastors and lay elders, some of which had to be members of the secular city councils and which met every Friday morning, liaising with the civic leaders in the governing of Geneva. The purpose of the body was to enforce church discipline, but it also became a very useful tool to instruct the population in biblical belief and conduct. Scrutiny of the population by the Consistory was systematic and thorough, with a public ban placed on all plays and music, and with church attendance made compulsory! This was a shock to the system of many, who had known no such restrictions prior to the city's reformation and it resulted in deep-seated opposition that was present throughout Calvin's life in the city. To many he became known derogatorily as "The Protestant Pope."

Preaching was of central importance in the life of the city. In the three urban congregations there were sermons preached every day of the week. On working days there were sermons at sunrise for the servant class and at 6 to 7 a.m. for all others, all of which were from the Old Testament. On the Lord's Day there were three sermons in each of the three urban churches—one at 8 a.m., a catechismal sermon at noon, and another sermon at 3 p.m., all of which were from the Psalms and the New Testament.

The Genevan Academy had been founded by Calvin in 1559 to specifically teach theology. In its first year it had 162 students, but by 1565 that number had risen to 1,600! As we noted above in the chapter considering the Regulative Principle, when all of Calvin's writings are studied together, his view of what ought to constitute worship pleasing to God is, in effect, what became known as the Regulative Principle. Calvin believed strongly that nothing ought to be introduced to worship that did not have scriptural authority, yet also believed that the religious observance of Christmas and other feast days did not contradict this principle.

For Calvin, Christmas appears to have not been a big issue and he was aware that the ban in Geneva had caused much uproar, so he adopted a conciliatory approach to the matter. He recommended that Christmas Day be observed in the morning only and that shops and trades resumed work as normal in the afternoon. He conveyed his view to Bullinger in Zurich who agreed with his approach. So we can trace a pattern of thought through Calvin, Beza, Bullinger, and Turretin, where with the removal of Roman Catholic superstitions and excesses, five major holy or feast days were retained.

However, the Company of Pastors and the Council of Geneva disagreed with Calvin and subsequently reintroduced the ban on all these holy days once again. In spite of the tremendous influence Calvin's theology bore on others, during and especially after his life, it is significant that on this issue of holy days, many theologians believed the Council of Geneva to have adopted the best policy. In doing so, the Company of Pastors were aware that other Reformed cities such as Bern and Zurich may have viewed them as acting too restrictively, therefore they issued the following judgement:

> In regard to the observation of the day of Christmas, things that are indifferent should not be formalised and we do not condemn [other reformed cities] that observe such a day, provided that they do so without superstition.[37]

What sort of Christmas Day was it in Geneva when Calvin's will prevailed, or rather, what sort of Christmas morning was it? We can be very certain that it was a very simple and conservative one, where the Word of God was central. As we have noted, Calvin and his colleagues were extremely strict. Attendance at sermons was compulsory and in 1547, a man who left during the sermon and made too much noise about it was imprisoned! There were over twenty executions that occurred in Geneva during Calvin's time there, for offences that would today scarcely be penalized in any Christian society, e.g., adultery where the married woman was drowned and the married man beheaded, or for the cursing/striking of a parent.[38] There was no "watch-night" service the night before, no Christmas carols sung, no Christmas tree in the churches, and of course no Santa at that time.

In 1547, Calvin opined:

> With respect to ceremonies and above all the observance of holy days [I offer the following]: Although there are some who eagerly long to remain in conformity with such practices, I do not know how they can do so without disregard for the edification of the church, nor [do I know] how they can render an account to God for having advanced evil and impeded its solution.[39]

The following is an excerpt from the regular sermon preached by Calvin in his congregation, on December 25, 1550:

> Now I see here today more people than I am accustomed to having at the sermon. Why is that? It is Christmas Day. And who told you this? You poor beasts.
>
> That is a fitting euphemism for all of you who have come here today to honor Noel. Did you think you would be honoring God? Consider what sort of obedience to God your coming displays. In your mind, you are celebrating a holiday for God,

---

37. Manetsch, *Calvin's Company*, 126.
38. Audin, *History of the Life*, 355.
39. Calvin, *Ecclesiastical Advice*, 90.

> or turning today into one. But so much for that. In truth, as you have often been admonished, it is good to set aside one day out of the year in which we are reminded of all the good that has occurred because of Christ's birth in the world, and in which we hear the story of his birth retold, which will be done on Sunday. But if you think that Jesus Christ was born today, you are as crazed as wild beats. (Sermon on Mic 5:7–14)

During the weekday services from November of 1550 through January of 1551, Calvin preached through Micah and so when December 25 came around, he preached from chapter five, picking up where he had left off the previous morning. He did preach a sermon on the birth of Christ on the next Sunday. Calvin, however, was not consistent in this practice. Between 1549 and 1554, Calvin sometimes broke off the series of biblical expositions that he was preaching on, to preach each weekday on themes that matched the incarnation around Christmas time and then the death of Christ around Easter time. This practice became less frequent as his time in Geneva went on.

The political factor we highlighted above with Zwingli and Bullinger, was of course true in Geneva as well. Humanly speaking, the support of the civil rulers was crucial to the success of the Reformation. The middle years of the sixteenth century were years of the greatest peril for the Reformation movement, which was then still in its formative stage and all of the Reformers were intent on protecting their churches from forces that threatened to destroy the edifice, which was being constructed with such great endeavor and labor. Accordingly, there was an exceptional sensitivity to the condoning of anything perceived to be unnecessarily controversial. Calvin had no sympathy for anything that was construed as being extreme and he was very conscious of the anger among the population over the banning of Christmas.

However, some of his fellow pastors in the city and of course a majority of the City Council disagreed with him and felt it was best to not recognize even a Christmas morning. There were numerous cases of discipline by the Council against citizens who breached the law and continued to celebrate the old Roman Catholic feasts such as Christmas and circumcision, etc., especially among the peasant class, which continued under Beza's tenure as leader.[40] The Register of the Consistory of Geneva records, for example, that with respect to Christmas observance, there were eighteen cases of discipline in 1562, twenty-one in 1565, twenty-three in 1566, and thirty-three in 1582.[41]

---

40. Manetsch, *Calvin's Company*, 138.

41. Kingdom, Lambert, and Watt, *Registers of the Consistory of Geneva*, fols. 24, 190v–191v, 197.

John Knox was in Geneva on four occasions between 1553 and 1559, having fled England upon the death of Edward VI and the ascension to the throne of his sister, Mary I ("Bloody Mary"). While in Geneva, he pastored the English congregation, was a member of the Company of Pastors and was acquainted with the City Council, all of which we have referred to above. His assessment of the Genevan church is well known: "The most perfect school of Christ that ever was in the earth since the days of the Apostles."[42] Knox was resident and ministering in Geneva on December 25 on three different years, so he had first-hand experience of the Christmas debate in the city. It is therefore of significance that on his subsequent return to Scotland, in the reformation of religion he led in 1560, he did not follow the view of Calvin, Beza, and Bullinger. Instead, he followed the majority view in Geneva and abolished Christmas and the other holy days altogether.

Calvin (1509–1564) had been the mentor of Beza (1519–1605). Turretin (1623–1687) succeeded Beza as the leading Reformed theologian in Geneva. Turretin's parents were Italian and in 1648 he became pastor of the Italian Congregation in Geneva.

Turretin's mentor was Theodore Tronchin (whose mother was Beza's adopted daughter), professor of theology in the Geneva Academy, and in 1653 Turretin was appointed as his successor, although he continued to pastor his congregation.

So Turretin came to prominence a full one hundred years after the Genevan ban on Christmas and times had changed! Until his death, Turretin battled against Arminianism, Socinianism, and Amyraldism, the former two we are probably more familiar with as distinctly wrong. The latter was a view of the atonement expressed within Calvinistic circles and which opposed extreme Calvinism. (It arose within a Huguenot theological academy in Saumur, West France, and centered upon the inscrutable order of events in God's eternal decrees, suggesting that he decreed to die for the sins of all mankind and *after* that decision, he then elected some to salvation. At the heart of the issue was the teaching by a Glaswegian, John Cameron, respecting the degree and type of control God exercised upon the human will. One of Cameron's students who championed the doctrine was Frenchman Moses Amyraut). Amyraldism was popular in Geneva, including among other faculty members of the academy and although opposed most vehemently by Turretin, was not considered heresy by him. Moreover, Roman Catholicism was reestablishing itself in the city, concurrent with growing French political and military interference and intimidation. Even the Mass was reintroduced in 1679 in the official French diplomatic residence! Even earlier, just prior

---

42. Knox, *Works*, 4:240.

to his death, Calvin opined that the entire European Reformation might come to naught. Within a generation of Turretin's death in 1687, his work was being undone, including by his own son, and another generation later, Deists (those believing that God created the universe, leaving it to run by natural laws without any direct influence by him in supernatural events or revelation in Scriptures) were teaching in the academy! Geneva became the city of its child Rousseau (1712–1778), with his humanist philosophy, and Calvin and Beza's vision for the city was lost. Turretin's *Institutes of Elenctic Theology*, in which we discover his acceptance of Christmas as a legitimate feast day of the church, were not a systematic theology but a response to issues confronting him from 1679 to 1685, a period where many more pressing issues and the forces of great cultural change were being felt in Geneva.

Therefore, to summarize our answer, religious endorsement of Christmas by some of the Reformers occurred in its own particular context, was inherited from Rome and not considered to be an issue of great significance in comparison to other issues. We would suggest that on this issue, some of the Reformers did not repudiate Rome's teaching clearly and robustly enough.

Reason 11

People come into church at Christmas-time who never do so at any other time of the year. It is, therefore, a great opportunity to evangelize, so that embracing Christmas is worth it in order to save a soul.

Answer

Evangelism is a very common doctrinal/theological reason for justifying the religious endorsement of Christmas. While the proclamation of Christ's claims upon sinners will never return void to him, being the fragrance of life to life for some and the fragrance of death to death for others (2 Cor 2:16), we noted that there appears to be a lack of tangible evidence, that he the Holy Spirit has blessed Christmas evangelism to unconverted communities and societies in the past or in the present. In the chapter above, "Significance for the Christian," under the subheading on the social significance of endorsing Christmas, we remarked upon the legitimacy of using any social season to preach the Gospel.

Indeed, the Calvinist ought to be the most prolific witness to Christ in all the world, as they know that the salvation of God's people is already guaranteed and the Word proclaimed will always fulfill a purpose that will glorify God, irrespective of the spiritual effect on the hearer. Consciousness of this fact surely explains the tireless ministry of Paul—if you did not know his doctrine, you might be forgiven for thinking that he was an Arminian who could save people by his own efforts and methods!

The Holy Spirit himself enlightens the mind and subdues the will of a sinner. He gives them that saving grace of a justifying faith, or to put it in another way, he effectually calls the sinner to himself. What we have just spoken about is the inward, invisible call of the Spirit, but it is, of course, usually accompanied by the outward, visible call to the sinner in the preaching of the Gospel. What is the cause of this effectual call? It is God's electing love. "And those whom he predestined, he also called" (Rom 8:30).

The shocking fact is that the world hates the Gospel and it hates those who preach the Gospel, and the reason for this is that it hates Christ of whom the Gospel speaks.

It hates to be told that it lies in sin, it hates to be told that its own righteousness is worthless in order to please God, and it hates to be told that it lies under God's anger and curse with a Hell looming. It hates God's person and God's work.

> If the world hates you, know that it has hated me before it hated you. If you were of the world, the world would love you as its own; but because you are not of the world, but I chose you out of the world, therefore the world hates you. (John 15:18,19)

In contrast to such hatred, we remarked in an earlier chapter about how the world does not hate Christmas but passionately loves it! Christ and him crucified is a truth that is quite unpalatable to the world, whereas in contrast, Christmas is very palatable. The mistake many churches make (perhaps unwittingly) is in trying to make Christ palatable to the world by means of Christmas! This is so incongruous for churches that purport to believe in the sovereign, electing, predestination of saved souls. We live in a day when evangelism has become the panacea for any criticism of church practice, whatever the practice might be. On the face of it, evangelism is an argument that sounds very proper, orthodox, and pious. What is the purpose of evangelism? Some may suggest that its purpose is in order to save sinners. The reality is, as with every aspect of the Christian life, that the purpose of it is to glorify God. This is, first and foremost, why we are to evangelize/spread abroad the good news of Christ and the salvation to be found in him. As with the type of worship we endorse, so Scripture acts as a guide as to how we evangelize. Forming a Christian heavy metal rock band to tour the secular circuit of rock concerts and festivals to save rock fans, or becoming an actress in seedy films to try and save some in that sector of the film industry, finds no warrant in Scripture for the Christian whatsoever. So our evangelism must be patterned after the example we have in Scripture.

The apostles did not build evangelism around an annual celebration of the birth of Christ (Christmas) no more than they built it around an annual celebration of Christ's death and resurrection (Easter). Virtually all of the traditions that the church decreed down the centuries were to fulfill the purpose of adding to the church. The usual supposition was that if one just added this and took away that, the gospel would be made more palatable to the world. In contrast, however, the usual result was that the gospel was increasingly obscured by a greater "farrago of useless observances" (to use Calvin's phrase[43]) and the traditions of men that the Pharisees exemplified.

John Owen stated:

> In things which concern the worship of God, the commanding power is Christ, and His command the adequate rule and measure of our obedience. The teaching, commanding, and enjoining of others to do and observe those commands, is the duty of those entrusted with Christ's authority under him. Their commission to teach and enjoin, and our duty to do and observe, have the same rules, the same measure, bounds, and limits. What they teach and enjoin beyond what Christ hath commanded, they do it not by virtue of any commission from him; what we do beyond what He hath commanded, we do it not in obedience to him; what they so teach, they do it in their own name, not His; what we so do, we do in our own strength, not His, nor to His glory.[44]

The twentieth century saw a steady growth, decade on decade, of churches with a Calvinist heritage that embraced Christmas to the same extent as Anglicans, Lutherans, and Roman Catholics. What was the result of this? Was it blessed by the Holy Spirit in revival and were communities transformed by the renewing of their minds? Was there even an outward temperance of moral behavior? The sad reality is that each passing decade has resulted in a numerically diminishing church and an increasingly bold defiance of biblical morality. The simple fact is that the Lord has given us all we need to set Christ before sinners, and when his glorious Gospel is preached faithfully, it is quite offensive to the natural man. The Lord certainly does not need us to use the sentimental romance of the Christmas season, as a tool to build his Kingdom, no more than he needed Israel of old to rely upon others apart from God. "Woe to them that go down to Egypt

---

43. Calvin, *Institutes*, book 4, ch. 10, sec. 19.
44. Owen, *Works of John Owen*, vol. 15, ch. 8, 59–60.

for help" (Isa 31:1). In the days of King Saul when "there was no blacksmith found throughout all the land of Israel," we are told that all the Israelites "went down to the Philistines to sharpen his plowshare, his mattock, his axe, or his sickle." (1 Sam 13:19–21).

Reason 12

Christmas is a fine tradition. The season brings families and friends together. Does it really matter if Jesus was not born on December 25, as long as he is being honored? Even if the holiday and artifacts used are based on false religions, ancient and more modern, surely the spirit of Christmas outweighs all of these?

Answer

Correct tradition *is* an important aspect of a godly life, as the Apostle Paul testified: "So then, brothers, stand firm and hold to the traditions that you were taught by us, either by our spoken word or by our letter" (2 Thess 2:15).

Paul clearly did not mean that every human tradition was appropriate, because he later wrote to the Colossians:

> See to it that no one takes you captive by philosophy and empty deceit, according to human tradition, according to the elemental spirits of the world, and not according to Christ. (Col 2:8)

In the famous musical and film, *Fiddler on the Roof*, the leading character—Tevye, the Dairyman—undergoes the dilemma of arranging marriages for his beloved daughters according to tradition, not according to their heartfelt wishes. When they question why the match-making tradition *must* be followed, all that Tevye can argue in support of tradition is . . . tradition! The famous motif of a fiddler playing and dancing on a high-pitched tiled roof, exemplifies the chief story-line, that depending on tradition alone to generate a positive outcome is a very precarious exercise indeed!

On the one hand, then, there are traditions we should hold to, and on the other hand, there are traditions that a follower of Christ should avoid. The Christian's aim must always be to generate an outcome that positively brings honor and glory to God. Some traditions are based on biblically sound doctrine, while others are based merely on human custom at odds with biblical teaching.

To appreciate the differences, it is helpful to review an example given by Christ himself. The Jewish religious leaders at the time were teaching their community, principles derived from oral tradition. Originally, these oral traditions were expansions of the law as given to Moses and the Israelites; however, over time they moved further away from the original intent, drawing more on custom than on Scripture. Jesus confronted the religious leaders over the matter of ceremonial hand-washing before eating. We see in Mark 7 that the Pharisees unashamedly referred to these washings as a "tradition of the elders."

Jesus' remarks were quite plain. He described the leaders as hypocrites for "teaching as doctrines the commandments of men," and added, "You leave the commandment of God and hold to the tradition of men." In other words, they can ignore the commandments if it serves their purposes, but apparently no one else can! Especially poignant was his remark that by superseding scriptural commandments with human traditions, they were worshiping God "in vain" (vs. 7). The clear message was that the commandments of God always override humanly devised traditions.[45]

The Bible nowhere identifies exactly when Christ was born, neither does it give any instructions for celebrating the day of his birth. This was not a tradition that any of the churches received from Paul or any other apostle. As we also noted previously, according to John 4:23–24: "But the hour is coming, and is now here, when the true worshipers will worship the Father in spirit and truth, for the Father is seeking such people to worship him. God is spirit, and those who worship him must worship in spirit and truth." As we highlighted in a previous chapter, many of the present day Christmas family traditions can be practiced and enjoyed to the full, without the inclusion of any religious element.

---

45. Orchard, "Christmas: Does it Matter?"

Conclusion

Origin

DUE TO A LACK of reliable data, it is impossible to determine the *exact* process by which December 25 first became regarded by the church as the day of Christ's birth. Was it universally believed by the immediate successors of the apostles and those that followed them throughout the second and third centuries, free from any influences outside of the church? No available evidence supports this. Was it believed by some during that period and adopted by many due to doctrinal controversy then prevalent within the church? Or was it believed by a few during the same period and adopted by many to displace long established pagan festivals around the same date? No definitive answer can be given. As the Roman Catholic Church developed and established itself, it certainly became routine to syncretize Christianity and paganism in order to extend the borders of the church.

However, we can determine two things with exactness. First, that the Lord, both in the days of his flesh and during the Apostolic era, has kept the exact date of his birth hidden, as he has done with the exact location of his birth, crucifixion, burial, and ascension, otherwise the blind idolatry and faith in the locations and dates themselves would have been an even greater means of Satanic delusion than they have already become. Second, the Lord did not commemorate his birth on any specific day or with any festival, neither did he instruct his apostles to do so for themselves or the future church.

Past Example

We all learn from the example of others and we have noted the attitude to the commemoration of the Lord's birth: in the early church fathers, in twelve hundred years of the Roman Catholic Church, and in the first Protestants and their successors, attitudes both for and against Christmas. We introduced this topic by noting that many of the Lord's people in previous generations, in various nations and at specific times, did not practice an annual celebration of Christ's birth. In the first and second centuries in the Middle East and Mediterranean Europe, from the sixteenth to twentieth centuries in Western Europe and North America (plus in the intervening period, groups such as the Waldenses), we have had brothers and sisters in Christ who did not endorse Christmas in a religious way.

What degree of glory did they deny to God by not practicing it? What benefit and blessing did they forfeit by not doing it? Was the worship of the apostles really incomplete? They never observed any of these holy days, so what has changed? These questions demand answers. The Bible has not changed and biblical principles have not changed. Society has changed and the church has changed with it. Is that change in the direction of holiness and greater conformity to his Word, or is it in the direction of sin and less conformity to his Word? The response of some to this book may be to suggest the impossibility of changing the present endorsement of Christmas by so much of the visible church. However, society and church have often changed direction in the past and will do so again in the future. We are reminded of one of Spurgeon's maxims:

> We shall not adjust our Bible to the age; but before we have done with it, by God's grace, we shall adjust the age to the Bible.[1]

We noted how the first-generation Reformers who had abandoned the church of their birth were sensitive to concerns from civil leaders and the populace that reform was going too far, whereby proposals such as changing the form and subjects of baptism and abandoning of holy days were very contentious and perceived as a threat to the success of the Reformation movement. We have also seen how successive generations of Reformed theologians built upon the study and formulation of doctrine and practice laid by their predecessors.

While our study has addressed the specifics of how it was that the vast majority of Reformed Presbyterians and Baptists came to celebrate holy

---

1. Spurgeon, *All-Round Ministry*, 230.

days when their forbears clearly did not, it does not tell us from where the psychological impetus for these changes came.

As Andrew Webb reflects, perhaps it was an unconscious desire to return to the comforting traditions and symbolism of medieval Roman Catholicism.[2]

The increasing willingness of Reformed congregations to observe holy days was ultimately the result of pressure from the laity, the movement toward the adoption of a common liturgy, and the pervasive atmosphere of pluralism, ecumenism, and liberalism in the Protestantism of the nineteenth and twentieth centuries. The statement made almost two hundred years ago by French statesman and observer of the new American society, Alexis de Toqueville, can be applied very accurately to many Reformed churches globally:

> All the clergy of America freely adopt the general views of their time and country and let themselves go unresistingly with the tide of feeling and opinion which carries everything around them along with it.[3]

History has shown that the acceptance of Christmas by Protestant churches has led directly to the adoption of more of, or the whole of, the liturgical calendar and there exists no evidence at all that its adoption has resulted in the tangible blessing of God. In his 1948 book, *The Pursuit of God*, A. W. Tozer noted the trend:

> Paul took up the cry of liberty and declared all meats clean, every day holy, all places sacred and every act acceptable to God. The sacredness of times and places, a half-light necessary to the education of the race, passed away before the full sun of spiritual worship. The essential spirituality of worship remained the possession of the church until it was slowly lost with the passing of the years.
>
> Then the natural legality of the fallen hearts of men began to introduce the old distinctions. The church came to observe again days and seasons and times. Certain places were chosen and marked out as holy in a special sense. Differences were observed between one and another day or place or person. The "sacraments" were first two, then three, then four, until with the triumph of Romanism they were fixed at seven....

---

2. Webb, "Why do Presbyterians Observe Holy Days?" December 10, 2009, http://providencepca.com/main/?p=105.

3. De Toqueville, *Democracy In America*, vol. 2, ch. 5.

> From this bondage reformers and puritans and mystics have laboured to free us. Today the trend in conservative circles is back toward that bondage again. It is said that a horse after it has been led out of a burning building will sometimes by a strange obstinacy break loose from its rescuer and dash back into the building again to perish in the flame. By some such stubborn tendency toward error, Fundamentalism in our day is moving back toward spiritual slavery. The observation of days and times is becoming more and more prominent among us. "Lent" and "holy week" and "good" Friday are words heard more and more frequently upon the lips of gospel Christians. We do not know when we are well off.[4]

In the seventy years since Tozer made this observation, more and more churches from a Reformed heritage, have embraced holy days such as Christmas. This has rendered the church collectively as increasingly sacral in nature, something most assuredly to be avoided, as it invariably stifles that which is authentically spiritual.

---

4. Tozer, *Pursuit of God*, 126.

Present Responsibility

To reiterate what we noted in earlier chapters, the adoption of the traditional Christmas season into society, together with its massive growth and importance throughout the twentieth century, was secular in origin and not instigated by any focus on the Bible or desire to bring God glory.

It must be recognized, however, that there are many Christian congregations all over the world, Protestant and Calvinist, for whom Christmas has become completely normal.

Irrespective of the rights or wrongs of their fore-fathers' adoption of December 25 as a hallowed/holy day in the nineteenth or early twentieth centuries, it is has become for them and the generations immediately preceding them, an intrinsic part of the Christian life.

Such brothers and sisters do not associate it with Roman Catholicism or with paganism in the slightest, as it has become part of their own heritage and as such is very precious to them. When challenged as to the propriety of endorsing Christmas as part of their worship, it is very clear that they have a strong emotional attachment to it, which is inseparable from the cultural traditions of the season. When this attachment is manifested privately in their homes, as to the Lord, no one has the right to censor them for it. Such believers should, however, be careful not to view celebrating Christmas as a prescribed religious duty or a necessity for holiness, nor censor those who do not endorse it.

For all that we may learn from our Christian predecessors, each successive generation of Christians has to appropriate the Bible for themselves. Each has to decide what the revealed will of God is, in order that they may seek to fulfill it in their own lives, individually and corporately, to God's glory on earth. Let us again ask questions of ourselves. Ought Christmas to have a religious place in a fellowship of God's people which has as its foundation, sole adherence to the Bible, by Scripture alone, by faith alone, and by grace alone? Is there any warrant from Scripture to endorse Christmas or to expect the Holy Spirit to bless that endorsement? History always shows us that no trend occurs in a vacuum. The current embracing of Christmas and other holy days in churches with a Reformed heritage, is symptomatic of a change of doctrinal emphasis. When the primacy of preaching and the special importance of the Lord's Day to facilitate this is misunderstood, then "special" days for evangelism will appear necessary and merge with what society recognizes, in a pseudo-religious sense, as "special" seasons of the year. Similarly, when the infinitely holy being of God is misunderstood, sensuality that entertains and satisfies human nature will manifest itself again and again. The Christmas season is exactly suited to facilitate this.

Consistency

There exists an obligation on the part of the Christian to be consistent in their lives, as much as is possible. God is consistent, the Lord being "the same, yesterday, today and forever" (Heb 13:8) and God's people are to reflect this. For example, the believer is to love consistently, God and man, especially their brothers and sisters in Christ and it is not something they can practice one week and relinquish the next. Similarly, they cannot decide to resist sin one day and then the next day, willingly countenance any and every sin that presents itself to them.

Yet, one obvious feature in many churches today that claim to be Reformed, is their inconsistency respecting their application of the Regulative Principle. We admitted previously that the principle has to be understood and applied carefully. God has not given us a New Testament rule book of worship, a sort of New Testament–styled Leviticus. It is a bad habit of mind to seek to label "biblically forbidden" what is really just unwise. It may not be the case that by endorsing Christmas in worship, a church is practicing something explicitly condemned in the Bible. It may not be the case that such endorsement is obviously and unquestionably contrary to a theological principle, such as the Regulative Principle. May it not be the case, however, that the religious endorsement of Christmas is simply unwise? Why? Because it mixes what is most precious with what is rubbish, what is true with what is false, what is godly with what is worldly, and what is sound doctrine with what is unsound. This is inadvertently admitted each year in Christmas sermons, tracts, newsletters, and social media submissions, by churches promoting Christmas, as they struggle to emphasize and prove what they perceive to be "the real meaning of Christmas," i.e., what is of supreme and lasting value, saving faith in a crucified and risen Christ, in contrast to what is ultimately of little value, everything else about Christmas! Wouldn't it be much simpler to just stop endorsing Christmas altogether and emphasize the crucified and risen Christ 365 days a year?

The inconsistency we refer to in applying the Regulative Principle is seen especially in the rejection of some worship styles against the acceptance of practising "holy days."

Churches will intuitively apply the Regulative Principle in respect to their chosen praise material, declining to allow those gathered to sing anything they want, from any song-book they want, and without any restriction upon the musical instruments and playing style employed. Instead, they will particularly endorse one or several praise books or type of praise-song, as well as the general style in which they are sung, all of which have met with the approval of the leaders and members, with content that they believe reflects the truth of Scripture. Halloween is no less Roman Catholic in origin than is Christmas, yet churches which annually oppose the former, heartily embrace the latter! Similarly, some churches will expect church members to conform to other practices, e.g., dress code or regular attendance at church services and a lifestyle that is consistent with a Christian profession. Some will also apply the principle to the question of the Apostolic gifts, maintaining a cessationist view that Scripture gives no warrant to include these in the elements of worship, believing that the gifts ceased with the original apostles. When it comes to Christmas, however, they are overtly inconsistent! They will not adopt other festivals instigated by the Roman Catholic Church, even although the festival is based upon a real, historically factual and biblical event in the life of the Lord Jesus. Yet with Christmas . . . they cannot resist it; indeed, the very thought of no longer embracing and endorsing it fills some with consternation. Where fanciful preaching and biblically inaccurate hymns are consistently rejected, fanciful Christmas hymns (carols) and inaccurate teaching are condoned. If it is permissible in God's sight to endorse Christmas as part of the worship of the church, then it cannot be wrong to endorse other days which the Church of Rome has decreed to be holy, provided it is in commemoration/celebration of a factual biblical event and no matter what pagan, mythological, or false paraphernalia are associated with it. Neither can it be wrong to criticize or prevent musical praise, irrespective of style or genre.

The fact is that with Christmas, Reformed churches are now adopting an interpretive principle generally embraced by those of a Lutheran heritage. Expediency is dictating practice more than theology! If you endorse Christmas in a religious sense, think for a moment of what it means to you. Could you equally celebrate these meanings that you hold during Christmas in, for example, August or February? If not, you may be more bound to the secularization of Roman Catholicism than you may be willing to believe! Or if when December 25 falls on the Lord's Day (as it does on average every seven years), would you feel compelled to adjust the normal worship routine out of deference to the "holy day"? Some probably feel that it is wise to have a day off on the 25th because, in imitation of Rome, they have been so busy with services on the 24th! If so, you may be in bondage to something, precisely when you think you are exercising free will!

God's Sovereignty

Is it the case that the main reason for endorsing Christmas is peer pressure? This alone seems to explain why there exists a departure from the example of so many spiritual forefathers.

It is not that believers have discovered something new in the Scriptures which those who went before them somehow missed, neither is it that they have discovered historical data that sheds a different light on the issue. It is just that everyone else is now doing Christmas and . . . they don't want to be oddballs in the eyes of their ecclesiastical peers or in the eyes of the world.

We noted the development of Protestantism through the first and second Reformation periods, culminating in the fixed dogma known as Calvinism, emphasizing the total sovereignty of God. The determination of the existence of all things to be created, of what is to be rose or buttercup, robin or hawk, deer or cat, and equally among humanity the determination of our own persons, whether one is to be born male or female, rich or poor, dull or clever, or even as Abel or Cain, is the most tremendous predestination conceivable in heaven or on earth and we still see it taking place before our eyes every single day. We are subject to it in our whole personality and entire existence. This all-embracing predestination is in the hand of Almighty God, Sovereign Creator and Possessor of heaven and earth. It is in the figure of "the potter and the clay" that the Bible has, from the time of the Prophets, expounded to us this all-dominating election. There is election in nature, election in providence, election also to eternal life. Election in the realm of grace as well as in the realm of nature. There is no other dogma that enables the Christian to defend the faith in the face of paganism. Let us never forget that this is the contrast, the light and the darkness, that has always been, is still and will be until the end at Christ's return—Christianity and paganism, worldview against worldview, principle against principle, spirit against spirit, the living God against idols! Concern about being an oddball, whether in the eyes of the visible church or the world, is not an honorable concern for the Christian whose interpretation of the Bible is Reformed.

Christmas and Salvation

There is a veneer about Christmas and its "spirit" that is platonic, vague, and hollow because in the final analysis, it has a foundation emanating from humanity and not from its Creator.

As people decorate outwardly their towns and homes and bodies to imbibe the spirit of Christmas, it is a reflection of the inward décor of all of humanity in a state of nature, lying amidst the ruins of the Fall and without any real sense of purpose or destiny beyond their own vain imagination.

Humanity's real need, as it always has been, is the Gospel of our Lord Jesus Christ and it is the duty of the Lord's people to tell it and live it. Let us not make the mistake of the church that went bad almost two thousand years ago and then tried to make Christianity attractive to the world by syncretizing what is true with what is false, what reflects the character of God with what reflects the character of Satan, and what is spiritual with what is worldly. "For what partnership has righteousness with lawlessness? Or what fellowship has light with darkness? What accord has Christ with Belial? Or what portion does a believer share with an unbeliever? What agreement has the temple of God with idols? For we are the temple of the living God; as God said, 'I will make my dwelling among them and walk among them, and I will be their God, and they shall be my people'" (2 Cor 6:14–16). Satan is described as 'the god of this age' or 'world' (2 Cor 4:4). The phrase indicates that Satan is the major influence on the ideals, opinions, goals, hopes, and views of the majority of people. His influence also encompasses the world's philosophies, education, and commerce. The thoughts, ideas, speculations, and false religions of the world are under his control and have sprung from his lies and deceptions. No less a part of this was Roman, Celtic, and Teutonic paganism, Roman Catholicism, and the false practices which evolved from them and which are, to a great extent, both embodied and reflected in what we know today as Christmas. Satan does not want people to think of Christ and him crucified, the glorious conqueror who bruised his head and destroyed his power. Satan would rather have people focus once a year on the helpless baby Jesus in combination with all the attendant festivities, designed to make people forget about death, judgement, and eternity.

To his people, is Jesus not "altogether lovely"? Lovely in his life, lovely in his death, lovely in his resurrection, lovely in his intercession now? Lovely and precious in his redeeming love? From every and any angle, to the eye of faith he is wonderful. Remember the Greeks who said to Philip that they really wanted to see Jesus (John 12:21). Why did they say this? Was it not because the Holy Spirit was at work in their hearts, impressing upon them something of the majesty of the Lord, something incomparably attractive and lovely that, for the first time in their lives, met the aspirations of their restless, sinful souls? Would we not want all others around us to want to see Jesus with a similar desire? Surely the answer is unreservedly in the affirmative. Do we then see Jesus—his person, life, and work—any clearer in Christmas? Does it really do anything to make him altogether lovely? We would suggest that, if anything, his person, life, and work are actually blurred, obscured, even distorted by it. One of the mottos of the

Reformation was *post tenebras lux* ("after darkness, light") but the practical effect of the increasing emphasis on Christmas is, after light, darkness! Can we with confidence go to Scripture, gather up all that we can identify of God's being and what he clearly delights in and conclude that the invention and practice of Christmas pleases him? On balance we would graciously and lovingly suggest, that we cannot attain such confidence.

Many Christians at the beginning of the twenty-first century feel the impact of living in an increasingly post-Christian society. Some note with objection the policy of many national, regional, and local governments to rename Christmas as the winter festival, in order to be politically correct and not offend non-Christian religions or atheists. Others are overwhelmed by the commercialization of it all. There exists, therefore, a desire by some of the Lord's people to champion Christmas and call on society to rediscover the "real meaning of Christmas" and to "put Christ back into Christmas." The only problem and reality is, that he was never in Christmas to begin with! It is never the easy option to change practices that so many in churches have become accustomed to, even if they are not most honorable to God and best for us. It was not easy for the first and second generation Reformers either; however, such change does have one notable advantage. It is the proper thing to do and doing what is proper tends to yield rich benefits in the long term. As the Puritan Thomas Manton said:

> This is the trial of our sincerity, to glorify him upon earth; in heaven we glorify Christ without opposition or interruption. It is easy to be good where that which hinders is removed, but our sincerity is tried by glorifying him now on earth.[5]

Does the church really think it honors her Master and is in step with the Spirit by becoming bound to an annual religious calendar of events, never given by the Spirit but invented by apostates? Do we really want to go backwards again, as some of the Galatians did? We have the reality, do we need symbolic shadows again? If so, we would humbly suggest that it is folly indeed on our part, and Tozer's analysis was spot-on, we really and truly don't know when we are well off!

Instead we would, in love, encourage the Lord's people to reconsider the issue of Christmas and follow the example of the New Testament saints who, led by God the Holy Spirit, celebrated the incarnation of our Redeemer every day throughout the year, with simple, sincere faith and who did not follow the god of this age or his ungodly innovations.

Soli Deo Gloria

5. Manton, *Complete Works*, 20:333.

Bibliography

Acts of the General Assembly of the Church of Scotland. Edinburgh: William Blackwood and Sons, 1922.
Ainsworth, Henry. *A Defence of the Holy Scriptures, Worship, and Ministerie, Used in the Christian Churches Separated from Antichrist: Against the Challenges, Cavils, and Contradiction of M. Smyth: In His Book Intituled The Differences of the Churches of the Separation*. Amsterdam: Giles Thorp, 1609.
Ambrose, Saint, Bishop of Milan. *De Virginibus*. Milan, n.p., 377.
Armitage, Thomas. *A History of the Baptists*. Watertown, WI: Baptist Heritage, 1988.
Armstrong, W. P. "Chronology of the New Testament," in vol. 1 of *International Standard Bible Encyclopedia*, edited by James Orr et al., 644–50. Grand Rapids: Eerdmans, 1949.
The Arraignment, Conviction, and Imprisoning, of Christmas. London: Printed by Simon Minc'd Pye, 1645.
Ashton, John. *A Righte Merrie Christmasse!!!*. London: Leadenhall Press, 1894.
Audin, J. M. V. *History of the Life, Works, and Doctrines of John Calvin*. Translated by John McGill. Louisville, KY: B. J. Webb & Brother, 1845.
Bailey, Kenneth E. *Jesus through Middle Eastern Eyes: Cultural Studies in the Gospels*. Downers Grove, IL: IVP Academic, 2008.
———. *Poet and Peasant: A Literary-Cultural Approach to the Parables in Luke*. Grand Rapids: Eerdmans, 1976.
Bannerman, James. *The Church of Christ*. 2 vols. Carlisle, PA: Banner of Truth, 1960.
Baptist History and Heritage Society. *Baptist Studies Bulletin* 9:8 (December 2010).
Barnes, Albert. *Barnes' Notes on the New Testament*. Edited by Ingram Cobbin. Grand Rapids: Kregel, 1962.
Barnett, Paul W. "Apograhe and Apographesthai in Luke 2:1–5." *The Expository Times* 85 (1974) 377–80.
Bauckham, R. J. "Sabbath and Sunday in the Medieval Church in the West." In *From Sabbath to Lord's Day: A Biblical, Historical, and Theological Investigation*, edited by D. A. Carson, 299–310. Eugene, OR: Wipf and Stock, 1999.
Beckwith, Roger T., and Wilfred Scott. *This is the Day: The Biblical Doctrine of the Christian Sunday in its Jewish and Early Church Setting*. London: Marshall, Morgan & Scott, 1978.

Bede, the Venerable, Saint. *Ecclesiastical History of the English People*. Translated by Leo Sherley-Price. London: Penguin, 1991.

Beitzel, Barry J. *The New Moody Atlas of the Bible*. Chicago: Moody, 2009.

Bennet, Richard. *Catholicism: East of Eden*. Edinburgh: Banner of Truth, 2010.

Blake, Thomas. *Vindiciae Foederis: or A Treatise of the Covenant of God Entered With Mankind, In the Several Kinds and Degrees of it*. London: Abel Roper, 1683.

Bock, D. L. *Jesus according to Scripture: Restoring the Portrait from the Gospels*. Grand Rapids: Baker Academic, 2002.

Brigden, Susan. *London and the Reformation*. Oxford: Clarendon, 1989.

Briggs, John. "The Influence of Calvinism on Seventeenth-Century English Baptists." *Baptist History & Heritage Journal* 39 (Spring 2004) 8–25.

Brodie, Brent J. "The Prevalence of the Magistrate in the Political Theology of Heinrich Bullinger." MA Thesis, University of Western Ontario, 2012.

Brook, Benjamin, ed. *The Lives of the Puritans*. 3 vols. Morgan, PA, Soli Deo Gloria, 1997.

Brooks, James C. *Benjamin Keach and the Baptist Singing Controversy: Mediating Scripture, Confessional Heritage, and Christian Unity*. Tallahassee: Florida State University, 2006.

Bruce, Malina, and Richard L. Rohrbaugh. *Social-Science Commentary on the Synoptic Gospels*. Minneapolis: Augsburg Fortress, 1992.

Bullinger, Heinrich. *The Decades of Henry Bullinger: The First and Second Decades*. Translated by H. I., edited by Thomas Harding. Cambridge: Cambridge University Press, 1848.

———. *On the Origin of Error*. Zurich, 1528/1539/1568.

The Bulwark: Magazine of the Scottish Reformation Society. (April-June 2011).

Burrage, Champlin. *The Early English Dissenters in the Light of Recent Research*. 2 vols. Cambridge: Cambridge University Press, 1912.

Calderwood, David. *The Perth Assembly, 1618*. Leiden, Holland: William Brewster, 1619.

Calvin, John. *Calvin's Commentaries*. 22 vols. Grand Rapids: Baker, 1974.

———. *Commentaries on the Epistles of Paul to the Galatians and Ephesians*. Grand Rapids: Baker, 1981.

———. *Commentaries on the Epistles of Paul to the Philippians, Colossians, and Thessalonians*. Grand Rapids: Baker, 1996.

———. *Commentary on the Gospel of John*. Grand Rapids: Baker, 1980.

———. *Ecclesiastical Advice*. Translated by Mary Beaty and Benjamin W. Farley. Louisville, KY: Westminster John Knox, 1991.

———. *Institutes of the Christian Religion*. 2 vols. Edited by John T. McNeill. Translated by Ford Lewis Battles. Philadelphia: Westminster, 1960.

———. *The Necessity of Reforming the Church*. Dallas: Protestant Heritage, 1995.

———. *Selected Works of John Calvin, Tracts and Letters*. 6 vols. Edited by Henry Beveridge and Jules Bonnet. Grand Rapids: Baker, 1983.

———. *Sermons on 2 Samuel, Chapters 1–13*. Translated by D. Kelly. Carlisle, PA: Banner of Truth, 1992.

———. *Sermons on the Book of Micah*. Translated and edited by Benjamin W. Farley. Phillipsburg, NJ: P & R, 2003.

Campbell, Ken M. ed., *Marriage and Family in the Biblical World*. Downers Grove, IL: IVP, 2003.

Canterbury Christmas. London: Printed for Humphrey Harward, 1648.
Chaffey, Tim. "Christians Celebrating Christmas at Christmas Town." Answers in Genesis, December 21, 2012. https://answersingenesis.org/holidays/christmas/christians-celebrating-christmas-at-christmas-town/.
Chaffey, Tim, and Jeremy Ham. "4 Misconceptions About Christmas." Answers in Genesis, December 28, 2010. https://answersingenesis.org/holidays/christmas/4-misconceptions-about-christmas/.
Chevallier, Temple. *Translation of the Epistles of Clement of Rome, Polycarp and Ignatius*. Edited by W. R. Whittingham. New York: Onderdonk and Co., 1846.
Cheyne, T. K., ed. *Encyclopædia Biblica: A Critical Dictionary of the Literary, Political, and Religious History, the Archaeology, Geography, and Natural History of the Bible*. 4 vols. London: Macmillan, 1902.
Chrysostom, John. *del Solst. Et Æquin*. (II, p. 118, ed. 1588[c. 400]).
Collins, Hercules. *An Orthodox Catechism: Being the Sum of Christian Religion Contained in the Law and Gospel*. London: n.p., 1680.
Cornwell, Francis. *A Conference Mr. John Cotton Held at Boston*. London: Printed by J. Dawson, 1646.
Cottret, Bernard. *Calvin: A Biography*, Translated by M. Wallace McDonald. Grand Rapids: Eerdmans, 2000.
Cramp, J. M. *Baptist History: From the Foundation of the Christian Church to the Close of the Eighteenth Century*. Philadelphia: American Baptist Publication Society, 1869.
Cranfield, C. E. B. "Some Reflections on the Subject of the Virgin Birth." *Scottish Journal of Theology* 41 (1988) 177–90.
Crosby, Thomas. *The History of the English Baptists*. 4 vols. London: n.p., 1738–1740.
Cunningham, William. *The Reformers and the Theology of the Reformation*. Edinburgh: Banner of Truth, 1989.
Curwen, J. Spencer. *Studies in Worship Music—First Series: Chiefly as Regards Congregational Singing*. 3rd ed. London: J. Curwen & Sons, 1901.
Dabney, Robert L. "Review of Dr Girardeau's Instrumental Music in Public Worship." *Presbyterian Quarterly* 3 (1889) 462–69.
Davies, Horton. *The Worship of the English Puritans*. Westminster: Dacre, 1948.
———. *Worship and Theology in England*. Vol. 1, *From Cranmer to Hooker, 1534–1603*. Princeton: Princeton University Press, 1970.
Davies, Samuel. "A Christmas-Day Sermon," in vol. 3 of *Sermons*, by Samuel Davies, 562–86. Philadelphia: Presbyterian Board of Publication, 1864.
Dawson, William Francis. *Christmas: Its Origins and Associations*. London: Elliot Stock, 1902.
De Greef, Wulfert. "Calvin's Writings," in *The Cambridge Companion to John Calvin*, edited by Donald K. McKim, 41–57. Cambridge: Cambridge University Press, 2004.
Delaune, Thomas. *A Plea for the Non-Conformists – Shewing the True State of Their Case: In a Letter to Dr. Benjamin Calamy*. London: James Marshall, 1683.
Denault, Pascal. *The Distinctiveness of Baptist Covenant Theology*. Birmingham: Solid Ground Christian Books, 2013.
Douglas, David C., ed. *English Historical Documents*. Vol. 8, *1660–1714*, edited by Andrew Browning. New York: Oxford University Press, 1953.
Dow, George Francis. *Every Day Life in the Massachusetts Bay Colony*. New York: Arno, 1977.
Drane, J. W. *Introducing the New Testament*. Oxford: Lion, 2000.

Dyck, John T. "Calvin and Worship." *Western Reformed Seminary Journal* 16 (2009) 33–40.

Dyer, T. F. Thiselton. *British Popular Customs, Present and Past*. Vol. 1. London: G Bell & Sons, 1876.

Edersheim, Alfred. *Sketches of Jewish Social Life*. Updated ed. Peabody, MA: Hendrickson, 1994.

Edwards, Jonathan. *Sermons and Discourses, 1720–1723*. Edited by Wilson H. Kimnach. The Works of Jonathan Edwards 10. New Haven, CT: Yale University Press, 1991.

Encyclopaedia Judaica. 16 vols. Jerusalem: Keter, 1972.

Evans, Craig A., and Stanley E. Porter, eds. *Dictionary of the New Testament Background*. Downers Grove, IL: IVP, 2000.

Finucane, Ronald. "The Waldensians," in *Introduction to the History of Christianity*, edited by Tim Dowley, 235–41. 2nd ed. Minneapolis: Fortress, 2013.

Firth, C. H., and R. S. Rait, eds. *Acts and Ordinances of the Interregnum, 1642–1660*. 3 vols. London: His Majesty's Stationery Office, 1911.

Forbes, Bruce David. *Christmas: A Candid History*. Berkeley: University of California Press, 2007.

France, R. T. *The Gospel of Matthew*. Grand Rapids: Eerdmans, 2007.

Garrett, James Leo. *Baptist Theology: A Four-Century Study*. Macon, GA: Mercer University Press, 2009.

Garside, Charles. "The Origins of Calvin's Theology of Music: 1536–1543." *Transactions of the American Philosophical Society* 69 (1979) 1–36.

George, Timothy. *Theology of the Reformers*. Nashville: Broadman & Holman, 1988.

Gies, Frances, and Joseph Gies. *Marriage and Family in the Middle Ages*. 1st ed. New York: Harper and Row, 1987.

Gillespie, George. *A Dispute Against the English-Popish Ceremonies*. Dallas: Naphtali, 1993.

Goldsmith, Oliver. *History of Rome*. In *Pinnock's Improved Edition of Dr. Goldsmith's History of Rome*, edited by William C Taylor. Philadelphia: Thomas Cowperthwait & Co., 1851.

Grant, Michael. *The Collapse and Recovery of the Roman Empire*. London: Routledge, 1999.

Grantham, Thomas. *Christianisimus Primitivus*. London: n.p., 1678.

Haigh, Christopher. *English Reformations: Religion, Politics, and Society Under the Tudors*. Oxford: Clarendon, 1993.

Haldane, James A. *Reasons of a Change of Sentiment and Practice on the Subject of Baptism*. Edinburgh: J. Ritchie, 1809.

Hall, Peter, ed. *The Harmony of Protestant Confessions: Exhibiting the Faith of the Churches of Christ, Reformed After the Pure and Holy Doctrine of the Gospel*. Edmonton, AB: Still Waters Revival, 1992.

Hardwick, Charles. *A History of the Articles of Religion*. Cambridge: Deighton, Bell & Co., 1859.

Harkness, Georgia, *John Calvin: The Man and His Ethics*. Nashville: Abingdon, 1931.

Hearn, Michael Patrick. *The Annotated Christmas Carol*. New York: Avenel, 1976.

Hill, Christopher. *The English Bible and the Seventeenth-Century Revolution*. London: Penguin, 1994.

Hooker, Richard. *The Works of that Learned and Judicious Divine, Mr. Richard Hooker: With an Account of His Life and Death*. 4 vols. Edited by John Keble. Oxford: Clarendon, 1836.

Hughes, Philip E., ed. *The Register of the Company of Pastors of Geneva in the Time of Calvin.* Eugene, OR: Wipf & Stock, 2004.

Hutton, Ronald. *The Rise and Fall of Merry England: The Ritual Year, 1400–1700.* Oxford: Oxford University Press, 1994.

James, Francis G., and Miriam G. Hill, eds. *Joy to the World: Two Thousand Years of Christmas.* Dublin: 2000.

Journal of Calendar Reform. 25 vols. New York: World Calendar Association, 1934.

Keach, Benjamin. *The Child's Delight.* London: n.p., 1702.

Kertzer, David I. *The Popes Against the Jews: The Vatican's Role in the Rise of Modern Anti-Semitism.* New York: Alfred A. Knopf, 2001.

King, Josiah. *The Examination and Tryall of Old Father Christmas.* London: Printed for Thomas Johnson, 1658.

Kingdom, Robert M. *Adultery and Divorce in Calvin's Geneva.* Cambridge: Harvard University Press, 1995.

Kingdom, Robert M., Thomas A. Lambert, and Isabella M. Watt, (eds.). *Registers of the Consistory of Geneva in the Time of Calvin: 1542–1556.* 10 vols. Translated by M. Wallace McDonald. Grand Rapids: Eerdmans, 2000–2016.

Knox, John. *Works.* 6 vols. Edited by David Laing. Edinburgh: Wodrow Society, 1864.

Leishman, T. *May the Kirk Keep Paschal and Yule?* Edinburgh: William Blackwood, 1875.

Letters and Papers, Foreign and Domestic, of the reign of Henry VIII, 1509–1547. 21 vols. Edited by James Gairdner. London: Her Majesty's Stationery Office, 1883.

Lewis, J. P. "Feasts." In *The Zondervan Encyclopaedia of the Bible.* Vol. 2, D–G, edited by Merrill C. Tenney and Moises Silva. Grand Rapids: Zondervan, 2010.

Loader, William. *The New Testament on Sexuality.* Grand Rapids: Eerdmans, 2012.

Luther, Martin. "On the Jews and Their Lies." Translated by Martin H. Bertram. In *The Christian in Society IV*, edited by Franklin Shermanm, 268–71. Luther's Works 47. Philadelphia: Fortress, 1971.

———. "An Open Letter to the Christian Nobility of the German Nation Concerning the Reform of the Christian Estate, 1520." Translated by C. M. Jacobs. In vol. 2 of *Works of Martin Luther*, 55–165. Philadelphia: A. J. Holman, 1915.

MacArthur, John, Jr. "A Son to Make Many Sons." Grace Community Church Sermon Catalogue, GC 80-76. Panorama City, CA, 1990.

Manetsch, Scott M. *Calvin's Company of Pastors: Pastoral Care and the Emerging Reformed Church*, 1536–1609. Oxford: Oxford University Press, 2013.

Manton, Thomas. *The Complete Works of Thomas Manton.* 22 vols. Edited by Thomas Smith. London: James Nisbet, 1874.

Marlow, Isaac. *A Brief Discourse Concerning Singing.* London: n.p., 1690.

Mather, Increase. *A Testimony against Several Profane and Superstitious Customs, Now Practiced by Some in New England.* London: n.p., 1687.

McBeth, H. Leon. *The Baptist Heritage: Four Centuries of Baptist Witness.* Nashville: B & H Academic, 1987.

McCrie, Thomas. *Lectures on the Book of Esther.* Edinburgh: William Blackwood & Sons, 1838.

McGrath, Alister. *Reformation Thought: An Introduction.* 3rd ed. Oxford: Blackwell, 1999.

McIver, Robert. *Star of Bethlehem, Star of Messiah.* Toronto: Lugus, 1998.

Merle d'Aubigné, J. H. *History of the Reformation of the Sixteenth Century*. Vol. 1. Translated by W. K. Kelly. London: Whittaker & Co., 1842.

Miles, Clement A. *Christmas in Ritual and Tradition: Christian and Pagan*. London: T Fischer Unwin, 1912.

Miller, Samuel. *Presbyterianis: the Truly Primitive and Apostolical Constitution of the Church of Christ*. Philadelphia: Presbyterian Board of Publication, 1835.

Minucius Felix, Marcus. *Octavius*. Rome: c. 160–250 AD.

Mullaney, James. "The Star of Bethlehem." *Science Digest* 80 (December 1976) 61–65.

Murray, John. *The Collected Writings*. 4 vols. Edinburgh: Banner of Truth, 1958.

———. *The Epistle to the Romans*. Grand Rapids: Eerdmans, 1965.

———. "Sanctity of Truth." Payton Lecture to the faculty of Fuller Theological Seminary, Pasadena, CA, March 1955.

Naphtali, Lewis, and Reinhold Meyer, eds. *Roman Civilization: Sourcebook*. Vol. 2, *The Empire*. New York: Harper: 1955.

Napier, James. *Folklore, or, Superstitious Beliefs in the West of Scotland within This Century: With an Appendix, Shewing the Probable Relation of the Modern Festivals of Christmas, May Day, St. John's Day, and Halloween, to Ancient Sun and Fire Worship*. Paisley, Scotland: Alex Gardner, 1879.

A Narrative of the Proceedings of the General Assembly of the Elders and Messengers of the Baptised Churches. London: n.p., 1692.

Neal, Daniel. *The History of the Puritans*. 3 vols. London: Printed for T. Tegg, 1837; rpt. Minneapolis: Klock & Klock, 1979.

Needham, N. R. "Musical Instruments in Worship: Historical Survey." *The Presbyterian* 32 (May 1990) 25–26.

Nevin, Robert P. *Misunderstood Scriptures: A Critical Examination of Some Passages in the Inspired Word, Respecting the Import of Which There has been Much Discussion . . . With a View to Establish the Real Meaning*. Londonderry: Montgomery, 1893.

Nichols, James Hastings. *Corporate Worship in the Reformed Tradition*. Philadelphia: Westminster, 1968.

Nissenbaum, Stephen. *The Battle for Christmas: A Cultural History of America's Most Cherished Holiday*. New York: Knopf, 1996.

Old, Hughes Oliphant. *Worship: Reformed According to Scripture*. Louisville, KY: Westminster John Knox, 2002.

Orchard, Brian. "Christmas: Does it Matter?" *Vision* (Fall 2007). http://www.vision.org/visionmedia/history-of-christmas_4116.aspx.

Orchard, G. H. *A Concise History of Baptists*, Texarkana, TX: Bogard, 1987.

Origen. *Against Celsus*, c. 248. In *The Early Church Fathers*. Vol. 4, *Ante-Nicene Fathers*, edited by Alexander Roberts et al. Peabody, MA: Hendrikson, 1994.

———. "Homily Eight," c. 245. In *Fathers of the Church*. Vol. 83, *Homilies on Leviticus 1-16*, translated by Gary W. Barkley, Washington, DC: Catholic University of America Press, 1992.

Owen, John. *The Works of John Owen*. 16 vols. Edited by William H. Goold. Edinburgh: Banner of Truth, 1968.

Packer, J. I. "The Puritan Approach to Worship," in *Diversity in Unity: Papers Read at the Puritan and Reformed Studies Conference*. London: Evangelical Magazine, December 1963.

Parker, T. H. L. *John Calvin: A Biography*. Philadelphia, PA: Westminster, 1975.

Pastor, Ludwig. *The History of the Popes, From the Close of the Middle Ages: Drawn from the Secret Archives of the Vatican and Other Original Sources.* 4 vols. Edited by F. I. Antrobus. London: Kegan Paul, Trench, Traubner, 1900.

Philo, of Alexandria. *Works of Philo Judaeus: The Contemporary of Josephus.* 4 vols. Translated by C. D. Yonge. London: Henry G. Bohn, 1855.

Pink, A. W., ed. *Studies in the Scriptures.* 17 vols. Lafayette, IN: Sovereign Grace Publishers, 2001.

The Records of the Parliaments of Scotland to 1707. University of St. Andrews and National Archives of Scotland.

Reisinger, Ernest C., and D. Matthew Allen. *Worship: The Regulative Principle and the Biblical Practice of Accommodation.* Cape Coral, FL: Founders, 2001.

Restad, Penne L. *Christmas in America: A History.* Oxford: Oxford University Press, 1995.

Richards, Katherine Lambert. *How Christmas Came to the Sunday-Schools: The Observance of Christmas in the Protestant Church Schools of the United States, an Historical Study.* New York: Dodd, Mead & Company, 1934.

Rihbany, Abraham Mitrie. *The Syrian Christ.* Cambridge: Riverside, 1916.

Robertson, A. T. *Word Pictures of the New Testament.* 6 vols. Nashville: Broadman, 1927.

Roney, John B., and Martin I. Klauber, eds. *The Identity of Geneva: The Christian Commonwealth, 1564–1864.* Westport, CT: Greenwood, 1998.

"Santa's Family Tree." *The United Church Observer,* December 1976.

Satlow, Michael L. *Jewish Marriage in Antiquity.* Princeton: Princeton University Press, 2001.

Scarisbrick, J. J. *The Reformation and the English People.* Oxford: Blackwell, 1984.

Schaff, Philip. *The Creeds of Christendom.* 3 vols. 6th ed. New York: Harper and Row, 1931.

———. *The Early Church Fathers.* 10 vols. Peabody, MA: Hendrikson, 1994.

———. *History of the Christian Church.* 8 vols. 5th ed., rev. Grand Rapids: Eerdmans, 1989.

Schwertley, Brian. *The Regulative Principle of Worship and Christmas.* Iola, WI: Reformed Online, n.d. www.reformedonline.com/uploads/1/5/0/3/15030584/christmas.pdf.

Shurer, Emil. *The History of the Jewish People in the Age of Jesus Christ (175 BC–AD 135).* 3 vols. Edited by Geza Vermes et al. Edinburgh: T & T Clark, 1973–1987.

Smith, Morton H. *How is the Gold Become Dim (Lamentations 4:1): The Decline of the Presbyterian Church, U.S.* Jackson, MS: Steering Committee for a Continuing Presbyterian Church, 1973.

The Southern Presbyterian Review 21:5 (December 1870).

Spijker, Willem van 't. *Calvin: A Brief Guide to His Life and Thought.* Translated by Lyle D. Bierma. Louisville, KY: Westminster John Knox, 2009.

Spurgeon, Charles Haddon. *An All-Round Ministry: Addresses to Ministry and Students.* London: Passmore & Alabaster, 1906.

———. *The New Park Street Pulpit Sermons and The Metropolitan Tabernacle Pulpit Sermons.* 63 vols. London: Passmore & Alabaster, 1855–1917.

———. *The Treasury of David.* 3 vols. Peabody, MA: Hendrickson, 1990.

Stipp, Neil. "Music Philosophies of Martin Luther and John Calvin." *The American Organist* 41 (September 2007) 68–72.

Stubbes, Philip. *Anatomy of the Abuses in England in Shakespeare's Youth, 1583*. Edited by Frederick J. Furnivall. London: Trubner & Co., 1877.

Supreme Court Reporter [Supreme Court of the United States of America]. Eagan, MN: West, 1983.

Tangl, Michael, trans., ed. *The Letters of Saint Boniface*. Berlin: Weidmannsche Buchhandlung, 1916.

Tappert, Theodore G., trans., ed. *The Book of Concord: The Confessions of the Evangelical Lutheran Church*. Philadelphia: Fortress, 1959.

Tertullian. *The Book of Apology Against the Heathen*. N. Africa, c. 198 AD.

———. *On Idolatry*. N. Africa, c. 200 AD.

Thompson, Ernest T. *Presbyterians in the South*. Richmond, VA: John Knox, 1973.

Thomson, William McClure. *The Land and the Book*. 2 vols. New York: Harper & Brothers, 1871.

Tocqueville, Alexis de. *Democracy In America*. 2 vols. Translated by Henry Reeve. New York: George Dearborn & Co., 1840.

Tozer, A. W. *The Divine Conquest* [later entitled *The Pursuit of Man*]. Westwood, NJ: Revell, 1950.

———. *The Pursuit of God*. Harrisburg, PA: Christian, 1948.

Turretin, Francis. *Institutes of Elenctic Theology*. 3 vols. Translated by George Musgrave Giger. Edited by James T. Dennison Jr. Phillipsburg, NJ: P & R, 1992.

Ulrich, Homer, and Paul A. Pisk. *A History of Music and Musical Style*. New York: Harcourt, Brace & World, 1963.

US Catholic Conference, Inc. *Catechism of the Catholic Church*. 2nd ed. Vatican City: Libreria Editrice Vaticanus, 1997.

Verduin, Leonard. *The Anatomy of a Hybrid: A Study in Church-State Relationships*. Grand Rapids: Eerdmans, 1976.

Victoria, Queen of Great Britain. *Journals of Queen Victoria: 1832–1901*. 141 vols. The Royal Archives, Windsor, London.

Voetius, Gisbertus. *De Sabbatho et Festis*. Utrecht: n.p., 1659.

Waldron, Samuel E. *The Regulative Principle of the Church*. Grand Rapids: Wisdom, 1995.

Wegman, Herman. *Christian Worship in East and West: A Study Guide to Liturgical History*. Collegeville, MN: Liturgical, 1990.

Weigall, Arthur. *The Paganism in our Christianity*. New York: G. P. Putnam's Sons, 1928.

Weightman, Gavin, and Steve Humphries. *Christmas Past*. London: Sidgwick & Jackson, 1987.

Wesley, John, ed. *A Collection of Hymns for the Use of the People Called Methodists*. London: John Mason, 1830.

Whitefield, George. *George Whitefield's Journals*. Edinburgh: Banner of Truth, 1960.

———. *The Works of Reverend George Whitefield*. 6 vols. London: Edward & Charles Dilly, 1772.

Whiting, Robert. *The Blind Devotion of the People: Popular Religion and the English Reformation*. Cambridge: Cambridge University Press, 1989.

Whitley, W. T., ed. *Minutes of the General Assembly of the General Baptist Churches in England*. Vol 1, 1654–1728. London: Kingsgate, 1909.

Williams, George H. *Radical Reformation*. Philadelphia: Westminster, 1962.

Williamson, G. I. "The Regulative Principle of Worship." Paper presented at the International Conference of Reformed Churches, San Antonio, TX, 2001.

Digital Sources

www.aavso.org (American Association of Variable Star Observers)
www.answersingenesis.com
www.archive.org
www.baptisthistory.org
www.biblearchaeology.org
www.bible-history.com
www.blueletterbible.org
www.bookofconcord.org
www.cafonline.org (Charities Aid Foundation)
www.carm.org (Christian Apologetics and Research Ministry)
www.catholiceducation.org/en/
www.ccel.org (Christian Classics Ethereal Library)
www.earlychristianwritings.com
www.earlychurch.org.uk
edwards.yale.edu
www.frame-poythress.org
www.hornes.org/theologia
www.icr.org (Institute for Creation Research)
www.monergism.com
www.parthia.com
www.particularbaptist.com
www.patheos.com
www.reformedonline.com (Brian Schwertley)

www.retailresearch.org
www.roman-empire.net
www.scottishreformationsociety.org
www.semperreformanda.com/
www.studylight.org
www.theoi.com
www.truthbeknown.com
www.uhl.ac (University of the Holy Land)
www.vatlib.it
www.worship.calvin.edu
www.wycliffe.org.uk

Index

Place Names in Bold

Abergavenny, 71
Advent, 21, 27, 114, 166
Ainsworth, Henry, 139, 140
Albigenses, 29, 139
Alexandria, 2, 13, 23, 25, 26.
Ambrose, 26
Amsterdam, 138
Amyraldism, 200
Anabaptist, 55, 138, 139, 141, 193, 194
angels, 58, 77, 89–91, 111, 166, 171, 181, 193
Anglican, 17, 33, 38, 42, 44, 46, 55, 56, 58, 61, 66, 68, 114, 121, 122, 136, 138, 141, 146, 158, 179, 188, 203
Ankh, xii, 161, 171
Antwerp, 138
Aquinas, Thomas, 16
Arian, 25, 27, 72
Arminian, 123, 138, 191, 194, 200, 202
artwork, 17, 103, 119
ascension, xv, 30, 37, 164, 175, 191, 200, 206
Ascension Day, 36, 105, 157, 196
Augsburg Confession, 124
Augustine of Canterbury, 18, 28
Augustine of Hippo, 28, 142
Aurelius, 1x, 4

Balaam, 92, 109
banned, xvi, 39, 50, 51, 124, 175, 176
Bannerman, James, 6, 7, 135
Baptist, xiii, 30, 53, 55, 56, 114, 115, 129, 122, 123, 126, 135, 138, 140, 143, 179, 188, 189, 192, 194, 196, 207
Bari, x, 72, 73
Basel, 122, 194
Basilides, 23
Bede, 18, 19
Beecher, Henry Ward, 187
Belgic Confession, 125
Bennet, Richard, 102, 103, 108
Bern, 34, 36, 194, 198
Bethlehem, 17, 26, 64, 77–79, 81, 85–87, 89, 92–96, 111
Beza, Theodore, 37, 142, 191, 197, 199–201
Boniface, 43, 70
Book of Common Prayer, 17, 136, 177
Boston, xii, , 39, 135, 142, 180
Brussels, 138
Bucer, Martin, 34–36 119, 137
Bullinger, Heinrich, 36–38 116, 118, 119, 191, 193–97 199, 200

Caesar Augustus, 79
Calamy, Edward, 50

INDEX

Calderwood, David, 60, 218
calendar, 4, 6, 8, 16, 34, 36, 40, 41, 51, 60, 61, 112, 146, 154, 155, 159, 161, 166, 167, 185, 186, 191, 208, 215
Caligula, 41
Calvin, John, xii, 16, 33–38, 116–20 122–28 130–32 136–38 145, 172, 191, 193, 196–201, 203
Calvinism/Calvinist, xv, xvi, 32, 38, 46, 47, 53, 55, 60, 102, 113, 115, 117, 120, 125–27, 138, 151, 200, 201, 203, 210, 213
Candlemas, 21, 30
Canterbury, 18, 28, 52, 53
Carnival, ix, 30, 31
carols, 22, 39, 48, 61, 66, 71, 107, 111, 112, 198, 212
Celtic Church, 28
census, 79–81 86, 90, 159
Charlemagne, 28
Christmas, x, xii–xvi, 1, 4, 15, 16, 21–45, 47–53, 55, 56, 58, 60–68, 71, 75, 76, 97–102, 105–13, 116, 121, 124, 125, 132, 135, 145–48, 151–53, 155–63, 165–69, 171–77, 179–84, 186–91, 196–205, 207–15
Christmas cards, 63
Christmas Carol, A, 66, 68
Christmas Day, 21, 28, 29, 36, 44, 48–53, 55, 58, 64, 66–68, 105, 113, 182, 186, 188–90, 196–98
Christmas Eve, xi, 21, 29, 70, 105, 113, 114, 174
Christmas tree, x, 41, 62, 63, 69, 106, 113, 156, 159, 163, 166, 170, 171, 188, 198
Chronographia, 24
Chronography, The, 26
Chrysostom, John, 27, 69, 183
Church of England, 54, 56, 113, 114, 123, 124, 139, 142, 177–79, 185
Church of Scotland, 37, 60, 61, 66–68, 177
Clement of Alexandria, 23
Coca Cola Corporation, xi, 76

coins, viii, ix, 11, 13, 19, 41, 74, 149
Company of Pastors, 35, 36, 38, 197, 198, 200
Constantine, IX, 3, 4, 15–17 19, 24–26
Constantinople, 25, 27, 43, 183, 195
Corinth, 146, 162
Cornwell, Francis, 142
Cotton, John, 135, 142
Council of Chelsea, 29
Council of Geneva, 36, 197, 198
Council of Mâcon, 27
Council of Nicaea, 25, 26, 72
Council of Tours, 21, 27, 41
Council of Trent, 102, 120
Cromwell, Oliver, 51
Cromwell, Thomas, 138

Dabney, R. L., 135, 190
D'Aubigne, Merle, 119
David (King), 85, 86, 129, 130, 172
Davies, Samuel, xii, 181, 186
Deists, 201
Dickens, Charles, 66, 68, 75
Directory for the Public Worship of God, 50
discipline, 36, 54, 113, 197, 199
divorce, 82–84, 139, 193

Easter, xiii, 4, 17, 20, 36, 37, 41, 50, 55, 56, 67, 99, 105, 125, 155, 157, 177, 179, 187, 190, 191, 196, 199, 203
Edersheim, Alfred, 148, 149
Edinburgh, 67, 68, 169
Edwards, Jonathan, 113, 181
Egypt, viii, , 9, 11, 23, 92, 96, 155, 203
Egyptian, viii, 11, 23, 40, 161
Elizabeth, 45, 46, 47, 78, 79, 81, 85, 100
England, xvi, 20, 28–30, 32, 39, 41, 43, 45–48, 51, 58, 62, 66, 67, 70, 85, 123, 136, 138, 142, 144, 176, 177, 180, 184, 200
Epiphany, 23, 27, 31, 105, 176
Episcopalian, 61, 75, 113, 114
Esther, 7, 92, 166, 167, 168, 169, 170
Eusebius of Caesarea, 26
Evangelism, 100, 122, 157, 201–3, 210

INDEX

Farel, William, 34–36, 137, 196
First Book of Discipline, 60, 176
Five Articles of Perth, 60
Formula of Concord, 16, 124
France, 20, 27, 28, 43, 46, 119, 200
Frankfurt, 46, 194
French (or Gallican) Confession of Faith, 125

gammadion cross, xii, 160
General Baptists, 55, 136, 140, 141, 142, 144, 145
Geneva, ix, xii, xvi, 34–38, 119, 120, 122, 136–38, 145, 191, 193, 194, 196–201
Genevan Consistory, 197
Germany, 20, 28, 30, 33, 39, 41, 43, 62, 63, 70, 74, 119, 124, 166, 192
gifts, 7, 24, 33, 34, 41–43, 63, 67, 72–74, 96, 98, 99, 101, 109–11, 168, 169, 211
Good Friday, 36, 38, 67, 155, 157, 209
Grantham, Thomas, 55, 56, 140–42, 144
Gregory of Nazianzus, 25

Halloween, 20, 44, 168, 212
Harper's Weekly, 75
Hebron, 79, 92
Heidelberg Catechism, 125, 141
Henry, Matthew, 98, 135
Herod, 24, 80, 81, 92, 94, 95, 149, 159
Hogmany, 42
holly, 21, 71, 163
Hooker, Richard, 123, 124
Huss, John, 33
hymns, 38, 39, 48, 56–58, 111, 126, 137, 140, 142–44, 152, 156, 212

idolatry, 2, 19, 24, 49, 106, 128, 160–63, 170, 172, 179, 184, 206
Incarnation, 25, 36, 74, 77–96, 101, 106, 163, 164, 175, 181, 199, 215
Independents, 55, 122, 141
Inn, 85, 89
Irenaeus, 23
Irish Articles of Religion, 125

Irving, Washington, xi, 75
ivy, 21, 71

Jacob, 66, 86, 162, 165
Jehu, 162
Jephthah, 87
Jeremiah, 69, 130, 159
Jerusalem, xi, 2, 21, 25, 78, 79, 85, 90, 92–95, 99, 103, 105, 129, 131, 133, 135, 146, 148, 149, 153, 167, 168
Jews, 6, 31, 77, 80, 81, 86, 92, 93, 110, 131, 138, 149, 154, 167–69, 181, 192
Job, 37, 94, 165, 172
John the Baptist, 23, 78, 79, 82, 159
Joseph (Mary's husband), 77, 78, 81, 84–86, 89, 92, 95, 96
Judah, 78, 79, 92, 93
Julius Caesar, 41

Kalends, 22, 27, 41–43, 49, 69, 70, 72, 173
Keach, Benjamin, x, 53–56, 141–46
Kent, 53
King Charles I, 21, 61
King Charles II, 140
King Edward VI, 45, 200
King George III, 63
King George V, 67, 100
King Henry VIII, 38, 139
King James I, 60
King James IV, 60
Knickerbocker History, 75
Knox, John, 37, 60, 117, 123, 165, 176, 200

Lambeth Articles, 125
Lancashire, 60
Leiden, 138
Libanius, 42, 69, 72
liberty of conscience, 151–58
London, 47, 50–53, 56–58, 63, 104, 120, 138, 141–43, 179
London Confession of 1644, 126, 141
London Confession of 1689, 126
Lord of Misrule, 7, 8, 30, 31

Lord's Day, 16, 24, 32, 34, 35, 49, 50, 60, 67, 107, 112, 118, 133, 152, 157, 162, 168, 171, 177, 178, 189, 197, 210, 212
Luke, 77, 78, 80, 85, 89–91
Luther, Martin, ix, 16, 32, 33, 55, 74, 117–20, 122, 192, 195
Lutheran, xvi, 33, 38, 42, 46, 63, 114, 115, 119, 120, 122, 124, 145, 146, 155, 156, 158, 172, 179, 186–88, 194, 203, 212

MacArthur Jr., John, 110
Magi, 29, 90, 92, 94–96
manger, 88–91, 96, 106, 111
Marlow, Issac, 143–45
Mary, viii, xi, 17, 18, 21, 41, 42, 49, 77–79, 81, 84–86, 89, 91, 92, 96, 103, 105, 157, 174, 193
Mass, xi, 2, 17, 24, 29, 32, 33, 65, 103–6, 112, 123, 157, 159, 167, 178, 200
Massachusetts, 22, 138, 180, 181, 186
Mather, Increase, xii, 39, 99, 180, 181
McCrie, Thomas, 169, 170
Methodism, 56
Middle Ages, 5, 39, 45, 71, 83, 159
Midwinter Solstice, 8, 17, 23, 40, 71, 173
Miller, Samuel, 186
mince pies, 51
mistletoe, 71, 163
Mithraism, xvi, 8, 12–15, 17, 25, 103, 173, 175
Moravians, 33
Moses, 4, 12, 60, 128–30, 133, 140, 149, 162, 175, 184, 205
music, xii, 39, 97, 101, 106, 114, 119, 135–37, 141, 142, 145–47, 152, 157, 158, 188, 190, 197, 204, 211, 212

Nativity Feast, 23, 24, 29, 37, 49, 50, 58, 60, 116, 169, 179, 191
Nativity plays, 29, 95, 96, 101, 105, 106, 113, 156
Nazareth, 77, 81, 84, 96, 101
New England, xvi, 39, 142, 176, 179–91

New Jersey, 39, 181, 188
New Year, x, xvi, 17, 20, 22, 24, 41–44, 48, 63, 67, 68, 99, 100, 113, 173, 196
New York, 39, 75, 189, 190
Noah, 8, 36, 109, 164, 165, 175
Noël, 29
North Carolina, x, 39
Normative Principle, 122, 123, 158
Nottingham, 71, 138

Oklahoma, 190
Origen, 23, 24, 174
Orkney, 75
Orthodox, 3, 30, 172
Owen, John, xiii, 135, 164, 203

paedo-baptism, xiii, 59, 115, 121, 135, 138, 142, 194
Parliament (English), 48, 49, 50, 51, 52, 55, 177, 179
Parliament (Scottish), 61
Parthian, 94
Particular Baptists, 126, 141, 142, 144
Passover, 24, 149, 154, 190
Paul, the apostle, 2, 4, 6, 24, 95, 96, 99, 112, 117, 120, 132, 150, 152–55, 162, 163, 182, 202, 204, 205, 208
Pennsylvania, 39, 114
Pentecost, 20, 24, 36, 37, 154, 157, 158, 185, 194, 196
Perth, 60, 189
Pharisees, 30, 131, 134, 154, 203, 205
Pink, AW, 107, 108
Plutarch, 13
Polycarp, 23
Pope Benedict XVI, 104
Pope Gelasius I, 27
Pope Gregory I ('The Great'), 18, 27, 28
Pope Gregory III, 20
Pope Gregory IV, 20
Pope Gregory IX, 30
Pope Gregory XVI, 31
Pope Gregory XIII, 41
Pope Innocent I, 27
Pope Innocent III, 30
Pope Innocent XII, ix, 20

Pope John III, 27
Pope Leo I ('The Great'), 27
Pope Leo III, 28
Pope Liberius, 21, 26
Pope Zacharias, 43
pregnancy, 77, 78, 81, 85, 96
Presbyterian, xiii, 55, 61, 67, 114, 115, 120–23, 136, 169, 179, 181, 186–91, 207, 208
Prince Albert, x, 63
Psalms, 39, 48, 66, 114, 135–37, 139, 140, 142–44, 156, 197
Purim, 148, 166–69
Puritans, xvi, 16, 39, 47–52, 55, 60, 61, 67, 124, 126, 133–36, 138, 159, 177, 179, 180, 191, 209, 215

Queen Anne, 62
Queen Elizabeth I, x, 45–47
Queen Elizabeth II, xi, 100
Queen Mary I (Bloody Mary), 45, 200
Queen Mary (of Scots), 46
Queen Victoria, x, 63

Regulative Principle, xvi, 116–50, 152, 197, 211
Reisinger, 134, 145
Roman Catholic, viii, xiii, xvi, 2–5, 11, 16–18, 20, 21, 27, 28, 30, 32–34, 37–39, 41, 42, 44, 45, 53–56, 61, 62, 68, 70–72, 74, 96, 99, 102–6, 108, 112, 113, 117–20, 122, 123, 134, 138, 146, 155, 156, 158–60, 164, 166, 172, 174, 176, 177, 179, 186, 190–92, 194, 196, 197, 199, 200, 203, 206, 207, 208, 210, 212, 214
Roman Empire, viii, ix, xvi, 2–8, 11–14, 16, 19, 21, 22, 27, 28, 41–43, 56, 60, 69, 70–72, 74, 80, 81, 85, 92, 94, 112, 159, 173, 195, 214
Roman religion,
Rome, viii, ix, 1, 2, 4–6, 9, 11, 13–15, 20, 21, 25–29, 31, 43, 56, 60, 72, 81, 94, 105, 146, 153, 173, 180, 183

Sabbath, 16, 38, 50, 67, 104, 132, 151, 152, 154, 168, 169, 178, 181, 187, 189
Santa Claus, xi, xii, 72–76, 100, 109, 110, 112, 166, 171, 190, 198, 216
Saturnalia, 7, 8, 24, 30, 31, 41, 42, 56, 71, 72, 162, 173, 180
Scandinavia, 9, 29, 41, 71
Schaff, Philip, 8, 15, 26, 120, 125, 172, 193
Scotland, xvi, 13, 29, 32, 37, 41, 43, 44, 60–62, 66–68, 75, 102, 113, 123, 165, 176, 177, 200
Scripture, xiii, xv, 2, 33, 36, 37, 46, 50, 54, 61, 81, 88, 91, 95, 99, 112, 116, 118, 122–27, 132–34, 136, 137, 139, 140, 142, 144–46, 149–51, 153, 155, 158, 169, 172, 176–78, 184, 187, 192–94, 201–3, 205, 210, 212, 213, 215
Second Helvetic Confession, 37, 116, 172, 191
Shepherds, 29, 48, 77, 89–91, 96, 106, 111, 159, 184
Smyth, John, 138–40, 144
Socinians, 194
Sol Invictus ('invincible sun'), ix, 4, 8, 13–16, 17, 19, 20, 173
Solemn League and Covenant, 60
South Carolina, 114
Spilsbury, John, 55, 141
spring, 17, 21, 40, 65, 70, 72, 159
Spurgeon, C. H., x, xiii, 64–66, 142, 207
Stable, 77, 85, 87–89, 96, 159, 160
star, 17, 29, 64, 77, 91–96, 111, 163, 174
St. Francis of Assisi, 29
St. Nicholas, x, 20, 33, 72–75, 188
Strasbourg, ix, 34, 35, 119, 137, 194
Stubbes, Philip, 47, 48
Sunday-school, 188, 189
superstition, 5, 17, 21, 35, 43, 44, 49, 50, 66, 70, 74, 113, 126, 162, 170, 174, 178, 181–85, 197, 198
Susa, xii, 166, 167
swaddling cloth, 90
Switzerland, 28, 119, 194

Ten Commandments, 16, 54, 104, 137, 155
Tertullian, 23, 24, 69
Theodosian Code, 195, 196
Thirty-Nine Articles, 124, 125
The Times, 61
Tozer, AW, xii, 101, 102, 208, 209, 215, 224
tradition, xiii, 2, 5, 16, 28, 30, 31, 33, 41, 42, 44, 46, 51, 62–64, 66, 68, 71, 72, 98, 100, 104, 112, 118, 123, 124, 126, 131, 134–36, 142, 147, 177, 182, 187–89, 194, 203–5, 208, 210
Turkey, 72
Turretin, xiii, 38, 116, 191, 197, 200, 201xiii, 38, 116, 191, 197, 200, 201
Tyndale, William, 117, 138

Vatican, 14, 18, 26, 103
Victorian, xvi, 61, 62–66, 69, 101, 112, 166, 186
Virginia, 181, 184

Waldenses, 29, 30, 139, 207
Washington, George, 39
Watch Night Service, 68
Wesley, Charles, x, 57, 58, 111

Wesley, John, 56–58
Westminster Confession of Faith, 55, 67, 141, 149, 168, 192
Whitefield, George, x, 57–59
Williamson, G. I., 147, 148
winter, 8, 17, 21, 23, 40, 44, 62, 63, 65, 70, 71, 74, 88, 97, 100, 113, 166, 173, 215
Woden, 73, 74
worship, xvi, 2–5, 7–9, 11–15, 17–19, 23, 33, 36, 37, 47, 50, 51, 53–55, 57, 61, 69, 71, 73, 102–4, 106, 112, 113, 116–20, 122–26, 129–40, 142–50, 152, 153, 156–59, 161–63, 165, 166, 168, 169, 171–74, 176–79, 181–83, 185–90, 197, 202, 203, 205, 207, 208, 210–12
Wycliffe, John, 85, 117

Yule, 8, 21, 29, 56, 61, 162, 204

Zacharias, 78, 79, 81, 85, 86
Zurich, x11, xvi, 34, 36, 37, 119, 120, 191, 192, 194, 196–98
Zwickau, 55
Zwingli, Ulrich, 34, 37, 117–20 137, 145, 191–93, 195, 196, 199

www.ingramcontent.com/pod-product-compliance
Lightning Source LLC
Chambersburg PA
CBHW070247230426
43664CB00014B/2438